Judge Luther W. Youngdahl

A CHRISTIAN IN POLITICS:
LUTHER W. YOUNGDAHL

A CHRISTIAN
in POLITICS

Luther W. Youngdahl

*A Story of a Christian's Faith
at Work in a Modern World*

by

ROBERT ESBJORNSON

*Department of Christianity
Gustavus Adolphus College*

Publishers

T. S. DENISON & COMPANY

MINNEAPOLIS

©, 1955, by

T. S. DENISON & COMPANY

Printed in the U. S. A.

By The Brings Press

* * *

International Copyright Secured

Library of Congress Catalog Card Number: 55-12294

Dedicated
To my father, Per Esbjornson,
who showed me what steadfast
devotion is
and
To my wife, Ruth,
who speaks her mind,
votes her ticket
and loves with all her heart.

Contents

Foreword

This book grows out of the author's conviction that illumination of "What, I as a Christian, ought to do in politics" comes to us most adequately by serious reflection upon what Christians actually do in a critical situation, rather than by focusing on the moral precepts and principles given in a religion. "What is the nature of moral decision in politics" is the key question of the book. And the answer is sought significantly in the career of one man, Luther W. Youngdahl, as he sought to understand American society, the meaning of his Christian faith, and the technical data relevant to particular decisions he had to make as a politician in Minnesota.

The approach of this book should aid men in public life and responsible voters in understanding the social implications of their faith better than most recent general books on political and social ethics. The man who lives in these pages is engaged in no neat deduction of a political position from a few general religious principles. We are asked by the author to place ourselves in the role of Luther W. Youngdahl and see how he had to live out his Christian commitments in full recognition of the need for reconciling various interests and of the tough task of securing the support of voters. These factors had to be considered along with his Christian principles as he made his decisions.

We learn that moral leadership emerges in the attempt of a person to bring to bear the whole of his loyalties and knowledge upon a problem. In every crucial decision of this man we see the complex confluence of habits of thought developed in a Christian family and church with hard economic and political facts.

This book is a new and welcome kind of essay in Christian ethics. It is a critical reflection upon the moral action of a Christian and the Christian community. And, given the tremendous resources and tasks of modern government, it is moral action in economic and political spheres of life that probably now has the greatest influence upon the lives and destinies of men.

KENNETH UNDERWOOD,

Associate Professor of Ethics and Public Policy
Public Affairs Center,
Wesleyan University,
Middletown, Conn.

Can Politicians
Be Christians?

More than 73% of American parents do not want their children to go into politics — if surveys are a reliable indication of their sentiments. Apparently this reflects an attitude characteristic of citizens of this country — a distaste for competitive politics. We argue about political issues; we vote, if the weather is pleasant and the campaign exciting. Then, having fulfilled what we think is our political duty, we settle back behind the Sunday sports page, into a comfortable pew in church, or in front of a 21-inch television screen; thus we are soothed into a mood of submissive lassitude toward the pressing responsibilities of citizenship.

Politics, according to many Americans, is a sordid, futile business; and they would rather not be involved in its conflicts and intrigues. They read about Tammany Hall in American history classes; they know about the corrupt boss rule of Hague and Pendergast; they remember the story of Huey Long; they listen with disgust to the exposé of five-percenters and the grain bin scandals; they listen to campaign speeches designed to revive their interest in politics long enough to get them to the polls — without getting them so stirred up that they begin to take positive action on "the Mess" in Washington, their state capitols or the large cities.

American voters are bewildered by the complexities, duplicities and ambiguities of American politics. They are frustrated

11

by the difficulty of fixing responsibility on anyone for actions of which they do not approve. In short, Americans don't like politics.

It is not surprising that they would be skeptical of a man who claimed that Christianity and politics could be intermingled and who has often been honored and gladly heard by church groups as a "Christian in politics." Luther Youngdahl, a Christian in politics? Is this not a contradiction? Surely, they decide, it must have been necessary for him to compromise his avowed Christian ideals in an attempt to win the votes necessary to hold power. How can a Christian, trying to apply his religious ethics to governmental affairs, be entirely successful? Is a firm declaration of Christian statesmanship popular with the voter — in Minnesota, or in any other state in the Union? Very seldom, says the disillusioned American citizen. Religion is divine, but politics — never!

There are two kinds of skeptical reaction to claims made for Luther Youngdahl as a Christian in politics. The politically-minded skeptic says, "Politics is a rough, dirty business. It requires that a man do things he never thought of doing before he entered the race for power. If a man is not corrupt before he enters politics, he does not long remain uncontaminated. If he is to be successful in politics, he must have the toughness to cope with the callous, brutal facts of political power — he cannot be squeamish." He would add, "Christian ideals, such as brotherhood, love, humanity and honesty, are window-dressing. A clever politician uses these lofty terms in speeches to convince the naive public that he is a good man, but idealism doesn't mean a thing in the struggle for power or the preparation of legislation. If the politician can display personal piety by going to church regularly, drinking milk, encouraging his staff to begin meetings with prayer, and contributing to churches and charities — so much the better, especially if religion happens to be in vogue." The politically-minded skeptic would decide that if Luther Youngdahl was a successful politician, his Christianity was just a front; that if he really is a Christian he would not have been a success in politics.

The other brand of skepticism is that of religious-minded

people. They would say, "A true Christian is not interested in the things of the world, like politics. He is interested in the things of eternity. He believes that he has 'only one life to live, it will soon be past, only what's done for Christ will last.' He dedicates his time and funds to the church's evangelization program and its related activities. He has no time for politics — the church needs him so badly." The religious-minded skeptic would have something more to say. "Politics is dirty. One must compromise his convictions so much that it would not be a calling worthy of a Christian who is supposed to keep himself "unspotted from the world." Such a skeptic would conclude that if Luther Youngdahl is a **true** Christian he would never have become involved in politics. He would have devoted his time to the Lord's work, not the Republican's.

Of course, no one is quite so obvious about his opinions as the hypothetical persons whose views were just stated. Yet, these prejudices exist. And where people holding them get together, Youngdahl's career makes an interesting conversation piece, because it does not fit into the pattern. Youngdahl was successful enough in politics to be elected three times to the governorship of Minnesota and to inaugurate important political and humanitarian reforms. At the same time he was Christian enough to be gladly heard by church people all over the country on the subject of Christianity and politics. He received such honors as the title, "Lutheran of 1950," given to him by the Missouri Synod Federation of Lutheran Clubs in America. He aroused the church people of his state to a new level of political activity. How can this be explained? Is Luther Youngdahl a unique phenomena — an item for a "Believe It or Not" column? Or have our prejudices about politics and religion obscured the fact that there are many conscientious Christian politicians?

This book is the result of the author's personal investigation into the relation of religion to politics — a study that began during World War II. When I was an undergraduate at Gustavus Adolphus College I believed that politics was dirty and surely no concern of mine. At its best it was a necessary evil and at its worst the arena of the devil himself.

Since I was brought up in a pious Christian home in which there was very little interest in politics, this is understandable. I believed that if the church worked hard enough to Christianize the world, such activities as "dirty politics" could be eliminated and a new world built on peaceful fellowship could be brought into being. World War II came, and my innocence about political matters began to disappear. I was dismayed by the fact that Nazism arose in the homeland of the Lutheran church to which I belonged. I wondered if there was a direct relationship between the kind of Christianity that had been taught to me and the rise of a totalitarian system that despised Christianity as the slave morality of weak people. It seemed that the Church had failed to teach a kind of Christianity that would prevent the ruthlessness and injustice that has plagued the world.

My studies at Augustana Seminary and Yale Divinity School led to the discovery that many churchmen were re-examining the question — Bishop Berggrav of Norway, Gustav Aulen of Sweden, William Temple of England, Reinhold Neibuhr of the United States, Karl Barth of Switzerland are only a few of them. The World Council of Churches' study commissions were struggling with the issue. The churches of Holland, Germany, Norway and Denmark were made aware of their failure by the fury of Hitler and his Gestapo and slowly began their bitter struggle against the powers that threatened them. I read the courageous, hard-hitting sermons of Kai Munk, the Danish country preacher and dramatist, whose words were such big guns that the Nazis had to liquidate him. The Church was beginning to discover — or perhaps re-discover — its proper role in relation to politics and the State. It was gaining a more realistic understanding of politics and it came to the conclusion that a more positive role by church groups and individual Christians would have to be brought to bear upon the political problems of our time.

I first became seriously interested in Governor Youngdahl's career while taking a course in Christianity and American politics under Professor Kenneth Underwood at Yale in 1950. I had heard about Youngdahl's crusade against gambling in

Minnesota but had not given it much thought until the class-room discussion one day turned to political leadership. Mr. Underwood raised the question as to what makes for moral political leadership — does it lie in the fact that a politician goes to church, does not drink or swear, is kind to ladies and does not approve of sin? Or is it present when a politician fights gamblers, horse-racing and the liquor crowd? Or is it manifest when a politician shows a keen awareness of the possibilities of justice and injustice in issues and programs that have no obvious relationship to morals and piety?

I began to wonder what kind of Christian politician Luther Youngdahl was. What was the story behind the headlines? What kind of political strategist was he? How did he manage the neat trick of winning elections and inaugurating legislative programs successfully without losing his reputation for integrity, honesty and humanity? What effect did his home and church training have on his political views and activities? Was his religion of the kind that merely expressed itself in church-going, clean language, abstemious habits, a kindly demeanor and the assertion that Christianity helped him succeed in politics? Or did he have a more involved understanding of the ethical problems of politics? Was he deeply aware of the moral dilemmas of politicians, of their involvement in the corrupting influences of intrenched selfishness and the agony of making decisions between alternatives that are not clear-cut and sharply contrasted? What Christian principles were basic to his program?

Youngdahl's career is a revealing study of the problems that arise when certain convictions of Christianity are taken seriously. This book is therefore neither a complete biography nor a full account of his administration. It is primarily a study of the relationship of Christianity to politics in a given situation. A theological analysis of Christian citizenship is brought to bear upon the activities of Youngdahl, other citizens and the churches. It is believed that the interplay of a theological analysis and an actual political situation will have worth by way of instruction to other Christians who look for guidance in applying Christian ethics to their political activities.

The story that follows is based upon the premise that Youngdahl's religious commitments are of central importance in understanding his career. His sincerity in trying to apply his Christian convictions to his political responsibilities is assumed to be genuine, although dissident opinions on that score are not ignored. The account is based upon newspaper and magazine accounts of events during his career, interviews with Youngdahl and many people closely associated with him and other participants in Minnesota public life, Youngdahl's speeches, autobiographical materials provided by Youngdahl and members of his family, documents published by the State of Minnesota and evaluations of his program in current periodicals.

I am aware of the delicate nature of writing about people who are still in the public eye and about events with which many readers of "A Christian in Politics" will be more familiar than I. New materials may keep turning up, so I shall be prepared to have people ask me, after they have read the book, why this or that incident was not included. I therefore offer my apologies to those who may have additional information they feel should have been included and to others whose participation in the events covered I have omitted or incompletely described. Revisions may be made in subsequent reprintings of the book.

If Youngdahl's career can throw light on the problem of the Christian's role in politics and the part the organized church can have in bringing greater justice and integrity into American life, he will have rendered his country a service, regardless of how his career or accomplishments might be otherwise evaluated. For these are vital questions concerning the welfare of the nation.

Acknowledgements

A book has one author but many contributors. I acknowledge gratefully the good graces and unrewarded help of many persons, without which this book would have been impossible. However, I keep for myself full responsibility for whatever limitations the book may have.

I especially want to express my appreciation of the valuable assistance of Judge Luther W. Youngdahl. In letters and interviews he has supplied important data unobtainable elsewhere and offered valuable suggestions after reading the manuscripts several times in its preliminary stages. Other members of the family have been generous with information and pictures— Mrs. Youngdahl, the Rev. William Youngdahl, Mrs. Margaret (Youngdahl) Peterson, Mr. David Youngdahl, Dr. Reuben Youngdahl and Mr. and Mrs. Ren Anderson.

Conversations and interviews with Minnesotans active in public life have been valuable sources of information, and I am thankful to each person who took the time to be helpful. The library file of the Minneapolis daily papers provided the bulk of the information about the day by day events during the Youngdahl administration. The St. Paul daily papers, the **New York Times, Range Facts, Minnesota Labor,** the **Chicago Tribune** and numerous periodicals and books (listed in the bibliography) were also consulted. The Rev. Emmer Engberg loaned me a valuable file on the Lattimore case.

The influence of those who have been my teachers and colleagues was obvious to me as I worked, and I salute all of them. I am especially indebted to Dr. Edgar Carlson, who has been my mentor in theology since 1939; and to Dr. Kenneth Underwood, under whose counsel this manuscript took its early shape.

Introduction

The Christian Faith and American Politics

Why Bring Faith into Politics?

Every man has political beliefs, whether or not he admits it and knows what they are. Every man also has religious beliefs, whether he acknowledges them or not. Even an atheist who denies God has a belief. His very denial is his belief. So a man may dislike government and believe it should be eliminated. His lack of faith in government is a faith in the possibility of a world without government.

Every reader of this book will analyze, approve and criticize the political activities of Youngdahl and others involved in the story by his set of political beliefs—whatever they are and whether or not the reader knows exactly what they are. It is not wrong to have beliefs, for beliefs are inescapable. What is unfortunate is not knowing clearly what they are.

A Christian, too, has beliefs—religious beliefs and political ones. All too often he never relates them to one another. When he reads about developments in Washington or interests himself in the President's press conference quotations, he interprets the material in terms of his political beliefs. When he listens to sermons, he filters the ideas of the preacher through

18

the sieve of his own personal religious convictions. If he fails to relate the two sets of beliefs, he should not be pleased with himself; faith in God should be so strong and clear to him that it influences his political ideas and actions (even though his faith must never be a substitute for his politics).

This book relates the Christian faith to politics. Although it has many practical implications, it is necessarily theoretical and therefore more difficult to read than the Youngdahl story itself. The reader may choose not to belabor himself with reading it, especially if he already has a Christian political philosophy adequate enough to satisfy him. On the other hand, he may want to read it—if only to understand the viewpoint used in this book to interpret the political situation in Minnesota and Youngdahl's career within it. This section may be worthwhile for some readers and not for others. If a reader decides it will not be of value to him, he can skip it and start with the story of Youngdahl's life on page 55—comforted by the words C. S. Lewis wrote about one of his chapters: "It is a very silly idea that in reading a book you must never skip. All sensible people skip freely when they come to a chapter which they find is going to be no good for them."

PART I

God's Law and the State

The fact that a Christian has a political philosophy does not necessarily mean that he starts with a representation of what ought to be, rather than with what actually exists. However, Christians often make this error. Faith is no substitute for an analysis of political life aimed at discerning its basic structure. We live in an environment that is not entirely of our own creation. There are facts of life that cannot be ignored. A political philosophy constructed in defiance of them comes up against the rocks and is wrecked. There are underlying facts about politics that must be faced, whether or not we are Christians.

Man's Social Nature

Political thought must not ignore the fact that man is by nature a social being. He lives in three "communities" which are expressions of his social nature. They are the family, the economy and the state; or the community of married love, of work and trade, and of political authority.

Each of these communities arises out of man's natural needs. Therefore, we cannot choose not to belong to them. Parents are a necessity none of us can escape. We need their care during a long period of comparative helplessness. The family exists, not just to propagate children but to surround them with affection and security.

The economic community is founded upon the need for food, shelter and clothing. Even in the family there is an interdependent exchange of services. One of the parents must care for the helpless children in order that the other might be free to provide for and to protect the family. As society becomes more complicated, the economic life becomes more inter-dependent and specialized occupations develop. It is not possible for one family to control and develop all the natural resources, so families begin to trade goods and services with one another. Each person specializes according to his abilities and the resources and opportunities available to him.

Another built-in fact of man's social nature is the power of some to exercise volition over others. This is political authority, and it produces the state. Even in the family there is a form of political authority. Usually it is the father who possesses the power to enforce his will; his superior physical strength gives him the initial advantage. (Of course, the wife has power, too. Few men can resist her tears). Because the necessity for standing together against a common threat to their safety and the need for order in their inter-related existence, some form of political authority is inevitable among people.

Elements in Political Authority

Political authority, the power to enforce one's will upon another, is dependent upon a leader's ability to command respect as well as fear. This observation can be illustrated in analyzing several types of political societies. The father, or whoever is entitled to the authority in a household, must earn the respect of his family. If he relied on strength alone and acted cruelly and unjustly, his position would be precarious. To earn respect, the head of the house must be able to protect his family and provide for its welfare. If he is wise and competent, he earns their regard; and they submit to his authority in order to benefit from his care for them.

Political authority in a tribe is vested both in strength and respect. A tribe is a combination of families banded together for mutual protection and interchange of services and goods. The question is, who gains authority and how? Several men are potential rivals for leadership. One of them might temporarily secure the upper hand because of his superior physical prowess, but he could not hold it long unless he earned the respect of the tribe. Tribal leaders are obliged to be not only strong but wise, not only cunning warriors but shrewd judges. They must have the strength and courage to win battles; and they must be adept in settling claims and conducting peace talks. An old chief can often hold the loyalty of younger and stronger men, because his wisdom and sense of justice command respect.

In larger political societies, in which authority is more centralized and the weapons of coercion more complicated, it becomes less difficult for leaders to maintain their positions by force. Yet even kings and modern dictators must have a measure of the confidence of the people. Irresponsible tyrants soon are overthrown.

Democracy is a form of government so organized that the people can reject irresponsible leaders, not by revolution but by elections. It uses no more belligerent methods than campaign mud-slinging, if it is working according to its structural principles. In a democracy, too, respect and coercion are the ingredients of political authority. The government uses laws, courts, police, prisons and even executions to force its citizens to abide by its policies. Yet the government cannot do just as it pleases; the people can oust from power the party it no longer respects. Authority shifts from one party to another, as each in turn convinces the people that it deserves control of the government and that its policies will contribute to their welfare. Ultimately it must fulfill its promises to secure their welfare. If the people become convinced that the governing party is merely making extravagant speeches and bungling badly, they will vote it out of office. Political authority is unreal in a democracy unless both coercive strength and respect are present.

International relations seem to be in a state of anarchy—nations in conflict for world domination, and no international agency or law strong enough to check them. A nation's power appears to depend upon its physical superiority. Each nation, governed by its desire for its own security, seeks to gain the geographical, military and economic advantage. Yet, even on the international level, mere military superiority is not enough. If brute strength were all that mattered, why would the United States and Russia seek allies, engage in diplomacy, and send forth propaganda? Even the great powers seek to convince others that their policies will benefit all of humanity. They are moved to make concessions; and a nation is never more dangerous to the peace than when it presumes to be so right that it will never budge from its position. To gain allies, a nation must win the respect of other nations; or they will join forces against it. No nation can monopolize political power.

The Law of Mutual Help

The foregoing analysis reveals that the inner structure of political authority is constituted of both coercive power and respect. Neither can be eliminated.

Now it is easier to expose the fact that there is a law at work in the political world and all human activities. It is the law of mutual helpfulness: in order to get, a man must give. He cannot live for himself alone, because he is dependent upon others who need him and make demands on him. Gustav Wingren has illustrated it succinctly:

"This worldly command, which holds sway on earth independent of the church, has this function that it constrains the individual to be of help to others, whether he wants to or not. In the home the father is driven to provide for wife and children; son and daughter are forced to subordinate themselves and serve the parents. The craftsman must seek to please his customers if he is going to get along. The prince (or politician) must look after his constituents' welfare, otherwise there will be a rebellion, and these in their turn must surrender themselves to law and ordinance, otherwise they will receive their punishment. However wicked and unwilling all these men still are in their hearts, they must still do that which is good toward one another." (Footnote: Wingren, Gustav, "The Church and the Calling," trans., Evert Olson, **The Augustana Quarterly, XXVI:4** (Oct., 1947, 307).

This command, in political language, is called justice. In order to receive, man is forced to serve his neighbor. Thus, justice is not different from helpful love. This command does not define what is helpful, yet it forces men to study the existing situation in order to determine what is most needed. The laws which are the outcome of this study are not rigid and absolute; they are subject to constant change because they are instruments which seek the welfare of the people and are not ends in themselves.

Laws can be unjust. They often are biased in favor of privileged, powerful groups or persons. The actual, positive laws passed by legislatures or executive orders are shaped as much by the will of strong, rich, vocal and well-organized groups as they are by the sense of justice—if not more. Justice remains basic, but legislation is usually only relatively just. Laws change, not only as human needs are more accurately defined but as shifts in power occur. (Labor legislation over the past fifty years is an illustration of this. As labor has become more powerful, laws more beneficial to labor have been passed). Laws are usually a balance, or compromise, achieved by the government in the interests of as many people as possible. Justice is thus at all times in danger of being over-shadowed by selfishly-used power. Despite its corruption, it is an ever-present leaven working within the political processes to correct wrongs. Demands for justice arise in individuals whose sense of fairness has been outraged or whose rights have been ignored. This is not just wishful thinking; it is an observable fact of political life.

The Function of the State

The state is not a lord but a servant. It exists because the people need it. In a negative sense the state serves to preserve order, to control the clashing self-interests in a society, to prevent anarchy and to protect the people from attack. By preserving order, the state creates conditions which promote the welfare of the people.

The state also has a positive function—promoting welfare.

There are sharp differences of opinion as to what extent the state should provide for the people; but it is a fact that the people can and do delegate certain tasks to the state. This occurs when there is no other agency for effective mobilization of resources to meet human needs. The state has been asked to educate the young, control prices, set up social security funds, pass traffic laws, build highways, carry the mail, and do many other tasks. In some situations the state monopolizes welfare activities; in others there is freedom for collateral activities by voluntary organizations.

The Demon in Politics

There is a "demon" in politics which has an opportunity to flourish because the state is given a monopoly on the power of the sword (or the use of penalty and coercion). Political power itself is not evil; but the lust for power, the will to dominate in order to realize selfish ambitions, is evil and dangerous. When government falls into the hands of power-mad men, it becomes tyrannical. When the governing party pretends to be omnipotent and takes as its absolute prerogatives matters which are delegated to it by the people, it has become tyrannical. It has presumed to be the lord, and it must then be opposed. Lust for power is the demon in politics.

The United States is a "multi-group society," a maze of inter-locking organizations and groups within which the political demon has many opportunities to work destructively. As George Graham has observed, it is in the conflict of organizations and organizational loyalties that many moral dilemmas of politics arise; and the economic groups (labor, industry, farmers, etc.) create the challenge to the freedom of all other groups. (George Graham, Morality in American Politics, N.Y., 1952, p. 302). The lobbyist who represents them has become the "bad guy" of American politics, because his activities are often the expression of the unchecked power lust of his group.

Economic organizations, like the National Association of Manufacturers, the Farm Bureau and the C.I.O. have gained a great deal of political power. The complexity of the legislative process, in which the actual work is done by committees, makes it impossible for the individual citizen to keep pace with developments. The lobbyist who represents groups knows how to exert influence at the right places, on the right people, at the right time. He becomes an expert in the intricacies of the legislative process and the manners and weaknesses of lawmakers. The groups with the greatest amount at stake are inclined to work most strenuously to put pressure on legislators; and the more money they have for lobbying, the more influence they can wield. It is not surprising that the most effective lobbying is done by well-organized economic groups; and it is not uncommon to find these groups using every means at their disposal, even corrupting public officials with bribes, to obtain their ends.

Lobbying in itself is not a corruption of the political process. It is a legitimate channel for the flow of information between constituents and legislators and a means by which a group can defend itself. Consider the example of a canning company. It is a servant of the community, because it preserves vegetables efficiently and economically. It is always possible that legislation that would hamper its operations could be passed. The company is entitled to representation, at the capitol, by a lobbyist who recommends or opposes legislation in the best interests of the company's responsibility to serve the community. It is protecting its right to serve, and from this right all other rights are derived.

Usually a company is more concerned about accumulating profits than about being a profitable servant, more worried about preserving its economic status than about human welfare, more apt to rationalize its self-interest than to look at a situation objectively. Thus there continues to be a clash between right and wrong, within every pressure group, over which ambition shall be allowed to dominate—the desire for profits, or the aim to serve the community effectively. Because each pressure group is made up of individuals who can influence policy, the root of the problem is in the individual. We must not lose sight of the personal nature of political activity, nor of the social effects of our individual decisions.

It is inevitable that special interest groups will rationalize their political objectives by identifying their own interests too closely with the general welfare. What is good for General Motors, or General Electric is not necessarily good for everyone. Industrial interests are tempted to argue that, because they produce jobs and low-cost goods for the benefits of all the people, they must be left free to conduct their own affairs. Organized labor advances the claim that it represents the masses and thus presses for legislation beneficial to its membership on the grounds that it will benefit a large majority. Professional lobbyists also develop vested interests. It is to their advantage to show results in terms of defeated legislation which would have been unfavorable to their employing company, whatever the social consequences of their activities might be.

The role of pressure groups is inevitable in a democracy. The problem is not to eliminate them but to devise political machinery that will prevent them from dominating American politics. It must be possible for all the people to have an influence on those in office. If a governing party becomes the captive of selfish and power-mad minorities, it must be possible for the people to oust the government by peaceful means.

Democratic Checks on Power Lust

In the United States, government is exercised in a complicated pattern of activities including voting, lobbying, jockeying within the party for leadership, legislative maneuvering, executive and administrative ruling, and judicial reviewing of legislation. In a democracy, no one man or one class of people is the "magistrate." Theoretically, all the people are magistrates, each in the measure that he aggressively seeks political power and participates in political maneuvering. This process of conflict and compromise, through party and pressure politics and the whole pattern of political activity, checks the power lust and the selfish ambitions of any one group or person.

Democracy—rule by all the people—is not necessarily an outcome of a belief in the benevolence of the people and their capability to rule. One may believe that all the people are subject to lust for power and selfishness; therefore, no one should be allowed to rule unrestricted by the discipline of the remainder. The more people there are who are active in politics, the less possible it is for a small clique to have the complete advantage. The groups counter-act one another.

The legislature was intended by the founding fathers to be the heart of the process. By its proceedings a self-governing people is supposed to make decisions that reflect public values and embody the best judgment of its representatives. The legislative process is supposed to get as close to the truth as human reason can, after the facts have been collected and studied and the criterion of the general welfare has been applied. (Graham, p. 68)

We are not heartened by what we see happening in legislatures today. They have relinquished their initiative in constructing public policy to the hands of the executive branch of government. They tend to be obstructive rather than cooperative when considering the executive program. Their chief work

is done by committees. Because the committees operate under
the seniority system, the legislatures are dominated by cautious veterans who have not offended powerful interests and
thus survive election after election. Because the committees are
easily subject to local and special pressures, the general welfare is cut up into small pieces of pork, just the size to fit
local pork barrels. The committees have more power than
they should have; because, in the legislative maze, the public
cannot keep track of legislation. As a result, lobbyists can
exert great pressure at opportune times; they are more familiar than the public with what transpires behind the scenes.

Even more disheartening is the discovery that the legislatures no longer are truly representative, especially state legislatures in which rural members have gained a preponderance
of seats by circumstances that are not only unfair but illegal.
Thus an element of disorder has undermined the power of the
legislative branch.

The two-party system in the United States makes available
another bulwark to check selfish minorities that endeavor to
dominate the government. The major parties are large and
inclusive enough to win the support needed to gain access to
the most powerful offices. They are able also to formulate
policy alternatives and, when out of power, to be energetic
critics of the party in power. The primary decisions about
candidates and platforms are made within party councils.

The parties, too, are subject to structural weaknesses that
limit their ability to hold power-lust in check. They are more
able to win elections than to govern. Once a man gains office,
it is difficult to hold him in line with party policy. The parties' dependence upon substantial contributions makes the
power of the groups that provide "the larder for the party
cupboard" a factor that negates the parties' control over its
chosen office-holders. Moreover, the parties are tempted to
consider their own survival above all other considerations. The
longer a party is in power, the more vested interests it has by
remaining in office. Thus the demon in politics corrupts and
introduces chaos into our political parties.

The executive has become more powerful with the passing

of the years. Popular interest is centered in him. People may not know who their senator or representative is, but they know their governor and call the president by his nickname. The executive is regarded as the spokesman of all the people. They look to him to champion their cause and do battle against the special interests that dominate the legislative branch and will often side with him against their local representative. The executive formulates a program and leads the fight for its passage. He supervises its execution and can often circumvent objectionable legislation by ignoring or impeding it on the administrative level. He can interpret his powers loosely in accordance with his aims. It does not take too much imagination to realize that the executive branch can become too powerful and that it is administrative red tape which provides the demon in politics with happy hunting grounds.

It is obvious that there is a need for continual analysis and reform of existing political institutions in American life. Channels permitting justice to flow into constructive policy must be kept open. Barriers to just laws must be exposed. The element of disorder and chaos must be reduced by periodic housecleaning.

God and Politics

Nothing has been said, thus far, about God and Christianity. Do the facts of political life change when God and faith are brought into the picture? Yes, and no.

Christians believe in God the **Father Almighty**. This means at least two things: that absolute power resides in Him and that God cares for his creatures. If man is by nature a social being it is because God created him that way and orders his existence by divine law. The family, economy and state are **orders of creation**, because they are created by God to order or govern human life. Man's membership in these orders cannot be evaded, and in them God's law of mutual help is at work. Men may not want to be mutually helpful; but their existence, within the orders of creation, makes participation unavoidable. It is naive to try to eliminate coercion from human institutions, when God Himself is the source of power.

A non-believer may conclude that these are natural orders and that God does not have to be brought into the picture. The Christian believes that they are divine orders. In his eyes, the state is the instrument of divine power and love designed to check sinfulness and promote human welfare. A Christian view of the state does not claim that politics is Christ-like; but it regards the political order as having been bestowed by God. It confesses that the evil in politics is a result of sin, and it warns that God rules over even those who rebel against him and that rebellion brings divine judgment.

In another sense, the facts are not changed. The Christian recognizes the elements of coercion and respect, as well as the presence of selfishness and greed for power under the primacy of the law. Perhaps his faith in God and his awareness of sin help him to accept these realities more graciously. He submits humbly to the fact that his life will always be under some authority. He acknowledges the presence of corruption and selfishness more realistically. He testifies to the sovereignty of law more fearlessly.

On the basis of the foregoing analysis, several concluding affirmations about God and politics can be stated.

1. Political authority is an inescapable fact of life, because God has created man as a member of society. It consists of coercion and respect, assertion of and submission to authority.

2. Politics operates under the law of mutual helpfulness which God has ordained. In order to obtain and hold the respect of those who submit to their authority, men in power must provide for the security and general welfare of the people; and the people must in turn obey the laws and the upholders of the law. The Christian politician accepts government as the instrument whereby God enforces his law of mutual help in human society. He therefore participates willingly, if not always light-heartedly, in the political process of conflict and compromise.

3. Because of human sinfulness, politics can become corrupt. Authority can be abused by leaders. Laws can benefit

the few at the expense of the many or ignore the interests of those who have no influence. Special interests can usurp the dominating roles in the political process. No individual or group is unambiguously good or evil. Even a Christian politician and a Christian group can be subject to the corrosive effects of self-interest and power-lust.

4. Because politics can become demonic, the Christian citizen acknowledges that the whole political process of conflict and compromise (the give-and-take in party and pressure group politics, as well as within the government itself) is an essential check on the self-will and power lust of special interest groups and individuals. He humbly accepts his role **within** the process and admits the necessity of having opponents and critics as a curb on himself and his party. (There is a good discussion of this point in "The Christian Faith and American Politics," **Social Action**, XVIII, No. 2 (November, 1951.)

5. The Christian citizen is aware of the need for political wisdom. He knows that he must be a political scientist in the broadest sense of the word. He must accurately take stock of the situation in which he is involved and adopt an effective strategy for achieving his goals. He knows that piety is no substitute for political shrewdness. To be effective he must know the facts. To the extent that he is naive, he is handicapped in his efforts to promote justice. God has given him his reason. It is his duty to use it in studying the political order.

6. Because the state can become tyrannical, the Christian acknowledges the right of rebellion, but he strives for a structure in which changes of government can be accomplished without violence. He does not ignore the problems of structure and system in his zeal to work for the more personal welfare of people. He knows that a faulty structure can frustrate justice. He realizes that when the structure of government prevents the people from having a voice in advising what the governing party should or should not do, and makes difficult the discussion and debate of public issues, conditions of disorder are created in the very instrument that is supposed to preserve order. For this reason the Christian politician constantly analyzes the political structure and suggests changes

that will remove the barriers to justice. His views reveal that he respects the government as God's instrument of order and realistically faces the corrupting presence of sin.

The Christian knows that man tends to exalt his own power to a place of dominating concern in his life and that the demonic forces are too powerful to be restrained completely by mortal man. Therefore, he seeks for the redemption of political life from **outside** the sphere of politics. He does not put complete faith in any form of government. He knows that justice will never be perfectly achieved by man. More than the humanist who believes in man's goodness, the Christian realizes the dangers of tyranny and man's helplessness to abolish evil by right thinking and strenuous work. He looks for the redemption of political life by the grace of Jesus Christ. His view of politics is not completely stated until he takes a look at the whole matter from the foot of the cross. How does God's redemptive work, symbolized by Christ's death and resurrection, affect politics?

PART II

The Grace of Christ and the Political Vocation

It is through Christians with a sense of vocation and a readiness to "go the second mile"—to do more than is demanded of them—that the redemptive grace of Christ enters the political arena to offset the demonic element in politics. Faith in God's redeeming love sets the Christian free from selfish striving, and he voluntarily commits himself to helping and befriending his neighbor in every time of need. This attitude brings Christians into political activity, because they realize that the complexities of their neighbor's needs, and the resultant social problems, make cooperative action and public regulation necessary.

The Christian in politics seeks aggressively to do **more** good than is accomplished by all the pressures of conflicting and compromising and bargaining self-interest groups. He is not content with the measure of welfare and justice attained

John Youngdahl and His Grocery Store

Baby picture of Luther Youngdahl

Taken at time of Confirmation

First Lieut. in U. S. Army, World War I

College graduation picture

along the first mile of conflict and compromise. He sets out on the second mile, speaking for the un-represented groups and demanding benefits for the under-dogs, even though they cannot help him politically. He appeals to the consciences of men, not just their self-concern. He sub-ordinates his personal ambition to his public duty.

This is the way the Christian acts, because he believes he is called by Christ to serve his neighbor. His earthly occupation offers the best opportunity for pursuing this course; because many of his neighbor's needs are of a temporal and physical type, the Christian finds it impossible to devote himself exclusively to spiritual matters. The Christian, like everyone else, might not always secure a job he thoroughly enjoys; yet his belief that every vocation is a place of service invests his work with a new spirit, a quality of holiness and significant purpose. Serving his neighbor becomes his primary business, but he does not take a "holier than thou" attitude toward the pleasures and profits of everyday life. If he is considerate enough of himself to acquire an education, increase his capital assets or go on a vacation, it is done because he thinks it will help him to be more effective in his calling.

What motivates him to accept Christ's call to serve his neighbor? Why does he look upon his life as a trust from God to be used according to divine command? Einar Billing has defined the calling as "life organized around the forgiveness of sins." (Note: "Our Calling," trans., Conrad Bergendoff, **The Augustana Quarterly**, XXVI, No. 2 & 3 (Apr., July, 1947) 99ff, 195ff.) Because the Christian believes that God's mercy is sufficient to cover his sins, his good works are not selfishly motivated by the desire to earn merit. The Christian loves his neighbor without calculating the reward or striving for his own salvation. His faith sets him free to devote his efforts to serving his neighbor—which is his calling.

A Christian's dependence upon God's forgiveness continues every day of his life. The temptation "to strike out on his own" and rebel against God is rarely absent, and he frequently sins. He is involved in a world of sinners and works side by side with people who are seeking their own selfish goals. In serving them, he indirectly contributes to the mutiny against God's precepts. Thus his new birth, or conversion, is only a prototype of what must continually happen as he daily turns to God to be forgiven. His life must be a continual cycle of sin, repentance and reassertion of faith.

As he goes about his business, the Christian is not so presumptuous as to believe that he is unambiguously good. Nevertheless, he participates boldly in the affairs of the world; because he knows that God employs even sinners to do His will and that his own salvation is not dependent upon his righteousness but upon God's mercy. Even when an individual contributes to his neighbor's welfare only to further his own personal interests, he is an instrument of God's rule. He is doing God's will in that he is rendering a service to others. When he is benefitting his neighbor, even though for his own selfish reasons, he is acting righteously. The Christian, however, acknowledges that it is God's righteousness, whereas someone else may boast of it as his own. The Christian also recognizes that his act is righteous, not because his motives are guileless, but because the act produces some good for the neighbor. This knowledge that God's will is done, even by sinners, not only heartens a Christian to be helpful even when he does not feel like it; but it also frees him to cooperate with those outside the church, in "secular" movements, when such cooperation will contribute to the welfare of his fellow human beings.

A Christian's vocation is founded on his belief in God's mercy. He sees this divine miracle revealed in Christ's acts, particularly his suffering and death. Jesus died for men. He bore the penalty of sin so mankind could be set free from sin's enslavement. He experienced separation from God so humanity might be reconciled to God. Since Christ did not deserve to suffer and die, his passion is a revelation of the true meaning of forgiveness and love. He could not have been seeking anything for himself, since he was despised and rejected and killed. He was giving himself for others in a spirit of forgiving love.

Jesus Christ is the only begotten Son of God—so the Christian confesses. Thus the sacrifice on Calvary is more than a noble human act. It is God who allows Himself to be nailed upon a cross. It is the means by which He upholds His law and reveals His love by taking the penalties of mankind upon Himself. The death on the cross is pleasing to God, not because He is cruel but because love is His nature. He cannot tolerate unloving behavior. The relentless opposition of a loving God to all selfishness is recognized as God's wrath. Selfishness in man must be punished, but in a loving way. The Law of love must be upheld, but God's love must not be obscured in the process. Christ's sacrifice is God's way of reconciling us to Himself without cancelling His Law. God Himself went "the second mile" of redemptive love up Calvary's hill to reveal that love is not only the law of creation but that it is His nature, too.

This revelation of divine love in Christ works a change in us, too. By faith we become grateful, obedient, trusting and loving persons—as long as we continue to believe. (No Christian is actually faultless enough to be the prototype or the model sketched in this part of the book.) Once hostile to God and defiantly disobedient to his law of love, we are now reconciled to Him and to our neighbor. God liberates us from the bonds of our own self-centeredness and makes us sensitively aware of what is right, so that we can love our neighbors without calculating the return or worrying about our salvation. By faith in Christ we are set free to serve our neighbor in our calling, and thus fulfill the command of God.

One of our callings is politics.

Choices of Political Activity Open to a Christian

When a Christian becomes interested in politics and in trying to participate conscientiously in public service, he must first study the situation to find out what his alternative courses of action are. There are several choices for him to consider. First, he must decide whether to be an independent, or a member of a political party. Then, he must decide what type of independent activity he will launch, or which party he will join.

The Christian may choose to be an independent, one who selects candidates and issues he can conscientiously and wholeheartedly support. As an independent he can limit his political activities to individual efforts, such as voting, and perhaps writing letters on behalf of candidates or legislation he favors. If he chooses the "lone wolf role," he must face the fact that his individual efforts in isolation are not very potent, and his views do not affect other people.

Another avenue is open to the independent—collective action with others in non-partisan committees organized to sustain candidates or legislation supported by the group. Usually the non-partisan committee chooses its program and uses it as a yardstick for deciding which candidates to support. This is the kind of organized action used by Americans for Democratic Action, the United Temperance Movement, the League of Women Voters and C.I.O.'s political action committees. The political effectiveness of the independent is thus enhanced by cooperative action. Effective, organized action may enable the independent to hold the balance of power in a close election.

The Christian may find the strategy of the independent very appealing. It does not implicate him in compromises with other groups whose programs he does not favor, as he might be involved if he entered a party. The committee is homogeneously organized, to promote a program which attracts like-minded people.

It is not too far-fetched to compare the independent in politics with the sectarian type of Christian. The sectarian Christian has several characteristics, some of which are his virtues and some his weaknesses.

1. He tends to over-simplify the ethical problems of life by defining morality in terms of private conduct—rather than complex, social evils—by constructing a code of precepts which clearly define Christian duty and by assuming that the defined duties are readily attainable by true Christians.

2. He is very zealous; in his whole-hearted devotion to the

Kingdom of God, he allows no faint-heartedness, divided loyalty, or toleration of sin.

3. Since there is a clear-cut difference between right and wrong, he has difficulty in seeing how the person who disagrees with him on ethical questions could be right; and he becomes intolerant of those who do not conform to the moral pattern he has adopted.

4. Exclusiveness develops as he seeks out the company of like-minded Christians who can form their own circles in which to carry out the kind of Christian life they all admire and where they can keep the holy zeal burning brightly.

5. The exclusionism of sectarian Christians tends to force the group into withdrawal from more worldly religious activity, partly because their zeal antagonizes others and partly because the group wants to keep itself unspotted from the world. The sectarian has little patience with the slow, often discouraging social processes that operate in heterogeneous groups. He wants action and is scornful of temporizing and compromise. To the extent that he withdraws, his opportunities and influence are circumscribed.

6. However, he wields an influence on the whole Church, because he stands for principles the Church has often forgotten and because the rest of the Church courts his support.

7. He is saved from complete withdrawal and ineffectiveness because of his intense concern for people. The love of Christ is so strong in his heart that it propels him out into the thick of the fight for human betterment, although he often conceives of human need in too-narrow terms.

8. The sectarian type of Christianity arises, most often, among laymen and members of the clergy not in positions of leadership. The officialdom of the Church does not usually rejoice to see it appear, although some of its effects are very salutary.

The political independent has many of the same characteristics.

1. He tends to over-simplify the political issues by picking out certain issues, such as personal corruption of politicians or Universal Military training, as being the "moral" issues,

and ignoring the more complex issues involving the whole structure of society, such as fiscal policy, tax programs, structural reforms.

2. He is often very zealous and whole-hearted in his devotion to the mission of obtaining passage of legislation in which he is interested. The zeal and success of the Anti-Saloon League is a good example of the single-minded fervor often found among independents.

3. The independent often has difficulty understanding how a person who disagrees with him, or opposes him, could be right. As his yardstick for measuring candidates, he appraises their attitudes toward his pet issue. In the days of the Anti-Saloon League, candidates could win the League's support by endorsing prohibition; it did not matter what else they supported.

4. The independent becomes impatient with the slow and discouraging processes of party politics, where there are many points of view, and a number of interest groups, to be considered. He wants action and scorns compromise. So he organizes his non-partisan conventicles to "back" certain candidates or issues he can conscientiously support.

5. His withdrawal from the party, which controls the major political offices and determines the future program of the government, lessens his effectiveness in the sense that he can wield political power only indirectly. His power is "second-hand," because he does not choose the candidates or the platform and cannot obtain a political office without the backing of a party.

6. The independent's influence upon the whole political process is not insignificant, however. Often he presents programs that arouse enough public interest to force the parties to adopt them. The political candidates, more and more frequently, must court his support during an election campaign.

The Christian may choose to join a political party. He may conclude that second-hand control of political power, such as the independent possesses, is not enough. To be effective, he must make his influence felt at the times when candidates for office are chosen by the parties—and be active within the parties which exercise the discipline that formulates and promotes a legislative program. He may conclude that, since the parties actually get the political offices and obtain control of the government, he never has "both feet in politics" until he is in a party.

The Christian is confronted by the question of which party to join. He must not think that he is faced with a choice between a party which is not working for the common good and one that is. Both parties must work for the welfare of the people; if they do not, they lose elections. Both parties are characterized by the self-interest and lust for power that corrupt politics; both tend to listen most attentively when powerful economic groups list their demands. The basic choice is that of deciding which party has the best method of achieving the welfare of the people.

There are two basically different approaches involved in the struggle for dominance in American political life. One faction declares that the commonweal is best achieved through allowing as much freedom to business and other groups as possible, governmental control of the economy and of social welfare being considered dangerous and inefficient. The views of big business interests coincide most closely with this political philosophy, for they believe that if the economy is left as free as possible to accumulate profits, all the people will benefit by the availability of jobs and goods. The philosophy of the Republican Party, with considerable modification, stems from this viewpoint.

The other approach assumes that the commonweal is best achieved, in a complex society, by governmental control checked by democratic processes. Society is too complex and men are too selfish to expect that the commonweal can be achieved by voluntary actions and the automatic functioning of the economy. This view is basic in the philosophy of the Democratic Party, although its philosophy is also considerably modified. The effect of the two-party system is to pull the parties closer to center, as each wants to appeal to as many people as possible. This must not obscure the fact that there is still a distinct choice available to the people.

A Christian may choose to join a third-party movement, but he should do so only if he decides that the time has come when a realignment of the major parties is both necessary and possible—unless he chooses to be cast in the familiar role of the independent, reform-minded politician whose views are not popular enough to enable him to gain an office.

The church member's choice of party may also be determined in part by expediency. Which party is in the best position to gain the power and appears most inclined to do something about the issues that interest him? If he is concerned about state issues, it is possible that the Republican Party is his best choice—even though, on a national level, it may promote policies with which he disagrees. In which party are there people with whom he could work most compatibly? In which party would he have more influence proportionately? Perhaps it would be clever politics to join the weaker party—obviously the one that is out of power. In due course, when the political situation deteriorates and his party wins an election, he would find himself in a position of greater influence.

If he decides to join a party, the Christian must be prepared for discouragement. Party politics are not always pleasant and nice. Ruthlessness has not disappeared from politics. He will often be forced to compromise and accept small gains as substitutes for the large ones he had been anticipating. Sometimes he will watch his party select candidates that he opposed in party councils. There will be hard work and few dramatic victories. He will know, at least, that he is in the thick of the fight.

Choosing one of these alternatives is a difficult and unavoidable decision for conscientious Christian citizens. They must be made individually, and there will be no universal agreement among Christians as to which is the most meritorious one. Taking the easy way out, by remaining aloof, is to walk the broad road to political perdition. The religiously-inclined commentator might well exhort, "God save the state from indecisive Christians!"

PART III

The Fellowship of the Holy Spirit and the Political Role of the Churches

"The churches should remain out of politics, and politics should be kept out of the church. When I attend church I don't want to hear about political matters."

People who utter this truism should stop and ask themselves, "What am I demanding? That preachers stop making naive statements about politics? That the churches should stop trying to 'throw their weight around' as pressure groups seeking to promote bills they favor? Or that God's Word be fenced in so that it does not apply to certain areas of life? That God abdicate from the government of certain areas of human affairs?" The truism is too ambiguous. Let people drop it from their conversation. There is a sense in which the churches should stay out of politics and politics be kept out of the churches; but from another point of view, the churches have a political role that is an unavoidable responsibility.

Alternative Roles for the Churches in American Politics

Four choices confront the churches in considering what their role shall be in American politics—defining the churches now as institutional, organized bodies acting as separate congregations, denominations or inter-denominational councils.

They can ignore politics as a part of the corrupt and perishing world. They can teach their members to withdraw from political life at as many points as possible. They can turn their eyes away from injustice and spend their time "evangelizing," saving people out of the world and fixing their hopes on a heavenly citizenship. They can concentrate on Christ's words, "My kingdom is not of this world," and ignore the implications of other Biblical truths concerning God's creative and providential rule of human life. They can work on the assumption that it is necessary to convert men to Christianity before there can be a righteous nation—to save the nation, it is compulsory first to save individuals. They can concentrate on preaching the Gospel and not waste time puttering in politics.

The churches can inspire their members to work actively for good government but, as institutions, make no direct contribution to the formulation of public policy. They can point out that Christians, because of their love for their neighbors and out of respect for government as a divine order, have civic duties originating in their commitment to God.

This program of "inspiration" can be implemented in several ways. The pastors can preach sermons in which they clarify the Christian and Biblical justification for participating in politics and sharing in the formulation of public policy. Church auxiliary organizations can conduct educational conferences, programs and forums at which political issues are discussed, and to which active politicians are invited—a reciprocal arrangement that would expose politicians to Christian thinking and church members to the realities of politics.

Should the churches choose this type of political role, which relies largely on the individual action of its members, it is imperative that they make clear the alternatives for the Christian individual. It must be recognized that legitimate political activity is not limited to voting and holding office, but includes participation in party politics, pressure groups, nonpartisan committees indorsing specific policies (such as mental health) and candidates, and holding civil service positions. They must urge their members to participate in politics wherever the opportunity best presents itself. Churches must discourage aloofness and indecision and must emphasize that the political process—comprising discussion, conflict and compromise—is a station in which the Christian can serve God. They must make clear the alternatives for political action that have been described earlier—political independence and partisan politics—and show the advantages and disadvantages of each.

The churches can participate directly as organized groups in formulating public policy through a process of discussion of

social issues and publication of the church's stand on those issues. This means that the churches must continually examine and study what is happening in the world, discuss politics in the light of God's Word and under the guidance of the Holy Spirit. They must formulate policy statements which call attention to injustices and totalitarian tendencies in the government and signify their approval of those which take a stand in favor of specific proposals that appear to be the best solution to the problems at hand.

There are three types of legislation in which the churches might choose to show interest: that directly affecting the churches and their activities (such as social security for the clergy); that affecting unrepresented or dispossessed minority groups (such as bills protecting migrant workers); and that affecting the general welfare of the country (such as tax policy and Hoover Commission reforms).

The churches would have to decide to what lengths they wanted to carry this type of activity. There are three stages, each successively involving the church more deeply in the process of policy formulation. First, the churches could formulate policy statements through discussion and vote, disseminating the conclusions among church members (including those in public office) only—and depend on these individuals to take a stand for them in their political stations.

Second, the churches could formulate policy statements and publicize them as widely as possible throughout the community and nation. It would be necessary to explain that the statements represent the conclusions of those attending the meeting and not the entire constituency; they would be expected to publish minority dissenting views when such exist; it would be imperative to indicate that the statement is an appeal from conscience to conscience and that its persuasive power lies not in the numbers sponsoring it but in the fact that it is the result of discussion based on the Christian faith in God's rule; they would have to emphasize that the corporate statement has more weight as an appeal to conscience than when individuals speak for themselves, because it represents convictions disciplined by discussion and exposed to the analysis of a whole group of Christians rather than just the private, undisciplined views of an individual. Failure to clarify these points would lead either to resenting the church's action as an attempt to indulge in political pressure, or to ignoring its proposals as inconsequential.

The churches could, thirdly, formulate policy statements through discussion and then, through lobbying, bring these statements directly into the legislative process by arranging for men to be employed by the church to make personal contacts for this purpose—and, while doing so, make it clear that no political pressure is being applied in the form of a threat to organize votes against the legislator or for bills in question, but rather that the appeal is from conscience to conscience with due respect to the power of reason. There are several ways of making these direct contacts with policy-makers: help draft party platforms, make friendly contacts with members of the government, draft legislation, furnish pertinent information to legislators by appearance at hearings and in personal conferences, work with administrators by providing them with information of assistance to them, and explain the views of the church on various government programs in progress.

If the churches are going to lobby effectively, they will need to organize special commissions or committees to study and interpret public affairs, prepare reports and proposals for the consideration of the churches and keep the constituency informed on public matters. While the churches could do this as individual congregations and denominations, they would gain in effectiveness by working together. Lobbying and study commissions are projects which require full-time legislative representatives and the financial support necessary for carrying on the work. Pooling their resources will not only increase the funds for the program but will help to unify the voice of the churches on public policy.

The churches could directly participate in the manipulation of political power—either as pressure groups lining up votes of approval or disapproval of candidates and programs, or as a political party aspiring to capture control of the government.

The churches have occasionally operated as pressure groups. Their pressure tactics are most outstandingly exemplified by the manner in which they operated through the Anti-Saloon League, which worked for the passage of the amendment on prohibition. Whenever a church group implies that it will marshall so many votes for or against a candidate or program, it is operating as a pressure group. Even letter-writing campaigns, organized by churches for informing church members of the voting record of legislators and exposing the political manipulation of specific administrators, are forms of political pressure. When a Swedish Lutheran pastor in Rockford, Illinois, collected all the men in his congregation and marched them down to the polls to vote for Abraham Lincoln in the election of 1864, he was using political pressure. This type of activity goes beyond moral persuasion to the extent of actually using the political power inherent in votes either for the purpose of perpetuating the party in power or overthrowing it by the revolution of the ballot.

The strategy of forming a Christian party is common in the multiple-party democracies on the continent of Europe, but it is hardly a feasible alternative in the American two-party system. Even if a third party would arise, it would not originate as a "pure" party but would come into existence because one of the two major parties had ceased to offer any worthwhile policy alternatives to the American people. It is unlikely that a Christian party could take shape here because of the deep conviction that church and state should be separate. To most Americans, this means not only that state support should not be given any religion but that the church should not become the government of the country.

Defense of the Church's Participation in Policy Formulation

Before we can present a convincing case for any of these four alternatives, it is necessary to understand the nature of the church and its mission in the world. One of the fatal defects in Protestantism is to regard the church as an encumbering addition to personal religion and to separate Christianity from the church. This has led to grievous errors in considering the church and its role in the world.

It must be remembered that the work of the Holy Spirit is to create the Church. Christianity is inseparable from the Church, for Christian faith is nurtured in the fellowship of Christians who are "called, gathered, enlightened and sanctified by the Holy Spirit." While it is true that not all church members are Christians, it is also true that all Christians are members of the Church, even though they are temporarily not registered in a congregation.

The New Testament has ample evidence to support the conclusion that the Gospel creates a fellowship, a corporate body of believers who are mutually dependent upon one another, each being endowed with different gifts to contribute to the common good of all. This "fellowship of the Holy Spirit" is most lucidly described in I Corinthians 12: "Now there are varieties of gifts, but the same Spirit; and there are varieties of service, but the same Lord; and there are varieties of working, but it is the same God who inspires them all in everyone. To each is given the manifestation of the Spirit for the common good . . . For just as the body is one and has many members, and all the members of the body, though many, are one body, so it is with Christ . . . Now you are the body of Christ and individually members of it." (Revised Standard Version)

The first significant statement to be made about the Church, then, is that it is not an optional aspect of Christianity. While it is true that there can be ecclesiastical organizations and fellowships that are not fully Christian, it is not possible to think of genuine Christianity apart from fellowship—and this means a church.

The Church is not merely an invisible, formless spiritual communion. Because it has a mission assigned to it by Christ, it takes on an institutional aspect. Its members have various gifts and functions in the Holy Spirit—teaching, preaching, prophesying, administering, giving to the poor, etc. (See Romans 12:3 ff.) Thus the Church becomes visible as an enlightened institution organized for effective witnessing in the world, and it grows and flourishes wherever the Word is preached and the Sacraments are administered.

The Church is the custodian of the Law and the Gospel. It is duty-bound to teach and preach the Law, clarify its content (justice or mutual helpfulness) and apply it to specific situations of human life. This it must do by word and action. Not only its preachers must proclaim justice, but each member must affirm that cardinal virtue by his own actions. The Church must also proclaim the Gospel, informing the world what God in Christ has done for humanity and urging that all men demonstrate His grace by loving their neighbor as Christ loves them. By preaching the Gospel of God's redeeming grace, the Church persuades individuals to regard their vocations as stations of service, to believe that Christ's death for them frees them from having to strive for their own salvation and sets them at liberty to serve their neighbor.

It is necessary to concentrate attention on the actually-existing churches when discussing the role of the Church in American politics. People know the Church only as they see it in operation and by participating in its activities. The Church in this country is not co-terminous with the community. All of the denominations operate within a free-church framework, and its congregations are composed of members who are more or less committed personally to Christ. Religious freedom has stimulated the separatistic tendencies within Protestantism; and, as a consequence, division and diversity are outstanding characteristics of church life. This has created a complex institutional pattern and has obscured the fellowship-creating character of Christianity.

The division of the American Church has weakened its witness within the nation, since it cannot speak with one voice about public issues. This witness has been further hampered by the churches' preoccupation with their own survival. Being free churches, without government support, they must raise their own funds and often become so engrossed with financial matters that their members have no time or energy for anything else. A third factor has weakened the churches' ability to witness in American society—the divisions **within** the denominations over the problem concerning the Church's relationship to the culture in which it exists. Within every denomination are groups which adopt the strategy of withdrawal from community affairs because they stress the cultivation of personal piety and the mission of the Church. There are others who are ready to accommodate the Church and its message to fit the culture, in order to be "successful" and "popular" and "respectable." The tension between these two parties occasionally becomes so great that new divisions occur. Only the existence of a large center party, which tries to relate the Church to society and Christianity to culture without destroying the tension between them, prevents a more divided Church. Efforts to bring the churches into fellowship with one another have been numerous during the past few decades, but they have succeeded more in organizational matters and cooperating on action programs than in resolving a theological basis for unity.

It is not easy to find a point of agreement on the role the churches should perform in politics, when the divisions and their causes are considered. Most of the alternative roles, described earlier, have been adopted by church groups. Perhaps this indicates that all of them are genuine alternatives. Therefore, to claim that any single one is the only legitimate Christian approach to the political situation would be arbitrary. This conclusion does not rule out the possibility of choosing one that would **normally** be followed by the churches. Let us therefore study each of the alternatives and advance arguments for and against them.

1. The churches can ignore politics. This is the strategy of withdrawal from culture, society and the world. It may be conceded that there are times when the situation is so odious that the churches must counsel retreat and adopt a policy of non-cooperation and protest. However, when the church withdraws from the political life and urges its members to take similar action, it will have to share the blame for allowing the situation to deteriorate. As long as there is a possibility of improving the situation, the churches should be whole-hearted-

ly active in the thick of it. On what grounds is such a conclusion reached?

First, the state is an order of creation, designed by God to regulate human life, to curb wrong and encourage the right. Government has a positive validity and is deserving of the respect and support of Christians. Second, the Christian's vocation is not fulfilled in keeping himself pure by withdrawing from sinful society, but in serving his neighbor in every way practicable. He is saved by faith and therefore is free to love his neighbor. Politics is a sphere in which he can organize his efforts, in cooperation with others, to serve his neighbor effectively. The strategy of withdrawal cannot be accepted as the normal pattern of the churches' relation to political life; it should be adopted only under extreme circumstances. In any case, complete withdrawal is not possible. Even pacifists pay taxes, and the most extreme anarchists benefit from the government to some extent.

2. The churches can inspire their individual members to participate in politics but have no direct role as organizations. This strategy accepts government as a divine order and politics as a vocation in which Christians can serve. Yet, it would not involve churches in committing themselves to support parties or policies. Thus its sponsorship does not give the dangerous impression that specific political policies or groups are completely right and just.

The chief objection to this strategy is that it fails to consider that the Christian is a member of a fellowship and therefore his witness in the world is not an individual and private one. There is no such thing as a private Christian conscience, free to make its decisions independently of the other members. This is a line of reasoning that leaves the individual church member too free to reflect the bias of the social or economic group to which he belongs whenever he acts or speaks outside the fellowship of the church. Further elucidation of this point will be made in defense of the third role.

3. The churches can participate as corporate bodies in the formation of public policy. This involves continual study of the political problems, discussion in the church of issues confront-

ing the citizens of the community, formulation of proposals for the best solutions possible, and taking a resolute stand on the proposals. In addition to inspiring individual Christians to be active in politics, Christian political instruction would be stressed.

This policy is based upon a complete acceptance of the definition of the Christian belief in the fellowship of the Holy Spirit, as it is applied to political life. Being a Christian means more than having a personal relationship with Christ. It also comprises membership in the Church, the fellowship of the Holy Spirit. A Christian's political convictions should be formulated as a result of his fellowship in the church, not just as a result of his private meditations. Each member has the social responsibility to contribute his ideas and proposals to the group—even as he has a Christian responsibility to be hospitable, sympathetic or generous. The Holy Spirit gives each individual his unique gifts for the common good, and among those gifts are insights into practical political problems that are a result of meditating on the Word of God and observing the social situation. However, his own opinions are not the only opinions, not any more than any of his talents are the only talents. Therefore, each Christian must be willing to submit his conclusion to the analysis of others, and to listen to and comment on the views of others. As all members submit to this discipline of discussion, the enlightenment of the Holy Spirit becomes a reality. The result is that the policy conclusions of the group will be sounder, and more representative, than the convictions of an individual. Each member goes forth armed not with his private convictions—but with the conclusions of the whole church.

The Church is in a very advantageous position to arrive at fair and just policies, because its membership is composed of people from all social, economic and political groups. No matter how devoted to Christ a labor union leader might be, his personal political views will be biased by his status within his own economic group; the same will be true of the farmer, the clergyman and the business man. In the Church these people from the various interest groups face one another, listen to one another with at least a measure of humility, and are certain to hear opinions that will counteract their bias. If they submit to the discipline of discussion under the guidance of the Holy Spirit, and it is a big "if," their views will be modified in the direction of the justice which God's Word commands; and they will become authentic representatives of Christ's Church within their economic and political organizations.

Just how extensively these conclusions should be publicized is a matter that must be decided in each situation—a matter of practical expediency. Sometimes it might be well to inform only the members of the churches involved in the discussion; sometimes it would be best to release the statements to newspapers and other media of public communication; often it might be most effective to make personal contacts with public officials and lawmakers. The basic feature of this strategy is not concerned with how the policies should be broadcast, but with emphasizing the fact that they are policies formulated by the fellowship of Christians, not just privately conceived.

In using this approach, it would be dangerous for the churches to forget that all policies are relatively fair—but that they may not be permanent solutions. The churches' proposals are not perfect, just because they are formulated by the churches. There is always the danger of absolutizing a policy and defending it when it is no longer valid—and the danger of blessing the status quo. The churches must always study the situation and be willing to change their positions as new situations develop. Another danger, especially if the churches use lobbying methods, is the temptation to employ pressures of various kinds to bend politicians to their will. The line between moral persuasion and political coercion is mighty thin in a democracy. It is very easy to shift into the latter if the churches are involved in the former.

4. Churches could participate directly in the manipulation of political power. Despite the fact that churches have indulged in at least some forms of pressure politics, there can be no sound defense of such actions unless one accepts the idea of a theocracy, government in the hands of or under the di-

rection of churchmen. Right-wing Puritanism and medieval Catholicism are two of the types of Christianity that have advocated and practiced theocracy. It is not defensible in the United States; because the free church idea and the principle of separation of church and state are too deeply intrenched.

The most serious objection to this strategy is founded on the fact that it has no basis in the nature and function of the Church. The Church is a fellowship, not a force; it has been entrusted with the Word, not the Sword; its methods should be persuasion and appeals to the conscience, not threats and penalties. While its members individually may take up the sword, assume the roles of judge, legislator and policeman, the Church as an organized group should not act in such capacities. In fact, the State must not allow the Church or any other group to use coercion and punishment to force acceptance of its ideas, or to prevent dissenters from worshipping or meeting together and propagating their ideas. One of the duties of the State must be that of preserving full religious liberty, including the freedom to arrive at conclusions and hold convictions. The State must prevent the Church from assuming the demonic roles of inquisitor and tyrant of men's consciences.

In conclusion, there are two aspects of democratic government which present a requirement that the churches can fulfill if they choose to assume an active role in producing conscientious citizens and formulating policy proposals by corporate discussion and decision.

In a booklet published by the Citizenship Clearing House, **Preparing College Men and Women for Politics,** a significant statement is found:

"... the demos cannot make up its mind in the same way as an individual but can only say 'yes' or 'no' to suggestions made to it by individuals. Not even the smallest and most homogeneous group can join hands and wait with any anticipation of success for an idea to emanate from their joint consciousness. This does not mean that a group through the interchange of ideas may not arrive at conclusions which no one had in mind at the beginning of the discussion. But to get action someone must say, 'Let's do this,' and somebody else say, 'Let's do that,' and the chairman, 'Those in favor of this say aye,' and so on, to a decision. This basic fact has important implications for the responsibility of leadership, **for the quality of democratic action depends largely on the quality of the suggestions made to it."** (Bold faced supplied.) (Note: Thomas H. and Doris D. Reed, **Preparing College Men and Women for Politics,** Citizenship Clearing House, New York, 1952, p. 2)

People make the suggestions. Government by the democratic process requires people with sensitive consciences and the ability to consider and discuss public questions. In a democracy, decisions are resolved by a process of discussion in which every individual has the freedom to express his convictions. By nurturing spiritually sensitive and responsible citizens, the Church contributes valuable people to the State—people who are equipped to make suggestions of a high quality during the discussion. As Bishop Berggrav has observed, Christians should be people informed by an awareness of justice and bolstered by a readiness to back up their convictions with suffering and sacrifice. The churches that inspire their members to take part in politics make a real contribution to the survival of democracy.

James Nichols has called attention to another basic feature of democracy defined by Principal Lindsay. Nichols writes: "Liberal democracy does not merely mean counting noses or establishing the strongest pressure group, even with due protection of minorities. Democracy means entering into discussion, the submission of diverse views to mutual criticism, with the intention of discovering something new." He further observed that genuine popular discussion of policy, through political parties, has not succeeded where the spiritual roots and presuppositions of democracy were not present. (Note: Nichols, James, **Democracy and the Churches,** Philadelphia, Westminster, 1951, p. 34)

A vital democratic process is dependent upon the willingness of the people to listen to one another and to advance by discussion toward new objectives. This kind of willingness is nurtured in churches where the fellowship of the Holy Spirit is taken seriously, where no man thinks he has a monopoly on wisdom or truth, and in which all members are willing to submit their views to criticism, as well as to contribute their ideas and opinions to the group. The Church can make a real contribution to the strengthening of democracy by encouraging respect for discussion and debate involving all individuals in the group. It will keep this procedure alive if it practices the method itself, not only in discussing its own affairs but in exercising concern about public issues of momentous importance to everyone.

CHAPTER ONE

Subject for Spotlight

On the platform of a Duluth auditorium stood a man who looked as though he could send a person flying across the room with one blow of his fist, or fell an acre of trees in a day. Standing over six feet in height and carrying his 200 pounds in a trim, well-groomed figure, he was vitally alive as he unfolded his ideas to a large group of people. Frequent and forceful gestures punctuated his speech. His ruddy face, framed by graying hair, was lit by the enthusiasm which inspired him as he discussed Minnesota's youth conservation program designed to prevent boys and girls from getting into trouble and to give delinquents a sympathetic chance for readjustment.

In the audience were a little boy of eight and his father. The little boy was impressed by the big man. "Who is that?" he whispered to his father.

"That man is Luther Youngdahl. He is the Governor of Minnesota."

"What is a governor?" the little boy persisted as little boys do.

"A governor is one who rules — like a king, like King Arthur. Do you remember the story we read the other night?"

The little boy nodded and listened with deepened interest as the Governor finished his speech. "A farmer was shown a gnarled and twisted tree and was asked for his opinion as to the cause for its distortion. His answer was, 'Someone must have stepped on it when it was young.'

"In Minnesota we place prime value on our boys and girls. We are determined that they shall not be stepped upon by an unthinking and unfeeling society. The operation of our Youth Conservation Act insures that we handle the lives of our youth as human personalities and not as de-personalized problem cases. The soul of the most reprobate child is fully worthy of salvation." The Governor sat down and then stood to acknowledge the sustained applause with a wave of his hand and a big grin on his face.

After the speech was over the father asked the boy if he would like to meet the Governor. The boy assented eagerly. While they were waiting their turn to greet him, the father briefed his son on proper procedure. "When he speaks to you, you must shake his hand and say, 'How do you do, your Honor.'" The boy nodded, and there was a rapt look on his face.

When he reached the Governor, he put his small hand in the Governor's big one as Youngdahl stooped down to talk to him.

He managed his line with a touch of awe in his voice, "How do you do, your Majesty."

Youngdahl laughed heartily. "Thank you, young man. That's quite an honor."

Luther Youngdahl, chosen three times by Minnesota's voters as the governor of their state, was not oblivious to the personal honors he had achieved as chief executive. He was proud of his record as a vote-getter, for he had often topped the entire ticket in an election. He enjoyed the experience of attracting the limelight by dramatic moves in the field of politics. His competitiveness was strong enough in him to give him a sense of satisfaction when he triumphed in a campaign or a controversy. However, to him being a governor was not just a personal honor but a serious responsibility. There was something majestic about the office. Government was not a thing to be taken lightly.

A Man with Reforms on His Mind

There were jobs to be done for human welfare — such as conserving the youth and curing the mentally-ill.

On October 31, 1949, a huge bonfire burned fiercely on the grounds of the Anoka State Hospital. Lighting bonfires, as pranksters are still caught doing, is an old Hallowe'en custom that originated when our pagan European ancestors followed similar procedures in the autumn, to keep evil spirits at a safe distance. After Christian missionaries came, the fires were lit on the eve of All Saints' Day to guide souls through Purgatory to Paradise.

The fire on the hospital grounds was not the prank of boys who saw no more meaning in it than a chance to harass the authorities. If anything, it was more closely related to the ancient act of driving away evil spirits. With a keen sense of the dramatic, Governor Youngdahl and the hospital authorities had planned it as an act to symbolize the end of the use of mechanical restraints on mental patients in Minnesota hospitals. The fire consisted of 359 strait-jackets, 196 cuffs, 81 straps and 25 canvas mittens. As he touched a match to the pile of discarded restraints, Youngdahl was fully aware that he was dramatizing the beginning of a new program for the mentally-ill that stressed rehabilitation. Before he lit the fire he spoke, "By this action we say more than that we have liberated the patients from barbarous devices and the approach which these devices symbolized. By this action we say that we have liberated ourselves from witchcraft — that in taking off mechanical restraints from the patients, we are taking off the intellectual restraints from ourselves."

The bonfire climaxed the Governor's two-year crusade to reform the state's mental hospitals. He had placed Minnesota among the first states to respond to the outcry against conditions in mental hospitals exposed by such books as **The Snake Pit,** which had been published in 1946.

This was not the first time Youngdahl had stirred Minnesotans since his inauguration as Governor on January 9, 1947. In the spring of 1947 he riled the still waters of a comfortablyintrenched Republican regime with a hard-hitting campaign to enforce the state's laws against slot machines and other gambling devices and the laws regulating the sale of liquor. There were laws on the books, but it was profitable to the tune of several millions yearly to ignore them. Youngdahl was making an issue of law enforcement almost four years before the televised hearings of the Kefauver committee on corruption in government dramatized it and aroused public ire against gambling syndicates. In doing so he stirred up one of the most violent controversies Minnesota has seen and placed himself squarely in the center of the spotlight.

But He Was No "Bluenose"

His law enforcement program earned him the label, "bluenose" — a puritan trying to reform the morals of the state according to his own strict religious beliefs. This charge irritated him. One day in 1949 he was addressing a gathering of the leaders of the Minnesota Council of Churches. He had been a guest at a dinner of the Twin Cities Newspaper Guild shortly before, and he told the churchmen about listening to someone sing a ballad of twelve verses picturing him as a "blue-nose." "Let them call me that, if it satisfies them; but it will not stop me from continuing to apply Christian principles in politics," he told the audience.

On another occasion at a reception Youngdahl came upon two of his friends drinking cocktails.

"Hide your drink. It's the governor!" one of the ladies said to the other in a half-joking way. If the remark was designed to get a rise out of the governor, it did as planned.

"No, listen here! I'm free to drink coffee, and I don't want people to meddle with your freedom to drink cocktails. But nobody is free to break the laws. I think I have heard that it is my job to enforce the laws of this state. That will keep me busy enough. Don't even think that my intentions go beyond that!"

The labels, "blue-nose" or "pietist" irked him, because he did not think of himself as a puritan who thought that enjoying life was a sin. He didn't smoke or drink cocktails or beer, but he had an un-ascetic capacity for drinking coffee. He preferred the whir of a fishing reel after a bass struck to the staccato slap of cards being shuffled at a poker game. But his preference for the outdoor life and coffee did not grow out of a belief that people who preferred the other were worse sinners than he.

There was nothing of the pale-faced, pinched-cheek look about him. A rugged, athletic man, he had an extravagant passion for physical fitness. He loved to outdo his friends in feats of physical prowess — revelling in a fast game of volleyball during the noon-hour at the Minneapolis Athletic Club, challenging newsmen **at a banquet** to do more sit-ups than he and then doing fifty of them himself on the cleared table before them all. Herbert Nelson, one of his friends who frequently went with Youngdahl on fishing excursions, learned to expect a wrestling match sometime during every trip. Youngdahl would not be satisfied until he had bested him — even if tables and chairs in their lodge were upended in the struggle.

He had been raised by strict Swedish Lutheran parents who frowned on worldly amusements, including sports. While he shared their Christian faith, he did not hold to all their views. They were stubbornly opposed to sports on grounds of principle, but Luther tried out for the South High (Minneapolis) football team and made it as its center. His triumph was brief. On the day before the first game his mother caught him taking a towel for a shower and soon found out he was playing football. He may have made holes in the opposing line on the football field, but he could not budge his parents an inch. He had to give up his coveted position. The parents fought a losing battle, however. There was too much of the competitive spirit in their children. Luther played football in college, and Reuben became a star basketball center. By the time that Reuben, the youngest son, was in college, the parents had become ardent, front-row fans.

His college frat brothers describe him and his brother Ben as "the Ukulele Kids," who used to serenade crowds gathered on the shores of Minneapolis' Lake Calhoun for a breath of air on a warm summer evening. They knew every hit tune, but some of their teachers wondered occasionally if they knew anything else and despaired of their accomplishing anything serious in the world.

His close associates, among them Ray Ewald and A. Herbert Nelson of Minneapolis, talk about his big laugh and his inclination for practical jokes. Once on a fishing trip he put some dead minnows under the sweat band of Nelson's hat. The weather was hot and the stench highly disturbing until Nelson discovered what caused it. It was characteristic of his pranks — nothing elaborate but effectively disconcerting.

He could not repress his delight in a joke even when giving serious speeches. His sermon, "Do Christianity and Politics Mix?" which he gave at the Chicago Sunday Evening Club is liberally sprinkled with humorous anecdotes. When speaking to college audiences he liked to tell them the story of a girl who got her pastor's advice about dating. The pastor told her that if her boy friend held her hand or put his hands on her shoulders, that was all right; but if he put his head on her shoulder she should stop him. "I would worry about that," the pastor concluded. After the date the pastor asked her how it went. She said, "He held my hand for a while and then — then I put my head on his shoulder and let **his** pastor do the worrying." He relished his stories and often repeated them.

If there were any who still wondered if he were a stuffy prude, they were usually disarmed when they heard Youngdahl lead a banquet crowd in the singing of one of the hits popular when he was a student — "Pull Your Shades Down, Marianne (if you want to keep your secrets from your future man . . .)."

Youngdahl's motivation for the law enforcement program has to be found in something other than a desire to cramp the style of fun-loving Minnesotans.

The Governor's Christian Faith

Did it grow out of basic Christian beliefs? There were those who believed that his law enforcement crusade and other aspects of his political program were the product of his Christianity. Frequently he was the featured speaker at church gatherings where he often elaborated on the subject of Christianity and politics.

Was it merely a shrewd awareness of the type of audience he had before him that moved him to express himself so adequately in the Cathedral of St. John's the Divine on November 2, 1947? He spoke that night at a Reformation service sponsored by the Protestants of New York City, his words echoing in the vast reaches of the unfinished cathedral as the large congregation listened to him say:

"Four hundred and thirty years ago Martin Luther erected three pillars which supported the partially destroyed structure of the organized church. He called for these three: the supremacy of the Bible, the supremacy of faith and the supremacy of the people. . . .

"I especially call your attention to the third pillar which Luther set up. It was known as the supremacy of the people and the priesthood of all believers. Luther advanced the proposition that Christian laymen have spiritual faculties and powers of the same sort as the clergy. He believed that they may feel, in all natural relationships, a spiritual dignity like that of the priest. He declared that it is not only at the altar and in the cloister that the work of God is done. He said it is also accomplished in honest toil, in the affairs of government, and in the institution of marriage and the home. . . .

"We must again stress that the Christian vocation encompasses all phases of living. We need to appreciate the Reformation tradition that we are personally responsible for the political conduct of our democracy. We must shoulder our obligations in keeping with our belief in the supremacy of the people. The Christian cannot keep his religion in a closed compartment if he is to keep faith with the teachings of Luther, Calvin and Zwingli."

He went on to assert that government is the machinery by which society makes its moral decisions and that people get just as good government as they are willing to work for.

From one to five years before President Eisenhower's emphasis upon religion had the whole nation talking, Youngdahl was making statements of this type. America's "new piety" had not yet taken a firm hold. Hollywood was not yet thoroughly convinced that religious themes could be turned into multi-million dollar extravaganzas. Articles on religion were just beginning to be seen in slick magazines. Novels about preachers and books on peace of mind were not firmly entrenched on best seller lists. Religion was not yet in style.

Center of Controversy

Youngdahl's record for gaining the spotlight by taking a controversial stand did not stop after he resigned from the governorship in July, 1951, to accept a Federal judgeship in the District of Columbia. National attention again swung in his direction on May 2, 1953. On that day he stepped into the District Court in Washington, D. C., and threw out the key charges of the government's indictment against Owen Lattimore, Far Eastern expert at Johns Hopkins University, whom Senator Joseph McCarthy had accused of being "the top Soviet espionage agent in America." Youngdahl's decision came less than five months after the new Republican administration had moved into Washington. The junior senator from Wisconsin was riding hard on his relentless hunt to rid the government of Red sympathizers, and the public still seemed to be with him. The televised "Army vs. McCarthy" hearings and the censure of the Wisconsin senator by the upper chamber were still two years in the future.

This man gives the impression that he thrives on controversy. He pulled no punches. His speech was blunt when he had a scrap on his hands — as it turned out at Little Falls during one of the campaigns. The Republican county organization had arranged an informal coffee party for the governor, and it turned into a gripe-session. The party members were disgruntled, because Youngdahl would not commit himself on patronage, special requests and favors desired by party workers. They told him so. Youngdahl wasted no time equivocating or apologizing. "I'm going to consider the needs of the people rather than those of political pros," he told them. This display of independence in the sphere of party politics often angered veteran party politicians, but the "independents" relished it and supported him in large numbers.

Sometimes his straight-talking was too tactless, as when he told a reporter something that no reporter likes to hear. "You just haven't got the facts straight, mister." On other occasions its bluntness was effective, as it was when a man of means asked Youngdahl to fix it so that a road could be built into his place in Northern Minnesota. Youngdahl told him, "No one else lives on that road. I would be giving you special consideration, and I can't do that. I have to consider all the people. Vote for me if you think I am right. Don't vote for me if you think I'm wrong." The man voted for him.

Yet underneath he was a sensitive person who longed for approval enough to fondly cherish the words of a boy of twelve who once rode in the governor's car during a parade as a representative of the school police.

As they rode along the boy suddenly asked, "Are you ever lonesome, Governor?" Here they were with crowds along the sidewalk and the governor in the spotlight, yet he seemed to have sensed that being governor had its moments of isolation.

"Indeed I am, boy. Many times."

The boy turned and looked straight into the governor's eyes and gave a solemn vow. "You don't ever have to feel that way again. I'll always be with you."

This is Luther Youngdahl — a man not cut to the cloth of any stereotype of a politician common to the American imagination, a man who claimed to apply Christian principles in politics, a man who was successful enough to be elected three times to the governorship of Minnesota, a man who had a habit of getting into troublesome spots and then out again with a facility for accomplishment while doing so.

What kind of a Christian faith did he bring with him into politics, and where did he get it? What strategy did he use to gain his ends successfully?

There's a story here, so let's get on with it.

Early Youngdahl family picture

Youngdahl children in later years

Gov. and Mrs. Youngdahl
visit their Alma Mater.

Gov. Youngdahl demon-
strates the technique he
used back in 1919 in pro-
posing to Mrs. Youngdahl

CHAPTER TWO

Son and Brother

"Let's see how fast we can get to the landing." Tired of sitting still while his older brothers rowed, Ben wanted some action.

Away they went, the waters of Lake Independence churning behind them. "Stroke! Stroke!" Ben commanded faster and faster. Suddenly Luther's oar slipped its lock, he lost his balance and fell into the lake. By the time Ben and Oscar got the boat around, Luther was in serious trouble. He couldn't swim. Oscar shouted for help.

A boat that had been anchored a short distance away had already started toward them. One of the men pulled the gasping, frightened boy out of the water just as he was going down for the third time.

Much subdued, the boys rowed carefully to their landing. When they got to the cottage, they had gained enough composure to explain Luther's soaked condition to their mother. "Oh, he just fell in near the landing."

That evening after fishing was over, there was a knock at the door. It was the man who had rescued Luther. He was a Canadian vacationing on the small lake, located about thirty miles west of Minneapolis. After learning that Luther was all right, he told what had happened. "It's funny," he said. "I had intended to go home yesterday, but on an impulse I decided to try one more day of fishing. Now I know why I felt I should stay over today, too."

What he could not have known, back there in 1910, is that he had saved a future governor of Minnesota from drowning.

This near-tragedy occurred during one of the many summers that the Youngdahl family spent at their summer place, located on two islands on Lake Independence near Maple Plain. Every June, after school was dismissed, the family loaded the buggy and made the trek out to the lake, where they lived all summer. John and Elizabeth Youngdahl believed in the outdoor life for their ten children, and the summer months at the lake were happy times of swimming on their island beach, fishing for crappies and picking berries. One of the islands was a fruit farm with apple trees and strawberry and raspberry patches. Mother Youngdahl, with the help of her children and a hired man named Ole, saw to it that the berries and fruit were picked and shipped off to the family's grocery store, the Washington School Grocery at 603 Eighth Avenue South in Minneapolis. While his family was at the lake, John Youngdahl kept the store going. He always came out to the lake on Saturday night to spend Sunday with them.

Father Seeks Opportunities and Rears a Large Family

Having ten children to support, John Youngdahl found that owning a grocery store helped him to keep the pantry filled. Like many another young Swedish immigrant, he had come to the United States seeking home and career opportunities that were highly superior to those offered in Sweden at that time. Born in Malmo, in the province of Skane, April 4, 1860, he came to America in 1886, at the age of twenty-six. After a brief stint as a commercial fisherman on Lake Superior, he moved to Chippewa Falls, Wisconsin. He worked there for a short time and then moved to Minneapolis. He tried his hand at several jobs. Finally, when he had managed to save $200, he opened a grocery store which was to be his business for forty years. Soon after moving to Minneapolis his wife died, leaving him with the care of two small boys, Peter and Carl.

While living in Chippewa Falls, Wisconsin, he had met Elizabeth Johnson, a widow with two daughters, Mable and Nora. Strangers in town, the Youngdahls had not known whom to have as the sponsors for Carl at his baptism. The Lutheran pastor had recommended Mrs. Johnson. This brief and rather casual contact was renewed after the Youngdahls had moved to Minneapolis. She wrote a letter to them asking for assistance. Her daughter, Nora, was in need of expert medical care, and Mrs. Johnson wanted their assistance in choosing a good doctor in the city. Unknown to her, John Youngdahl had become a widower, but he took time to help her locate a doctor. Her coming to Minneapolis on this errand resulted in the renewal of their friendship and soon they were married. Whether it had occurred to them or not, and it probably had, it was fitting and proper that little Carl's godmother should become his step-mother. The Lutheran baptismal services lays upon the sponsors the responsibility of caring for the child in the event of the death of the parents. Thus John and Elizabeth Youngdahl began their married life with a family of four children — Carl and Peter from John Youngdahl's previous marriage and Mable and Nora from his wife's.

It was into this combined family that Luther was born on May 29, 1896. In addition to himself, five more children filled the ranks of the family — Oscar (who preceded Luther), Benjamin, Myrtle, Ruth and Reuben.

There were times when arguments and competition for the attention and affection of the parents threatened to disrupt the family. A story used to circulate around Minneapolis that John Youngdahl looked out upon a group of fighting youngsters one day and said to his wife, "That looks like your children and my children fighting our children!" Often the boys' arguments were settled in customary American-boy style — by fists and wrestling. The family record is held by Luther and Ben, who had about fifty fights.

As the children grew older, there were frequent and vigorous discussions with scarcely any unanimity of opinion. The parents not only allowed freedom of discussion but encouraged it. In fact, they participated in the arguments as vigorously as their children.

One Sunday Ben invited one of his college friends home for dinner after they had attended services at Messiah Lutheran Church. The conversation turned to the question of which forms of fun were proper for Christians. The parents, especially Mrs. Youngdahl, had strong opinions on the subject. "Worldly" amusements like shows and dancing were absolutely forbidden. Girls should not wear lipstick. Men should never drink. Soon she was arguing as vigorously as anyone else. When the discussion shifted to the question of whether football should be allowed at the college the boys attended, the debate became heated. Ben's friend was amazed as he watched several members talking at once with arms waving and voices rising. Suddenly Mrs. Youngdahl, feeling that things were getting out of hand, called the discussion to a halt.

"Quiet! Everyone — keep still now! It is time now that we pray." With no apparent difficulty in transition the whole family joined reverently in the prayer as the meal came to an end.

"You mustn't think we are a quarrelling family," Ben explained to his friend later. "We just love to argue." The Youngdahl children still claim that a good, vigorous discussion is one of their favorite sports. When they gathered for family reunions, there was always an argument about something — sometimes just for the pleasure of a stimulating debate.

When the discussion turned to politics, sharp differences of opinion became apparent. Oscar, who was a Congressman from Minnesota's Fifth District until defeated by Dr. Walter H. Judd, was a conservative Republican. He was one of the few men in Congress who remained a thorough isolationist at the outbreak of World War II. On the other extreme was Ben, a passionate New Dealer and internationalist, with a great admiration for Franklin D. Roosevelt. He also was appointed by Floyd B. Olson to a high administrative position in the Farmer-Labor party's relief program. In between was Luther, sometimes accused by his brothers in the heat of a family debate of being a fence-straddler but in reality a Re-

publican whose liberalism made him scarcely distinguishable
from a New Dealer. The sisters often jumped into the argument on the side of the one who seemed to be "taking a
licking."

Basic Family Unity Produces Leaders

For all their arguments, there was a basic family unity.
They loved to sing together around the living room piano and
often forgot that they were half-brothers and half-sisters. The
children cherish the memory of their parents' fairness. "We
learned some basic principles of justice. Father had to rule
with a stern hand at times, but his discipline was tempered
with love," Luther has recalled. "Mother made a special effort
to treat each child as an individual and often leaned over back-
wards to be fair to the step-children."

To what extent this family situation stimulated the competitiveness and intense ambition to come out on top that
characterizes some of the children, including Luther, is hard
to determine. But it is true that several of them became outstanding leaders. Within one week, in 1950, articles about
Benjamin, Reuben and Luther appeared in three leading magazines. **Newsweek** carried a story on Reuben and his newly-
dedicated Mt. Olivet Lutheran Church in Minneapolis. Since
becoming its pastor in 1938 he had built a congregation of
over 7,000 baptized members and in addition found the time
for two radio programs a day, a weekly television appearance,
the writing of four books, and a full schedule of speaking
engagements outside his parish.

Time reported Benjamin's successful efforts to open the
George Warren Brown School of Social Work of Washington
University in St. Louis to Negro students. He became dean
of the school after a career of teaching, social work and government service that was climaxed by his appointment as the
director of displaced persons for the United Nations Recon-
struction and Relief Administration at the close of World
War II.

Collier's featured an article on Luther's program of social reform in Minnesota, which he had administered while being governor.

Others in the family have not been idle. Oscar became a lawyer and served in the United States House of Representatives for several terms. Peter became a successful lawyer in Los Angeles. Carl was for twenty-five years the Director of Music at Augustana College, at Sioux Falls, South Dakota. Ruth married the Rev. Clarence T. Nelson, pastor of the Augustana Lutheran Church in the nation's capital. In addition to her duties as a pastor's wife and a mother of four children she has a full schedule of speaking engagements all over the country, has authored a book, and recently served as the chairwoman of the Council of Church Women in Washington. Mable (Mrs. Alfred H. Anderson) has been active in civic and church affairs in Minnesota. Myrtle died at the age of eleven, and Nora was an artist before her death.

Religion, Education and Work

"Religion, education, and work" were stressed so emphatically by John and Elizabeth Youngdahl that those words became a family motto for the children.

Religion was the most important. Both parents were devout Lutherans. Like many other Swedish immigrants they had been deeply influenced by the evangelical revivals that swept over Sweden during the middle decades of the nineteenth century. These revivals, frequently led by laymen, stressed personal religious experience, prayer meetings and Bible study in the homes. They led to a real concern for one of Sweden's chief social problems, alcoholism, and the formation of temperance societies. When the Youngdahls established their home in Minneapolis they joined the First Augustana Lutheran Church, one of the congregations of the Swedish Lutheran Minnesota Conference of the Augustana Synod. This church body was founded in 1860 by immigrants, most of whom had, like the Youngdahls, been influenced by the revivals.

John Youngdahl was a staunch supporter of the Church. He gave it the first fruits of his labor and often participated vigorously in the business meetings of the congregation in support of projects that would further the work of the Church. It was not unusual for him to take charge of the Thursday evening prayer meetings in the absence of the pastor. He was an advocate for the use of English rather than Swedish in church and was one of the leaders of a group that left the First Augustana Church in Minneapolis to form the Messiah congregation where English was to be used.

Luther and his brothers and sisters got religion in large measures, sometimes too large, they felt when they were young.

One Sunday night, just as the family was about to have its devotions, someone came to the door. One of the boys went to answer.

"Dad, a couple of the boys want us to go skating tonight over at the park," he announced when he returned. "Please let us go — just this once."

"You know that there is church tonight. You will have to tell them you can't go."

"Ah, Dad," one of the other boys pleaded. "We have been to church three times already today." It was a regular routine for the family to attend English Sunday school, Swedish worship services and Swedish Sunday school. They were in church from 9:00 A.M. to 1:30 P.M. Despite their pleas, the parents did not yield, and the children were in church that night as usual. They did not always like this routine, but it succeeded in giving them a deeply rooted religious heritage.

There were moving and happy experiences at church, too — events, sounds and sights they never forgot. In those days the Sunday school picnic was one of the year's highlights. The entire Messiah congregation gathered at Spring Park. There was an outdoor service under the trees. Fidgety and eager, the children wondered if the preaching would ever end so they could get at the big picnic basket dinners their parents had brought. In the afternoon there were games for all — with prizes for the winners. Then ice cream cones were passed out to the children by the Sunday school superintendent and his helpers, sweating as they worked furiously to keep up with the demand.

The Youngdahl children are just as moved as any other family of Swedish background when they hear the stately strains of "Var halsad skona morgonstund" ("All hail to thee, O blessed morn"), the chorale that was invariably sung at "Julotta" services on Christmas morning by all Swedish Lutheran congregations. It brings back memories of getting up while it was still dark and walking to church in the crisp, cold Minnesota air, of the stars shining brightly in the sky above and of the sound of snow crunching under each step, of the church all lit up with candles and a huge Christmas tree, and of the subdued, festive air of a Lutheran Christmas service.

There were Christmas programs with Swedish "pieces" for each child; with parents craning their necks to see if their youngsters bowed properly to the pastor and congregation before reciting, and settling back with satisfaction if they recited loudly enough for all to hear; and at the end of the program there were boxes of hard candy and small Swedish story books as gifts from the teacher.

Luther's confirmation came when he was about fifteen. For an entire year he attended classes held by Pastor C. O. Lundquist every Saturday morning. He and his classmates were required to study the Lutheran catechism, memorize it and review it again. They reviewed Bible history, and for good measure the pastor exhorted them about the things of this world. He warned them of the dangers surrounding the dance hall, the gambling room, the saloon, the theatre and the latest device of the devil, the "movies." But most of all he impressed upon them the holiness of the Lord's Supper of which they would partake for the first time on their confirmation day. Before Communion they must examine themselves and confess their sins to God. If they were not properly prepared, they should not partake of the Sacrament.

The important day arrived. Luther was worried about whether he would remember the answer when Pastor Lundquist quizzed him on the catechism, and relieved when he answered his question on what is God without a miscue. He was excited about his new confirmation suit. But his deepest impression was the sacred feeling he had as he knelt for his first communion.

The Luther League at the Messiah Church was chief center of the Youngdahls' social life during their teens. Though religious in intention and program, the League meetings also gave the youngsters an outlet for their gregariousness. There were skating parties, sleigh-rides, ice cream socials and hay-rides as well as prayer meetings, song festivals and talks on religious matters. Luther was president of the group for several years. One year, under his leadership, the Leaguers worked to gather funds to buy lights for the church. When the time for presenting the lights approached, Luther suggested that they invite Lieutenant-Governor William Nolan to speak. When he accepted, the Leaguers exerted themselves to have a full church in attendance to celebrate the occasion.

Moral and Religious Code is Observed

John and Elizabth Youngdahl were not content to shift the responsibility of the religious training of their children to the church. Devotions must be conducted in the home every day, "as regular as clock work." After supper the father got the Bible, read from it and prayed; and then there were prayers from other members of the family. Mrs. Youngdahl often used a hymn she loved as the theme of her prayers:

"Just as I am without one plea,
But that Thy blood was shed for me,
And that Thou biddest me come to Thee,
O Lamb of God, I come, I come."

When Luther was growing up, one of his older brothers, Peter, became a leader in the Minnesota organization of the Anti-Saloon League. It was a high-powered, well-manned pressure group supported by the churches and was successful enough in its campaigning to get the Prohibition Amendment passed. The Youngdahls approved of Peter's activities. They believed that liquor was a deadly evil and drinking a sin. Their church bolstered their beliefs. Since its founding, the Augustana Synod had consistently and frequently expressed its opposition to the liquor traffic.

The moral code instilled in the children was not all in negative terms. There was to be no compromise with sin. There is a sharp line between right and wrong, and it was a poor Christian who diluted his religion or was afraid to stand up for his beliefs. One's entire life was a trust to be spent in responsible service to God.

One day Luther and one of his brothers came home from school. As they munched some of their mother's freshly-baked buttermilk-and-sugar cookies they complained about one of the teachers. "If only she knew how to teach . . ."

Luther hadn't finished the sentence when his mother cut him off. "That's enough of that, boys. Instead of criticizing, go out and do better. How many times have I told you you must respect those in authority, not only your parents? Don't you remember your catechism?" (The catechism interprets the commandment, "Honor thy father and thy mother," to include all those in authority as recipients of honor and respect). The Youngdahl children learned that it was right to respect not only their parents and teachers, but the pastor and the policeman.

Another admonition they repeatedly heard was that they should respect all people, regardless of their status, and be concerned about their welfare. One day there was a knock on the kitchen door. Mrs. Youngdahl opened it, and there stood an unkempt, rough-looking man. He had a peg leg and looked every inch what he was, a hobo looking for a hand-out. Mrs. Youngdahl welcomed him into her kitchen and treated him as a guest. The white table cloth was spread and an appetizing lunch of home-made bread and other delicacies from the grocery store were set before him.

After he had gone, one of the children exclaimed, "He scares me. I'm afraid of bums."

Mrs. Youngdahl explained, "He is a human being like you are and deserves to be treated with as much respect as I show anyone." For all her kindness to him, however, there is no record that she ever succeeded in "converting" the hobo from his wandering ways. "Peg-Leg John" made regular visits to the Youngdahl door after that.

To give their children the advantages of all the education they could possibly acquire was a primary ambition of the Youngdahls. Everything was done to make this possible; and with ten children to support, it was not easy for them.

Luther attended South High School in Minneapolis and graduated from there in 1915. Forty years later, the school's annual was dedicated to him, the first time in its history that an individual had been honored in this way. The **Tiger** citation called him South High's most prominent graduate and described his high school years: "An ambitious student at South, Judge Youngdahl participated in debates and the Senior Class play; and was an active member of Hi-Y's predecessor, the Bean Club. Moreover, he relinquished his position as center on the football team for a paper route which helped pay his school expenses."

The students and teachers in South High forty years ago probably would not have chosen Luther as the senior most likely to succeed, his high school career having brought him no special recognition for outstanding achievement. His parents' strictness seemed to have a restraining influence on his development. He felt sluggish and unsure of himself. It was not only that his parents forbade him to play football, but he was uncertain of himself. He was not sure about his future career. He took part in debate, but his skill as a speaker was a development of the future. He had not yet learned the secret of social poise and the well-tailored look, which were to be his hall-marks later.

Luther Trained to Respect Work

Part of his difficulty was rooted in the limited financial circumstances of the family. Luther had to spend most of his spare hours working in the grocery store and delivering papers. There was little time or money for the frills of high school life. John Youngdahl was a hard worker and his wife a tireless and efficient manager of the large household. They did everything possible for their children. The grocer was willing to forego vacations for forty years in order to feed, clothe and educate his children — a record his children recite now with pride. He also had some stubbornly-held convictions about money and work. He believed in honest and persistent industry, and made certain that his children became personally acquainted with work and financial obligation. He refrained from buying anything on a conditional sales contract, and insisted on the children learning to save their money until they had enough for what they wanted. The discipline of childhood paid off in later years for Luther. He developed an amazing capacity for getting work done. But at the time it curtailed his participation in high school activities.

Luther remembers an incident that taught him the value of money and revealed the grim fact that everyone in the world was not as trustworthy as "Honest John," as Minneapolis businessmen called his father.

With typical teen-age intensity, he wanted a bike so he could finish his paper route faster and go with the other boys on their bicycle jaunts. For months he saved his earnings until he had enough to purchase the bike he wanted. It was a happy day when he and his father went down town to buy it.

About a month afterward he rode his bike to the newspaper office. Leaving it outside, he went in to settle his monthly accounts.

When he came out, the bike was gone.

He ran quickly to the corner to see if he could spot the thief — but no bike was in sight. He rushed into the office to ask if anyone had seen someone ride away with it — but no one had. Sick with anger and loss, he trudged home — a pedestrian again. Advertising brought no results. The bike was never found. There is only one thing to do, his father told the disappointed boy. Luther started saving again. Months later he had enough for a bike — and a good, strong lock.

Perhaps it was not so hard to trudge day after day on a newspaper route — nothing like walking Betsy for 29 miles twice in one summer. Betsy was the family cow. The journey extended from the red brick barn on Eleventh Avenue to Lake Independence. Luther and his brothers learned a lot about perseverance as they kept the placid animal moving toward their destination.

There were many good times in the Youngdahl home — life was not all work. The summers at the lake were filled with happy memories. There were strawberries and raspberries to be picked and crated for shipment to the store, but there were crappies to be caught, too. Mother Youngdahl delighted in getting her limit before anyone else. It was worth the walk to have Betsy at the lake. She kept the family well-supplied with milk and cream, and there was plenty of ice cream from her milk and the hand-turned freezer.

In the evenings the family assembled on the large screened porch overlooking the lake. Often the Youngdahls would gather around Ole, the hired man, as he played his guitar and led them in one song after another — the haunting melodies of old folk songs, hymns, whichever tune was requested. Sometimes there would be a game of Rook, a card game that somehow escaped the censure of the usually-strict Mrs. Youngdahl. She played it with a fierce competitiveness, hating to lose especially when the winners would be treated to "black cows" (root beer floats) by the losers.

One day in 1911 a Ford drove up to the big house on Eleventh Avenue. It was one of those early models, open to all the elements and not even having doors for the front seat. On the front seat beside the driver sat John Youngdahl. "How do you like it?" he asked. "It's ours!" The children were almost beside themselves with excitement, and the Youngdahls and their new Ford became the sensation of the neighborhood. There were very few automobiles in Minneapolis at that time. Successive Sunday afternoons found the whole family crowded into the Ford for a ride. There were special "touring bonnets," replete with long chiffon ribbons, for each of the girls, and plenty of activity for the boys when a tire went flat or the radiator boiled.

One day Luther and several other members of the family were returning to Minneapolis from Lake Independence. Luther sat on the back seat wedged in between some luggage and his brother Oscar. It was raining, not very pleasant to ride in the open Ford. Once in a while the car swerved on the slippery road. The unpleasantness of the trip was not enough to spoil Luther's contentment. The youngster had on new shoes, and getting new shoes was an occasion in his life. "Watch out, Occie! You're stepping on my new shoes," he would exclaim; and he would often steal admiring glances at them. Suddenly the car lurched and skidded out of control. Luther felt himself tossed and turned and bumped with relentless force in the next chaotic seconds. When the violent motion stopped, his first sensible, but incongruous, thought was, "I hope my shoes aren't ruined." The dazed and bruised family crawled out of the Ford that lay overturned in the ditch — all but Oscar. They discovered that his leg was broken. The car was a wreck. The sensation of Eleventh Avenue had come to an untimely end. Luther's shoes were — muddy but unscratched.

Those were the days of Luther Youngdahl's youth — the events the family likes to remember — the days described by his sister as "good, memory-packed, character-making days."

CHAPTER THREE

Orator, Lawyer and Judge

"Why don't you study dentistry, Luther?" his father suggested one day. "You'll make good money, and I think it is a career within your capacities."

Still unsure of himself, and lacking encouragement to do otherwise, Luther followed the parental advice and enrolled in the University of Minnesota in the Fall of 1915. He soon discovered that his heart was not in dentistry. He detested chemistry so violently that even his sleep was disturbed. The night after he registered in the School of Dentistry he had a nightmare about test tubes, hydrogen chloride, Buntzen burners and all the other paraphernalia of the chemistry lab. He spent a sleepless night, squarely facing the origin of his unhappiness and searching for a solution. Not only did he dislike his course of study but he felt lost in the crowd at the University and had no opportunity for leadership there. By morning he had resolved on a new approach to a future career. The next day he cancelled his dentistry courses, and registered in the College of Science, Literature and Arts. A year later he transferred to Gustavus Adolphus College in St. Peter, Minnesota — with his parents' blessing, since this college was a Lutheran school supported by their church. Two brothers had attended the college before him; Benjamin enrolled the same year and Ruth and Reuben were to attend later.

College Days

Luther wasted no time getting into college life. Having an enrollment of about 500 students, Gustavus gave its students ample opportunity for leadership and participation in a variety of activities. One of Luther's professors, Dr. Conrad Peterson of the history department, remembers that Luther Youngdahl came to Gustavus full of enthusiastic ambition to lead and direct student activities. The chronicle of events from 1916-1919 in College Breezes reveals that he took part in several college activities.

Speech Training at College

He blossomed as a speaker during his college days. Forensics was an activity with a high student rating at the time. Several debating societies flourished on a lively program of oratorical contests, debates, after-dinner speeches and occasional picnics on the hills across the Minnesota River valley or out at Lake Emily, about three miles from town. Luther and Ben were admitted to the Ephronian debating society soon after they came to Gustavus. The Youngdahl name was already known in college forensic circles, Oscar having won the state college oratorical contest in 1916.

Ben and Luther picked up valuable experience in debate, oratory and extemporaneous speaking at the meetings of the Ephronian society. In December, 1916, both of them entered the intramural oratorical contest. Luther's oration, "Barriers Burned Away," dealt with "hyphenated Americans," the problem of national loyalties made urgent by the World War. The oration itself rated publication in the December (1916) issue of College Breezes, but Ben won second place over his brother's third. Luther's delivery, according to a critic's article in the magazine, was unpolished and his voice too high-pitched.

Luther's college career was interrupted by a short stint in the Army. His desire to get to the top was not frustrated by being drafted. On the contrary, he seemed to gain maturity and self-confidence while in the service. He vowed he would not come home on furlough until he had received a commission as a Second Lieutenant. After his promotion to corporal, he was given the opportunity to attend officers' training school at Louisville, Kentucky. He worked hard enough to be first in his class and merited the honor of marching to the platform at graduation as the head of a contingent of Field Artillery — as a Second Lieutenant. Before he had a chance to see service overseas, the war ended and he was mustered out in time to enroll for his senior year with the class of 1919.

Upon his return to the campus he took up oratory again. His oration, "An Enduring Democracy," took first place in the intramural contest, and he earned the privilege of representing the college at a contest at Rock Island, Illinois, against contenders from Augustana and Bethany Colleges. He triumphed there, too, and thus achieved his peak as a college orator. Leonard Kendall, who later became his pastor in Minneapolis, took second place. "Youngdahl was quite an orator," is his pithy comment about the occasion. College Breezes printed "An Enduring Democracy" and the following comments, which show that his hearers had noted a marked improvement: "Mr. Youngdahl is a forceful and convincing speaker and displays great skill and ability in his masterful oration. . . . The admirable theme lays down the just and practical basis upon which an enduring democracy must be realized. He tersely defines the intent and meaning of the principle of liberty with a logical and coherent shaping of his plea. Throughout the splendid oration the speaker dramatically and vividly describes those menacing and relentless forces which have sought to blot out the true democratic sentiment." (p. 197, April, 1919)

Luther led two lives at Gustavus. The one was legitimate and respectable in terms of the fond hopes and dreams the administration had for its students; the other, not particularly shocking, but nevertheless out of bounds when judged by the same standards! He was the despair and joy of President O. J. Johnson and the faculty — and he was not alone in this distinction. The faculty once put him on probation for several weeks.

He belonged to the Ephronian society, over which the faculty beamed in approval of its fine forensics program. He also belonged to a secret fraternity called "the Greys," driven underground by a faculty ultimatum outlawing its existence. Its membership was drawn from all other campus organizations and included students who are now regarded by the college with pride as "leading alumni." Its happy and clandestine activities were marred only by its having to cope with a rival and equally clandestine fraternity known as "the Reds." There was no love lost between them. At one time the rivalry was so intense that the basketball team began to lose too many games. The Reds on the team refused to pass the ball to the Greys. Even the girls had to be careful. No Grey would speak to or date a co-ed who was indiscreet enough to wear a red tie with her middie blouse.

Experience as An Athlete

Luther played football — both before and after it was authorized by the Board. Athletics was a controversial issue at the college. From 1905 to 1910 all intercollegiate sports had been banned, because of disapproval of the Lutheran Minnesota Conference that supported the college. Some church leaders considered sports sinful; football especially was regarded as a game unsuitable for Christian gentlemen. At the time football was quite a brutal sport, and there was a nationwide outcry against it, leading to a revision of its rules. In 1916, the year Luther enrolled at Gustavus, the students were agitating for its sanction — and playing while waiting for official approval.

The students exaggerated the importance of football, demonstrating a readiness to be outspoken about their views, even though they did not agree with the authorities of the church — as one of the editorials in **College Breezes** reveals:

"First of all **vade mecum** to our athletic pasture where you see several husky young lads, battling against odds (the Minnesota Conference and the Augustana Synod) in an endeavor to develop themselves into manhood; where 'Blondy Barney' alias Prof. B. E. Anderson, our athletic coach, molds raw human material into football machinery; which, if it were permitted by the above mentioned dignitaries, would make other colleges feel like a maiden's sigh in a hurricane. Yet these 'low brow toughs, **cum laude**,' as some ultra-refined people would call those who play football at our cultural cannery, have made the best of existing conditions. . . . Football is the game which puts a school on the map during the fall season. It is a game which starts the college spirit aright and unites the old and the new students in united efforts for their Alma Mater. As it is now, we have no common bond by means of which the new students can acquaint themselves with our college and its traditions. The result is that the campus is permeated with a droll and drowsy spirit. Probably it is not well to advertise the fact, yet such it is that we have a smaller freshman class than those of recent years while the other colleges in this state show a decided increase above former years. May the powers that be take heed and stop this retrogression while it is yet time. INTERCOLLEGIATE FOOTBALL WILL DO IT!" (Oct. 1916, p. 31)

Football did not gain official approval until June, 1917, when the Augustana Synod decided to leave the issue with the college boards. Students at Gustavus were playing football among themselves without official approval before this time, and Luther Youngdahl was an active participant. The sports editor of College Breezes reported a game between two intramural teams, the T.M.T.'s and the I.B.'s, which were sponsored by two sororities, the Tau Mu Tau and the Iota Beta. The T.M.T.'s won, 15-0, and Luther was one of the stars. Playing halfback, he recovered one of his team-mate's fumbles across the opponents' goal line, to score one of the touchdowns. He also played fullback on the intramural championship team of the sophomore class. Upon his return from the army, he played on the football team which was the first to be fielded after intercollegiate football was reinstated at the college. Since the team had no more than twelve or thirteen players, he was shifted from one position to another — fullback, halfback, center and guard. He recalls to this day a practice game with Pillsbury Academy of Owatonna: "An old pair of pants had been assigned to me — all the college had. When I caught the kickoff as halfback on the team, one of the opposing tacklers grabbed my pants and ripped them wide open. Because some of the co-eds were on the sidelines, I became so embarrassed and frightened that I scooted like a rabbit and made about forty yards more than I would have ordinarily made!"

One day it looked as though the opponents of football on the faculty were justified. The team was in South Dakota for a game. A telegram came to the college:

"Youngdahl injured. Broken leg. Will arrive
Sunday night."

The campus was in a furor. Talk of abolishing football again was revived. A girl with a passion for Youngdahl prepared a sweet note and sent it to comfort him. The platform was crowded when the train pulled in the next day. A hearse, doubling as an ambulance, stood ready to take the wounded warrior to the hospital.

Jaws dropped when Youngdahl appeared and walked off the train under his own power.

He had a hard time convincing the president that he knew nothing of the faked telegram.

In 1916 the alumni began to raise funds for a new Gymnasium; and after the War was over, this cause became the most important project on the campus. Again Luther Youngdahl revealed his capacity for leadership. It was he who presented the proposal that the students set up a pledge system for collecting contributions from the campus family at a mass meeting of the student body and faculty, after chapel exercises on the morning of February 19, 1919. He was appointed to the constitution committee and thus continued to play an important part in furthering the project. About $13,000 was pledged by faculty and students. Most of the student pledges were about $40.00, with a few as high as $100.00. Luther pledged $60.00 to the fund. Despite opposition around the

Minnesota Conference, the fund continued to grow until it was possible to put up a $150,000 building in 1922.

Luther was a member of the Lyric Male Chorus the year it joined forces with the Schumann's Ladies Choir to go on tour as a representative of the college. It was the first time in the history of the college that the men and women singers had travelled together — and the last for quite a while. The innovation apparently was too audacious for the administration — perhaps evoking too many disapproving letters from supporters — and the combined tour was abandoned after that one bold adventure. An extended and lively chronical of the trip was written by official diarist, Luther Youngdahl.

His singing was not limited to vocalizing with the chorus. As one of the "Ukulele Kids," he did a bit of serenading on his own under the windows of the girls' residence halls and led song-fests at Euphronian picnics at Lake Emily. His involvement in campus social life may have disqualified him for top honors in his class, but he won another first place more satisfying.

Romance on the College Campus

He began to take a special interest in an organization known as the I.B.'s. (Iota Beta, the oldest sorority on campus). He was attracted to one of its charming members, Irene Engdahl, a Lutheran minister's daughter, whom he began to see more and more frequently. After enjoying her company on hikes along the river and among the hills near St. Peter, and on picnics at Wolfe's Resort on Lake Emily, Luther was convinced that he liked Irene — very much.

Then he loved her.

One day they went out to Lake Emily.

"How about a boat ride, Irene?"

Her consent came quickly, perhaps because she did not realize what was coming — or perhaps because she knew very well.

When they were an appropriate distance from shore, Luther

popped the crucial question, and Irene gave the only satisfactory answer.

"What could I do but say yes?" she has protested often since. "I didn't know how to swim!"

She taught school while Luther finished law school, and they were married June 23, 1923.

In one area of campus life, Luther apparently had no active role. The records do not indicate that he held positions of leadership in religious organizations, and his name is never reported when speakers at religious meetings or delegates to church conventions are mentioned. It was not because there was a lack of opportunity. Religious activities during this time were coming more and more under student control. There was a Luther League for women and a Lutheran Brotherhood for men. The Missionary Society created a lively interest in missions, and the classes from 1910 to 1922 furnished sixteen workers for the foreign field, as compared with only two from all previous classes. More frequently than ever, the Saturday Night Prayer Circle was being conducted by students. Luther's apparent lack of interest in the religious program at Gustavus may have been a temporary rebellion against his strict upbringing. His non-conformity was not an isolated phenomenon at Gustavus.

In later years he has looked back on his college career and discovered that its religious emphasis has had an impact on him. Recently he acknowledged that the guidance and inspiration of the professors had been especially important.

"The professors were all dedicated and consecrated men working for a small salary, but realizing they were helping to create lives of influence for a better world. Dr. J. P. Uhler had a great influence on my life because he taught not only astronomy, but he taught life itself. His whole personality radiated the qualities of a Christian gentleman. He had a good sense of humor; he encouraged romantic activities; and all the students loved him. Part of my social philosophy was inspired by Dr. Conrad Peterson, my instructor in history and economics. In my earlier years I was more conservative in my political philosophy; but as I came to study history and came into contact with some of the wrongs of our society, I became more progressive in my approach. I am strongly in favor of the denominational college for at least part of the education of every boy and girl."

Begins the Study of Law

Having decided while at college to go into law, Young-dahl spent the summer after graduation selling kitchen cleanser from house to house to earn his tuition and going to night school to learn typewriting and shorthand. In the Fall he got a job with five lawyers as a stenographer and enrolled in the night school of the Minnesota College of Law in St. Paul. He finished his legal training in two years and hung up his shingle.

About a month after he had opened up his office, he met one of his former classmates from law school. They began to talk shop. "There will be a civil service examination soon. Why don't you take it?" Youngdahl's friend suggested.

"Oh, shucks! That's all politics."

He decided to participate, despite his skepticism. He amazed himself by being top man among the fifteen who took the test. There was another surprise awaiting him. The City Attorney recommended the top man on the list, despite the fact that some of those who took the test had worked in his office for several years. Youngdahl was sworn in as his assistant. This first contact with the civil service system gave him a great faith in it that he never lost. He was convinced that if political influence had been the decisive factor, one of the men known to the City Attorney would have secured the post.

While he was Assistant City Attorney he had his first brush with gambling. One day someone came to him with a complaint. "Did you know there is gambling going on in one of the night spots down town?"

"Is that so? Where?"

The informant named the place.

"Why don't you go to the chief of police? The department has a squad to take care of that."

"He won't do a thing! I don't trust him. For all I know he may be in cahoots with the club. I think you should use the sheriff instead!" Further explanation convinced Youngdahl of the necessity of the action. He made arrangements for the raid and planned to accompany the deputies.

The raid was a complete success. No tip-offs. Thirty astonished people were caught in the "back room" playing craps and other games of chance. Gambling paraphernalia was found. The lawbreakers were loaded into the Black Maria and taken to jail. The next morning they pleaded guilty in Municipal Court.

In 1923 Youngdahl was invited to enter a law partnership with Judge M. C. Tifft, with whom he remained until 1930 when he was appointed to the municipal judgeship. He credits Judge Tifft with making him the beneficiary of worthwhile bits of legal advice and common sense that have served him well during his career.

One day after the mail had come, the judge walked into Luther Youngdahl's office and showed him a letter. Youngdahl read it and then exploded.

"Who does he think he is! After all the work we did for him — after winning the case — he writes a letter like this." It was a sarcastic message of complaint about the fee. "I thought the fee was too low for all the work we had to do. Why don't you tell him a thing or two?"

The judge took the letter back without comment. A few days later Youngdahl chanced to see it lying on his partner's desk, still unanswered.

"Aren't you going to answer that letter?"

"Luther, when I get a letter like that one, I generally wait a few days. By that time I have simmered down enough to write sensibly. If I had answered that letter when I got it, I would have said something rash and hot. That would have accomplished nothing."

Youngdahl became active in the Republican Party during the gubernatorial campaign of 1924, when Theodore Christianson opposed Floyd B. Olson, the candidate from the Farmer-Labor Federation, which was the successor to the Non-Partisan League and forerunner of the Farmer Labor Party. Youngdahl campaigned in the solidly-Swedish community of Scandia. In 1928 the Republican State Central Committee organized "the Minute Men for Hoover," a group of people who would be available on call to fill speaking engagements all over the state. Both Oscar and Luther Youngdahl were Minute Men and took an intensely active part in that campaign. Luther's political activities were strictly non-partisan during the thirties, because his judicial offices were non-partisan.

Appointment as Municipal Judge

Youngdahl was not reluctant to let his ambitions be known. Members of the legal profession remember him as a young lawyer who was determined to use every situation as an opportunity to advance. Some believed he had early set his heart upon becoming a member of the State Supreme Court. The first step was to be a Municipal Judge. Governor Christianson had considered him, but others took precedence for natural or political reasons. Finally, after Christianson had . been defeated by Olson in 1930 and a vacancy on the Municipal bench had been created by Judge Manley Fosseen going to the Probate Court and Judge Selover to the District Court, Youngdahl received his appointment from Christianson.

It came as a surprise. The Youngdahl brothers were great ones to tease each other with practical jokes. One night, as Youngdahl sat in the living room of his home at 3933 Zenith Avenue South, the phone rang.

"Mr. Youngdahl? This is Governor Christianson calling," the voice said. "I would like to have you come to the Capitol in the morning to pick up your commission as Municipal Judge."

"Oh, quit kidding me!" Luther exclaimed. The voice sounded just like Oscar's, who previously had teased him about his ambition to be a judge. This was just another of his practical jokes.

"The Governor repeated, "I don't think you heard me. This is Governor Christianson calling, and I would like to have you come over to get your commission."

Again Youngdahl said, "Don't kid me. I know who you are." Finally the Governor had to explain the facts in detail over the phone, whereupon a much subdued young lawyer meekly promised to come to the Capitol in the morning. He still could not believe it and called Judge Fosseen to verify the story. Needless to say, his apologies were ready when he went to the Capitol the next day.

Interested in the Problems of People

After he went on the bench, Youngdahl undertook other community activities, in addition to his church work — Y.M.C.A., the Boy Scouts, Parent-Teachers' Association, and the Big Brother movement. His contacts with all kinds of people and their problems deepened his interest in human welfare, especially that of youth. It was while he was Municipal Judge that his interest in mental health awakened. As he dealt with people in court he realized that many of them were in difficulty because they were not well adjusted emotionally and needed psychiatric care. "I found that there were more sick people outside the hospitals than inside," he told Jack MacKay during his crusade for mental health, years later. He established a friendship with Dr. Alexander Dumas, a Minneapolis psychiatrist, who became a voluntary psychiatric adviser to the judge. Together they were able to provide rehabilitation or treatment for many who would otherwise be doomed to unhelpful incarceration.

A striking example of Youngdahl's humanity is the case involving a University student who was hailed before the court and accused of stealing a car, and possessing and distributing pornographic literature. Some of the authorities at the University pronounced him an incurable sexual psychopath. If this were true, he would be liable to life commitment in the ward for the dangerously insane of the state hospital in St. Peter. Attorney Leslie Anderson, who was representing the youth, tried to get Youngdahl's permission to have another psychiatrist examine him. For some reason this was impossible, but Youngdahl took a personal interest in the youth. He saw to it that he got individual attention at the work farm and continued to give him encouragement. The young man eventually was released, became a captain in the air force, married, and is now a father of two children and is a professor in a large Eastern university.

Since those days Youngdahl has continued to take an active and personal interest in boys through the Big Brother movement. Recently the **Saturday Evening Post** told the story of Freddie, whom Youngdahl helped to rehabilitate during the days he was a judge in Minneapolis. (Issue of Feb. 5, 1955) The Big Brother movement strives to interest responsible men in serving on a continuing basis, as friends and counsellors of boys in danger of becoming delinquent. The task is neither simple nor short. The story of Freddie is a case in point.

"One day Freddie, a short, thin-legged boy of ten, marched across a crowded playground in Minneapolis brandishing a revolver and threatening to shoot his playmates. Freddie's mother, a woman of some education, was embittered by her husband's desertion of her and her three children. She complained that she was overworked; she denounced the Government because relief payments were small. Perhaps unconsciously, she directed most of her complaints at the children and, if something were missing, she almost automatically accused Freddie of having stolen it. Often he had.

"The effect of all this was that the children, especially Freddie, who wanted adult love, got no recognition at home and tended to feel like misfits at school. Freddie desperately wanted a bicycle, so he stole one from another boy, fell off and broke his leg. His mother felt her past complaints fully justified. When Freddie stole a revolver and carried it to the playground, he was rebelling against the down-graded position he occupied at home. He wanted to attract attention and show he was a big shot, but, of course, he also might have killed somebody. Instead, his shooting rampage was happily interrupted and, a short time later, he came to the attention of Judge Youngdahl. Freddie was invited to the judge's chambers in the courthouse. Youngdahl talked to the boy about his misbehavior and his good behavior, too, and made a standing date for a conference each Saturday morning.

"Thereafter the frail, thin-faced boy would come whistling into the judge's chambers once a week, wave his hand and say, 'Hi, Judge!' in a friendly, yet offhand way. Then he would start talking about what he had been studying and what he did after school. Many times he ended up with something like, 'Yeah, I stole a pair of gloves from an automobile.'

" 'You can't do things like that,' Youngdahl would reply. 'If you want my help, you've got to play the game. You've got to show good faith.'

" 'Yeah,' Freddie would say, 'I know it, Judge. I believe in you.'

"But a couple of weeks later he would steal something else. Youngdahl didn't see much future for the boy except at Alcatraz Prison, but he didn't give up. Freddie finally was sent to the County School for Boys. Judge Youngdahl kept in touch with him. And when the boy got away from his disturbing home atmosphere, he began to make progress in school. Later, the judge helped him get a job and continued to write to him. The last letter from Freddie said he was in the Navy, married and had a child."

One of the boys who received Youngdahl's assistance repaid his "Big Brother" in a startling way. The judge had befriended the boy when he was on the way toward serious delinquency. A few years later the young man was married and a son was born to him and baptized in the Catholic Church. Out of gratitude for Youngdahl's efforts on his behalf, the father insisted that his son be named Michael **Luther** O'Hara!

While he was Municipal Judge, Youngdahl suffered a discouraging experience with the problem of law enforcement. It happened during the prohibition era, when a bootlegger was to appear before his court. One day there was a knock on the door of his office just before court was to convene. A cub reporter from one of the papers appeared.

"I came to tip you off. I have reason to believe that if you talk to this man charged with bootlegging, you will get some dope on certain police officers whom he had paid off weekly."

Youngdahl immediately called the man into his chambers and took a statement from him. Then he telephoned the newspapers and pleaded with the city editor to withhold the story until the grand jury could get it.

Instead, the paper rushed a reporter to the bootlegger's home, and the story burst forth in the Sunday paper. That caused furor behind the scenes. By the time the grand jury met, the accused refused to testify.

Youngdahl was further disconcerted to find an editorial in the paper, soon after, charging "certain persons" with making accusations before they were sure of the evidence. He knew what the facts were and that an indictment could have been made, and he knew that the paper's untimely story had prevented it. It was a disillusioning ordeal for a young man wanting to see the laws enforced, an experience which has been neutralized only by the perspective of the years in which he has observed the integrity of the great majority of the police force.

Campaign Methods are Tested

Youngdahl's long association with Ray Ewald, prominent Minneapolis dairyman and civic leader, began while he was Municipal Judge. Serving as campaign manager and money-raiser, Ewald was Youngdahl's top lieutenant in every campaign until the judge ran for the governorship in 1946, when the Stassen organization took him over. Ewald was one of the independents who gave Youngdahl substantial support during his political career. When Youngdahl decided to line up with the G.O.P. in 1946, Ewald took no part in the canvassing. He renewed his activities in the next two campaigns, however, serving as treasurer of the Volunteers for Youngdahl Committee. Apparently Youngdahl's actions in office convinced him that he had not lost his independence.

It was during the years that Youngdahl ran for municipal and district judgeships that he learned how to solicit the support of the people. Ewald remembers that he and Youngdahl conducted very active and versatile campaigns, their duties ranging from tacking up posters to attending gatherings involving any number of people — from two or three, to thousands. In one of the early campaigns Youngdahl and Ewald and his other aides made a decision that affected his campaigning methods throughout his career. Youngdahl's supporters offered him the use of their homes as neighborhood campaign centers. Someone suggested, "Why don't we serve beer in the basement room?" It was a common procedure during campaigns in Minneapolis—even during prohibition.

"I don't like the idea," Youngdahl replied.

"I doubt you will get enough votes if you don't do it. You know people. It takes all kinds to make a world. All kinds vote, too. Your opponents will serve it."

The arguments did not succeed in overcoming Youngdahl's scruples about liquor. He was never a party to serving free drinks, yet it did not seem to hurt his prospects. He led the ticket in number of votes polled in every primary and general election while he ran for judicial posts. His reputation for vote-getting began to look very appealing to Republican leaders.

Youngdahl was a candidate for the District bench for the first time in 1936. He won the election and held this position until he became a member of the State Supreme Court in 1942.

Shortly before he became an Associate Justice of the State Supreme Court, he tried a case that attracted widespread attention and is still cited by his associates as an illustration of his willingness to sustain the cause of labor, despite heavy pressure from other groups, when the working man was right before the law. Powerful interests were arrayed on either side of the conflict — the Minneapolis Star and Tribune Company on the one hand, and the Minneapolis Newspaper Guild on the other. In 1940 the Minnesota Tribune Company sold its interest in

The Minneapolis Tribune to a new corporation, the Minneapolis Star and Tribune Publishing Company. Some of the employees were dismissed by the old corporation, and others were given new contracts and retained by the new company. Among the latter were two employees, Matthews and Campbell. Along with others in the same situation, they were not paid severance wages by the Minnesota Tribune Company, since they had been rehired by the new concern. However, the contract with the Minneapolis Newspaper Guild required payment, so Matthews and Campbell brought suit. An amount of about $80,000 was involved in wages to all employees who had been treated similarly. Before Judge Youngdahl, the plaintiffs contended that a real sale had taken place and new contracts had been issued. Therefore, the old corporation owed them severance pay, even though they had been hired by the new corporation and had continued to work with no loss of time. Youngdahl handed down a decision in favor of the plaintiffs and thus won the respect of labor leaders in the city.

When he decided to run for a Supreme Court post, Youngdahl was unable to get Governor Stassen's public endorsement, so he decided to conduct his own campaign. Herbert Nelson, one of his friends and a Minneapolis insurance agent, became politically active in Youngdahl's behalf at this time. They had become acquainted at the Minneapolis Athletic Club, where they had adjoining lockers and their friendship had developed around a common love of hunting and fishing and a mutual regard for each other. Nelson served as chairman of the Volunteers for Youngdahl during the three gubernatorial contests.

By this time Youngdahl was adept in the art of campaigning, and he labored tirelessly to cover the state in a supreme effort to win the election. His increasing reputation as a speaker had flourished with the years, and the assistance of Ewald and Nelson were advantages that helped him not only win the election but to poll more votes than Stassen himself in that particular election.

Distinguished Record as a Member of the State Supreme Court

While on the Supreme Court bench, Youngdahl wrote an opinion which revealed his characteristic concern for the home and family. In his opinion on the case of the City of Minneapolis vs. Rutland, decided by the court on June 11, 1943, he protested the order of a lower court removing Agnes Rutland and her children to Whitefield Township from Minneapolis on the grounds that "it tends directly to sever family ties and is against public policy. We concur whole-heartedly in the sound and well-established rule that ordinarily families should not be separated and that the home, which represents the very foundation of our social existence, should be protected and preserved by the courts."

While on the Supreme Court bench, he also became acquainted with the complex problem of taxation of the state's iron ore deposits — one of Minnesota's most vital economic and political questions. In March, 1944, he delivered the opinion in the case of the Village of Aurora vs. Commissioner of Taxation, upholding the decision of the Board of Tax Appeals which stated that the properties of three mining companies had been under-evaluated by the Commissioner of Taxation and ordering a higher evaluation for tax purposes.

Youngdahl's court opinions are very different from his public speeches. They reveal a mind capable as much of careful, discriminating legal analysis as his speeches do of popularizing his ideas of government. In the taxation case just cited Youngdahl showed a penetrating understanding of and respect for the jurisdiction of the courts in relation to the executive branch of government.

The taxpayers contended that the Board of Tax appeals had erred in ordering the Commissioner of Taxation to increase the valuation of the properties of the three mining companies involved. Youngdahl dispensed with the taxpayers' contention that the case should have been heard directly by the Supreme Court by stating that the function of a special board of appeals is to relieve the courts of the burden of research on highly technical and specialized matters. The board is com-

An award presented to Luther Youngdahl designating him as the Lutheran man of the year

Gov. Youngdahl visits with a Sunday School group

Gov. Youngdahl signs the anti-slot machine bill.

posed of impartial experts, and its judgments are to be respected as long as they have a reasonable basis in the evidence presented and the laws applicable to the case. Some of the data presented by the disputants conflicted which made it necessary for the Board to make its own reasonable conclusions based on a careful study of the problems involved. Youngdahl wrote:

"We cannot substitute our judgment for that of the board. It is the trier of the fact, and it determines the probative value of such conflicting testimony. Sitting in review, our jurisdiction upon fact questions is limited to the determination of whether there is reasonable evidence to sustain the findings. There is nothing to indicate that the board did not give due consideration to the fact that the witnesses for the taxpayers had the additional mining experience and background heretofore mentioned. We believe that the testimony of witnesses for the municipalities was competent and proper to be considered, together with all the other evidence in the case, in the determination of the discount rate. . . ."

He went on to say that it was apparent that the board had considered the testimony carefully and that the Supreme Court sustained its decision. He further pointed out the great possibility of error and miscalculation in computing the taxation of iron ore and that it was the function of the Supreme Court to ascertain whether the Board's decision had a reasonable basis in law. (Note. Village of Aurora and Independent School District No. 40, St. Louis County vs. Commissioner of Taxation. Oliver Mining Company, Lake Superior Consolidated Iron Mines, and St. James Mining Company, Relators. 217 Minnesota Reports 64, 14 Northwestern Reporter, 2d series).

The Luther Youngdahl that Republican leaders offered to support as a candidate for governor in 1946 may not have had much experience in party politics, but he brought into this new phase of his career a veteran's knowledge of Minnesota law, a solid reputation as a vote-getter well versed in the strategy of campaigning, and a deep interest in the human problems confronting the state. His early career had groomed him well for the highest political office in the state.

CHAPTER FOUR

Family Man and
Church Member

"Hello, George. It seems good to be back here again."
Youngdahl looked around the familiar setting. The Rainbow
Grill in Minneapolis was one of his favorite eating spots.

"How are you, Judge?" George Legeros greeted his well
known customer warmly and ushered him to a booth. "Where
is Mrs. Youngdahl? She is usually with you when you come
in here."

"I had to leave her home this time. I'm just passing through
on the way to a speaking engagement in Fargo. I wish she
were here. I haven't seen much of her for the last couple of
days. This Lattimore case has really tied me up." (That day
he had prepared and delivered the memorandum stating his
reasons for refusing to step out of the case and denying that
he was biased in Lattimore's favor.) "I have talked with her
several times today though — never too busy for that!"

Youngdahl has relied much on his wife's companionship
and encouragement. To one who has observed him casually
in public situations, he seems quite capable of standing all
alone. He is aggressive and bold in action and speech. His
reaction to challenges and criticism is quick and blunt. Members
of his family know him as a man whose very boldness
gives him the need for the encouragement and affection of an
intimate group of persons who are aware that his confident
manner cloaks a sensitive personality.

Mrs. Youngdahl Has Been a Source of Inspiration

Irene Youngdahl has given him the inspiration and affectionate understanding he has needed; and ever since they met and fell in love in college, he has thrived on it. It was she, according to one member of the family, who helped him more than anyone else to find himself — even in such matters as the way he wore his clothes her woman's touch became evident, and Youngdahl now is a model of good grooming. Their daughter Margaret wrote recently of their relationship to one another. "I feel that Mother was a big factor in Daddy's life. She was always ready to listen to him, encourage him, and say just the right thing. They were and are a great team and enjoy each other and life together thoroughly." Youngdahl once told Brenda Ueland, a reporter, that his wife was one of the reasons he was willing to go into politics. **(Minneapolis Tribune)** "Sometimes you feel kind of alone in politics, but she backs me up." She often went with her husband on his frequent jaunts to party caucuses, campaign rallies and civic events. A quiet, friendly person with an alertness in sensing the feelings of others, Irene Youngdahl does not give the impression of being a kitchen adviser to her husband on professional problems. She is not a sleeve-tugger, ready at his arm to direct him this way and that. What she did, her son William remembers, was to smooth the feathers her husband occasionally ruffled. "Dad is not the most tactful man in the world. He could be severe and blunt and at times gave the impression of being formal when dealing with individuals. Many times Mom would soothe offended newsmen or party workers with just the right words. She was a real diplomat." Mrs. Youngdahl enjoyed sharing the political life of her husband and recently she admitted, "When an election campaign starts, my husband and I are like a couple of fire engine horses who hear the siren—raring to get in the race again." And her husband agreed.

Three children were born to the family, Margaret, the oldest is married to a hospital administrator and is the mother of a son. William was ordained as a Lutheran pastor in 1955. David is a hospital administrator in Houston, Texas.

Youngdahl has taken his responsibilities as a parent seriously. In 1938 he was approached about becoming a candidate for governor. He discussed it with his wife and also talked to his pastor, Leonard Kendall, about it. The opportunity challenged him, but he finally decided not to run. He was aware that his children were at an age when they required a great deal of his companionship, and that he might deprive them of it if he became involved in politics.

When Margaret arrived, the Youngdahls — like most young parents — were determined to make no mistakes in raising her. They were more strict with her as a consequence.

Margaret was allowed her first bike much later than the other children in the neighborhood. "Why can't I get a bike? The other girls have bikes," she pleaded.

"When you are a little older. I want to be sure you will be careful with one." Her father did not yield either, until he felt she was old enough. One day, after she had turned eleven, he came up the block wheeling a brand new bike. When Margaret saw it, she was so thrilled she burst into tears. This was too much for her father. His eyes grew moist, too.

"Somehow the bike seemed more precious because I had to wait," Margaret recalls. Her father's inflexibility did not prevent a strong bond of affection from developing between them. "I had a wonderful sense of security in Daddy," she writes. "I always felt he could do or take care of anything that happened and that we could always depend upon him."

To his political foes Youngdahl often appeared brusque and unyielding when he was defending a policy in which he had faith. His daughter sees him as a tender and very sentimental person. He always remembered special events and anniversaries. He sent her beautiful letters on her birthday and on Valentine's Day.

She especially remembers her eighteenth birthday. Shortly before that important day, she developed severe abdominal pains. Appendicitis, the doctor's diagnosis stated. The operation was routine, but it disrupted the family's plans for the celebration of her birthday. They always made a noteworthy

occasion of it, because it occurred so close to Christmas that it was likely to be subordinated in the holiday rush.

"I know what we'll do," Youngdahl told his wife as they discussed plans for making the birthday seem extra special this time. "I'll cut off the top of our Christmas tree and bring it to the hospital." That is just what he did. Margaret had a part of the family Christmas tree in her hospital room to help her feel a part of the family. Little gestures of this nature were characteristic of her father. He had always shown concern about her. When she used to awaken at night feeling ill or frightened, it was her father who arose from his bed to comfort and reassure her, no matter how tired he was.

Devoted Companionship with His Children

William and David tell of the companionship their father gave them. David writes: "It is extremely hard for a man, who must be so active in his work, not to neglect his family life. This trait of always being ready to listen to our many small problems, that were big to us at the time, is the essence of Pop's success in carrying out his dual role of being a community leader and a real father to his family."

It was not easy. In addition to his demanding professional and civic life, Youngdahl was active in church, sang tenor in the Odin Male Chorus, became a thirty-second degree Mason and often went hunting, fishing and golfing.

Summers were not such a problem. While he was a judge, he had a two-month summer recess. He had plenty of time for recreational activities with his family at their cabin at Gull Lake, which they built in 1937. The family enjoyed doing many things together, including swimming, fishing, picking berries, playing golf and hiking.

"Mother became an expert fisherman," Bill remembers. "She actually learned to put a minnow on the hook."

He remembers even more vividly his father's lack of mechanical ability.

"One morning as we loafed around the table after breakfast, Dad left to putter around outside. Soon we saw him with a birdhouse and hammer. He climbed up to fasten it in place. Out came the hammer, but he seemed to have trouble. He fumbled around for a while, until finally the hammer went up and descended. The bird-house seemed to disintegrate under the blow and fell to the ground in pieces. Dad threw his hammer down in utter disgust. Then he saw us watching, and we exploded with the laughter we had tried to hold in. He began to laugh, too. Dad couldn't even drive a nail, he was so clumsy with tools."

It was another matter where his major horticultural interest was concerned. He planted a grove of pine trees on the property by the lake and nursed them along like babies. If one of them appeared to be dying, he carried water to it. "He was so fussy about those trees," Bill remembers. "He would even talk to them as he worked among them." If the children got too exuberant in their play and forgot about the little trees, he warned them to be careful. Every tree was important to him. "I can picture him anytime wandering through his little trees and caressing each needle," Margaret recalls. Today a beautiful pine grove on the property is testimony to his efforts.

Anything that involved physical exertion he enjoyed, too. He got the boys out with him to saw wood. "It wasn't enough to have wood for the next five days," Bill says. "Dad wanted wood cut for the next five years — or so it seemed to us boys after we had sawed wood for awhile with that Swedish saw of his!"

Friends and neighbors often dropped in for a visit at the cottage and they were always urged to stay for a snack. Maybe it would be fresh blueberry pancakes or fried wall-eyes that had been caught that morning. "Dad used to show people how he steaked wall-eyes. That's one feat he could do with his hands, and he was proud of it," Bill recalls.

An Auspicious Hike

One summer Bill was working on his first class Scouting requirements. Active in the Scouting movement as a member of the Court of Honor, Youngdahl was interested in his boy's progress. One evening they were discussing the next requirement Bill had to pass, the fourteen-mile hike.

"Why don't you take a practice hike one of these days?"

"Why don't you go with me, Dad — tomorrow? Dave can come, too." It was agreed; and the next morning, equipped with a lunch packed by Mother, they set out about ten-thirty. After they reached Pine Beach Hotel, the half-way mark where they ate their lunch, the boys got up to begin the return journey. Seeing a sign pointing to the road which continued around the lake, they started down this road rather than taking the return route.

"Wait a minute," their father said, "Don't you realize how long a hike this is?"

The boys taunted him, "Can't you take it, Dad?" After that challenge to his innate competitiveness, there was nothing for him to do but follow along. As they walked they composed a song to the melody of "God Bless America":

"We love to take a hike   To the lake shore with white
All around Gull Lake   sand
Just the three of us   We love to take a hike
With our lunch packed   All around Gull Lake.
We pause to take a rest.   We love to take a hike
"O'er the hill-tops,   All around Gull Lake."
Through the valleys,

By six o'clock in the evening they were very tired, but after eating dinner at a resort they continued to walk until nearly midnight.

This hike produced an encounter with one of Minnesota's wide-open gambling spots. Several miles before they would reach home, they had to pass a place called Bar Harbor, a night club built out over the lake, with a long bar, a big dance floor and several batteries of slot machines. Youngdahl later described the scene: "Drunken drivers were tearing up and down the road in their automobiles, which swayed and swerved so dangerously that my sons and I had to leap into the ditch several times. We could hear the raucous laughter and see the great crowd at the bar and hundreds lined up to get at the slot machines. Young women with pockets full of money walked about ready to make change."

Finally at 11:30 P.M. the hikers reached their cabin. Bill described the last mile: "I was about one hundred yards out in front. Dave was next, and Dad came last. Mother and Margaret were worried and scolded us for not coming home, but they immediately brought a pan of hot water for Dad's feet. The next day we clocked the hike by car and discovered that we had walked exactly 34.1 miles."

Judge Youngdahl's description was more terse: "It almost ruined me!"

In the winter time it was more difficult for him to find time for his boys, but he arranged his schedule to spend as many hours with them as possible. Every Saturday morning he took them down town with him. While he went to his office they had a work-out in the gym and pool of the Minneapolis Athletic Club. At noon he called for them and took them to Lee's Broiler for lunch. Often he took along a couple of boys he and his wife had taken under their wing through the Big Brother movement. They spent the rest of the afternoon playing baseball or touch football or hiking. In the winter they went skating, skiing and tobogganing. Often Mrs. Youngdahl and Margaret went along for the afternoon's activities. "We'll never forget the Saturdays and Sundays on the snow-covered hills around Minneapolis," Bill wrote, "nor the rides into the country or to Lake Minnetonka for picnics in the summer."

Youngdahl also found time to be with his children by taking them with him when he went on a speaking engagement. He was much in demand for commencements, father-and-son banquets and other affairs.

One night Youngdahl came home early to go to a fathers and sons banquet. "Do you boys want to go along?"

"Sure, Dad. Let's see — that makes 147," Bill mumbled.

"What are you saying?"

"I've been to 147 banquets so far, as closely as I can remember."

"You don't **have** to go tonight, you know."

"I don't want to stay home, Dad. I might miss that joke about the Irishman and the Swede," Bill kidded.

As they drove along, Dave said, "I betcha we have ham." It was a routine wager they always made.

"Roast beef," said Bill.

"Swedish meatballs," their father predicted. "Loser buys Cokes on the way home."

As they sat down to the table and waited for the food, they watched to see what the meat dish would be.

Meatballs.

Their dad turned to them and grinned triumphantly.

One day when David was fourteen, Youngdahl decided to have a frank talk with him, as he had done with the two older children. He took his son with him to Milaca, where he was to give a commencement address.

"Well, Dave," Bill inquired the next morning, "did you have a good trip last night?"

"Very good."

"What did you do?"

"We talked."

"What about?"

"Oh, the facts of life."

"Did Dad tell you all about it?" Bill was leading his brother on.

"Well, I just listened and when he got all through, I told him a few," Dave quipped.

The many talks the boys had with their father through the years gave them confidence in his advice.

When Bill was in the Navy he went through a rather serious religious crisis. One day a letter came to his father from him. When Youngdahl had finished it, he passed it to his wife. "It sounds to me like he is finding it difficult to live the kind of life he is used to," she remarked after she finished. The letter reflected Bill's confusion about the sort of life a Christian should live. He had come into contact with a religious group characterized by its zealous but negative pattern of behavior. "Perhaps my faith is weak. I want to be a Christian and yet I want to enjoy the things they condemn. They seem so sure of themselves."

That night Youngdahl composed a letter to his son, which Bill still cherishes as an example of his father's understanding and practical good sense. In substance he wrote: "If a person cannot enjoy life and still be a Christian, there is something wrong with his faith. There is nothing wrong with going to a good movie, setting the hook on a wall-eye or playing a round of golf. A Christian's faith is not bound by a petty, pietistic legalism."

Recently Bill wrote, "Whenever I have been faced with an important decision, I have sought Dad's advice. This may sound unbelievable, but he has never been wrong in these situations." If the Youngdahl children felt so much confidence in their father, it was because they sensed his concern for them. Theirs was no father whose "successes" cost the family dearly, no selfish, egotistical parent who might leave in his wake a trio of bitter, resentful children who felt robbed of a father's attention. In his speeches, they had heard him use a poem that expressed his sentiments about fatherhood, and they had reason to believe he meant it.

> "A careful man I want to be,
> A little fellow follows me.
> I do not dare to go astray,
> For fear he'll go the self-same way.
>
> "I cannot once escape his eyes,
> What e'er he sees me do, he tries.
> Like me, he says he's going to be,
> That little chap who follows me.
>
> "He thinks that I am big and fine,
> Believes in every word of mine,
> The base in me, he must not see,
> That little chap who follows me.
>
> "I must remember as I go,
> Through summer suns and winter snows,
> I am building for the years to be,
> That little chap who follows me."

Church Member

Important as the companionship of their parents was to them, the children value even more the religious training they received. Margaret writes about her father: "I think perhaps the greatest thing he gave us was a love for our God, a love for the family and the home, and the great basic principles of honesty, loyalty and the true moral values of life." David comments in a similar vein: "The most important thing my folks did for us kids is awaken in us the real need for a basic Christian faith and the place of the church in the home." William, now a pastor, stressed the importance of religion in their family. "Both Dad and Mother have such a strong Christian faith, and I am convinced that the years of family prayer and Bible study have been largely responsible for this."

From the age of three the children were taken to church as well as Sunday school. "I don't think the children ever felt church-going was compulsory, though," Mrs. Youngdahl says. "No one ever asked, 'Are we going to church today?' It was a part of our way of life, which we did as naturally as sitting down to dinner each day."

Margaret remembers dawdling on Sunday mornings, but she did not get away with it. "It's just as important to be prompt for Sunday school as public school," her father reminded her.

For twelve years during and after the depression, Youngdahl was a member of the Board of Trustees of Messiah Lutheran Church and served his turn as its chairman. His pastor remembers he was progressive and optimistic in his thinking about church affairs. His son Bill remembers something quite different — sitting in the car after church waiting impatiently for his father to finish counting the morning offering so they all could go home and eat. Mrs. Youngdahl continued taking her turn to serve refreshments and wash dishes for the Ladies Guild every year while her husband was governor.

Youngdahl and his wife saw to it that a religious atmosphere gave their home its character. Family prayers were conducted every morning after breakfast. They read from the

Bible and a book of meditations and then prayed, sometimes with a free prayer from every member of the family. One of Bill's most vivid memories is an appealing mental picture of his mother on her knees in her room, praying for her husband during particularly critical days when he was governor.

Christmas holidays were happy times for the family. The children remember the china closet in the corner of the dining room, and for a good reason. It was there that the presents were hidden, presumably without their knowledge. But they knew, and they snooped—and they crawled right into the large closet to hide when they heard someone coming. They also remember singing around the piano — Christmas carols, their favorite hymns, popular tunes. They had a jolly time of it when their father got out his old ukulele and revived some of the tunes from his college days. Often Bill got out his trumpet, and Dave his clarinet, to join Margaret at the piano for some ensemble numbers. Christmas eve reached its most solemn and beautiful moments for them when their father read the Christmas story as they sat by candle light at their supper table or in the living room around the tree.

It was with an authority gained by the practice in his own life and family that Youngdahl urged young people to take time for daily Bible reading and an active church life. In one of his baccalaureate sermons he said:

"Regardless of where you may be or how busy, a few minutes spent in meditation and a consideration of the eternal truths of God will return rich dividends in renewed strength and enthusiasm. I urge you to form the habits of regular worship in the home. . . . And be willing to get up and testify for Christ in the daily affairs of your life. Place Christ ahead of everything else and your individual contributions will be great and lasting ones. Identify yourself with the Church. Join the church of your choice and fulfill your obligations of stewardship to it by faithful attendance, by willingness to teach in Sunday school, and by participation in the many other activities of a vigorous church program." (from "A Governor's Baccalaureate Sermon.")

Youngdahl Declares His Personal Faith

Youngdahl made his personal faith a matter of public witness. His speeches frequently stressed the theme of the relationship of religion and politics. His policy statements reflect his attempt to bring his faith to bear, as directly as it is possible to do so, upon the problems of public life. In his first inaugural address he spoke of his faith in God as a sustaining power in his life: "I would feel very insecure were it not for my faith in God, and the fact that I shall be able to rely upon Him for guidance and support when uncertainty and discouragement come."

People are inclined to be skeptical about politicians who mouth religious words in their speeches and make a public display of their personal faith. One writer recently reminded his readers: "God, says the unwritten glossary of American politics, is a word in the last paragraph of a political speech." (Hutchinson, Paul, "The President's Religious Faith," **The Christian Century**, March 24, 1954, Vol. LXXI, No. 12, p. 362.) It is one thing to have a devout personal and family religion, but can a man make a public witness out of it and be so presumptuous as to think he can apply his Christianity to politics? Is there not a danger of identifying himself and his program too closely with the Almighty God and His will? Even Adolph Hitler used to close his speeches with a reference to the Almighty. What did Youngdahl's personal faith mean politically? Was his religion, as one Minnesotan put it, just good politics? Were his frequent references to Christian principles and morality a play for the church vote? What kind of a personal faith did he bring with him into Minnesota politics?

The following description of Youngdahl's faith is based upon his public utterances, and the assumption is that he was sincerely expressing religious and moral truths that were meaningful to him in his political life.

The significance of what he said stands out more clearly against the background of his religious heritage. The Lutheranism of his home and church were deeply influenced by the evangelical revivals of Sweden and therefore had a strong pietistic strain. This pietism expressed itself in various ways: emphasis upon personal religion characterized by repentance, conversion, zeal and a devout prayer life; the informal prayer meeting with laymen taking part; the leadership of laymen in the church; prohibition of "worldly" and sinful activities such as drinking, gambling, dancing, and the theater; a zealous concern for preaching the Gospel and saving souls and a resultant indifference toward most social and political issues. The church body (Augustana Lutheran) that nourished the Youngdahl faith was saved from becoming a revivalistic emotional sectarian group because of its concern for preserving a loyalty to the Lutheran confessional writings. The stress on salvation by faith in the Book of Concord, as well as on other classic Christian doctrines, prevented the church from becoming exclusive and barring members who showed no evidence of an emotional conversion or a sufficiently high level of moral perfection. The group found a precedent for its recent concern about social issues in its traditional readiness to speak out on the liquor problem and to support movements that attempted to remedy it. Since its Commission on Morals and Social Problems was established in 1937, the Augustana Church has issued studies and resolutions on a variety of questions; capital-labor relations, gambling, race relations, use of public funds for parochial schools, Universal Military Training, Ambassador to the Vatican, status of conscientious objectors, marriage and divorce, war, disarmament, outlawing the use of nuclear weapons, birth control and dancing, as well as its favorite issue of liquor have come up for discussion. However, suspicion of the "social gospel" and a reluctance to participate in political action programs have cultivated an attitude of non-intervention in partisan political activities.

At one of the prayer breakfasts attended by government leaders in Washington recently, Youngdahl described the legacy of faith that has motivated his career by recounting a conversation he once had with his mother. She was very ill with a heart condition and could be out of the oxygen tent to visit with members of the family for short intervals only. Her

son was at her bedside telling her of his ambition to win the
election to a district judge's bench in Minnesota. When he had
finished she said quietly, "Luther, I know you will win the
election. But I want you always to remember that winning
elections is not as important as winning souls for Jesus Christ."

Respect for People Dominates His Actions

Youngdahl never forgot that counsel of his mother's although he probably did not interpret the charge in quite the
same way as his mother had. He translated it into the terms
of his political vocation. In a speech urging that the Youth
Conservation Act be strengthened he said, "The operation of
our Youth Conservation Act insures that we handle the lives
of our youth as human personalities and not as depersonalized
problem cases. The soul of the most reprobate child is fully
worthy of salvation." At Mankato in observance of Health
Day he said, "The basis of our democracy is that the lives of
our people are worth saving — that is the philosophy that is
at stake in the world." Youngdahl also linked up Minnesota's
mental health program with love for people: "Yet the care of
these patients is the most accurate barometer I know, of our
real concept of human values. It is an indicator of the weak-
ness or the strength of such a moral counterpart as we may
have to the totalitarianism which holds the individuals — particularly the weak individual — insignificant. . . . Even the
most hopeless patient in our hospitals has something so precious
that he cannot be judged in values other than human or divine.
. . . 'If we can love' — this is the touchstone. This is the key
to the entire therapeutic program of the modern psychiatric
hospital." Mrs. Clarence T. Nelson, his sister Ruth, believes it
is the key to his humanitarian program and his political ethics.
"When my brother was a judge dealing with delinquents, they
were never cases but always persons who could be redeemed
if people cared enough about them. If he was willing to risk
his political fortunes rather than do something dishonest, it
was because he was conscious of his duty to bear witness for
his Lord in such a way that people would be won for Christ,

not driven away. His legislation reflected his dominant concern for human lives."

This respect for people, rooted in his family training, may explain Youngdahl's disdain for class or race distinction. George Leonard, veteran Minneapolis lawyer and close friend of former governor, Floyd B. Olson, said that he had never seen Youngdahl kow-tow to anyone. "As a young lawyer he never showed any signs whatsoever of the adulation of the rich and the successful that so many lawyers show." One of Youngdahl's favorite fishing buddies was Bill Williams, a Negro who worked as an attendant at the State Capitol. An incident in Washington during the Mid-Century Conference on Youth revealed his impatience with the color bar. He and a Negro lawyer, whom he had come to know and respect during the conference, were about to enter an elevator in a hotel. The operator opened the door and, seeing the colored man, was about to say that he could not enter. Youngdahl immediately sized up the situation. Before she could speak he threw his arm over his friend's shoulder and said, "I am the Governor of Minnesota. This man is going to ride up with me. He is my friend." Perhaps there was something in Youngdahl's eyes that defied opposition. Nothing more was said, and they entered the elevator. This was one occasion when the "don't-you-know-who-I-am" routine was worthy of applause.

Youngdahl believed that the nation was in need of a moral and spiritual regeneration. In many speeches, including his inaugural addresses, he expressed this belief when he told a graduating high school audience at a baccalaureate service: "You are going out to take your place in a world that is in crisis. It is a world in which man has achieved almost unbelievable success in pushing back the frontiers of science and technology. But while he has advanced in that area he has lagged sadly in the acquiring of moral and spiritual understanding." He went on to plead for personal zeal and commitment as the beginning of the solution: "It is my earnest conviction that the world is in its present predicament because of our unwillingness to really accept Christ. We have tried to gain hold of heaven without losing hold of the earth. . . . We haven't been willing to become the hands of Christ. We haven't been willing to pay the price of living the Christian way of life. Too many people profess to be followers of Christian principles but give only lip service. This is a dangerous attitude at a time when the Christian faith in the world faces its most crucial test. The call, then, is for a fiery, zealous devotion to Jesus. There was never a time when the ardor of true discipleship was more needed than now. . . . If the world is changed for the better, it is going to be done by each of us taking the slow, hard, rugged road of discipline and unselfishness. The great power of Christianity comes only as one person and another person and another is willing to put the teachings of Christ into actual practice in daily life."

Another frequent theme in Youngdahl's faith was his belief that Christianity works in the practical affairs of life, including politics. When pressed to explain what he meant by such a statement he said: "I believe the key to success in politics is the following of one's conscience in doing what one thinks is best for all the people. People soon learn whether their leaders are sincere. When I say that Christianity works in politics I mean applying the Christian conscience to every decision one makes and every act one performs." (Letter of June 25, 1952.)

At the outset of his career on the bench Youngdahl applied the rule of following his conscience regardless of consequences. He frequently refers in his speeches to an incident that took place after he had tried his first case in the municipal court in Minneapolis. "I called my reporter into my chambers and said to him, 'We're going to try cases with lawyers on both sides of the table with whom we are personally acquainted. Many times we will know the litigants. There is only one proper rule to follow and that is to let your conscience decide from the evidence what is just and right and not try to satisfy both sides.' I have found that to be the only safe rule to follow, not only in the law but in politics as well."

He once stated that the Lutheran teaching of which he was most aware while in politics is "that there is a right and wrong and a sharp line between the two; that sin cannot be compromised with." While he did admit that human selfishness makes it more difficult to get humanity in government, his realism was not so overbearing that he could not be optimistic about the prospects for justice when the "good people" would become active in government.

In a Chicago speech, delivered on May 7, 1950, he expressed his confidence that one could successfully follow one's conscience in politics and that basic compromises could be avoided: "I can give a positive answer to the question tonight, 'Do Christianity and politics mix?' I can say very definitely that they do mix. You can sleep much better at night if you follow Christian principles in public life. You don't have to worry about the votes or the next election. All you have to worry about is if you're on the right side of an issue. You don't have to satisfy the people. What you'd better be concerned about is whether you are right with your own conscience."

Youngdahl developed an early distaste for competitive politics and frequently expressed his disapproval of the artifice, intrigue, bickering and bargaining that characterized political canvassing. What made him change his mind and decide to run for office? There are those who would explain his career in terms of a powerful ambition to get to the top and an egotistic confidence in himself, but it would not be easy to convince the church people of Minnesota that he was not motivated by a religious sense of vocation. They have heard too many of his speeches, in which he expressed his belief that politics is as sacred a calling as church work. In urging his fellow Christians to reverse their indifference to government and step into the thick of politics, he was revealing his own sense of obligation. On what idealistic foundation did that obligation rest?

Probably most prominent in his mind were the Protestant beliefs in the sacredness of all vocations and the priesthood of all believers. In a speech, "Politics — A Challenge to Christian Youth," he referred to the doctrine of the calling: "Many Protestants have never learned, or have forgotten, that the early days of Protestantism emphasized the importance of the role of political duty. Martin Luther declared that it is not only at the altar and in the cloister that the work of God is done. He said that it is also accomplished in honest toil, in the institute of marriage, the home and parenthood — and in the affairs of government."

In one of his Reformation Day addresses he linked up the doctrine of the priesthood of all believers with political duty: "Four hundred and thirty years ago, Martin Luther erected three great pillars which supported the partially destroyed structure of the organized church. He called for these three: the supremacy of the Bible, the supremacy of faith and the supremacy of the people. . . . I especially call your attention to the third pillar which Luther set up. It was known as the supremacy of the people and the priesthood of all believers. Luther advanced the proposition that Christian laymen have spiritual faculties and powers of the same sort as the clergy. He believed that they may feel, in all natural relationships, a spiritual dignity like that of the priest. He declared that it is not only at the altar and in the cloister that the work of God is done. He said it is also accomplished in honest toil, in the affairs of government, and in the institution of marriage and the home. . . . We must turn once more to the teachings of the great reformation leaders. This means a greater recognition of the fact that the Protestant vocation encompasses all phases of living. We need to appreciate the reformation tradition that we are personally responsible for the political conduct of our democracy. We must shoulder our obligations in keeping with Luther's belief in the supremacy of the people. The Christian cannot keep his religion in a closed compartment if he is to keep faith with the teachings of Luther, Calvin and Zwingli."

A definition of politics that Youngdahl often used was that it is "the machinery by which society makes its moral decisions." He did not elaborate upon it, but the implication is that he had a positive view of the value of the State as the order which upholds the moral principles held by society. It did not operate automatically, however. Youngdahl often said that "we get just as good government as we will work for and just as bad government as we will allow." He urged people to renounce their contempt for politics and government, an attitude which — more than anything else — was encouraging corruption in government.

What did Youngdahl believe the role of the Church should be? While he stressed the importance of Christians' participating in politics, Youngdahl never advised the organized church to do more than inspire its members to go into politics. He believed that church people had been appallingly indifferent towards politics, but he did not suggest that the church organize itself into a pressure group. He was a member of the Board of Trustees of the Minnesota Council of Churches while he was Governor. Apparently he knew of its social action program, yet there is no record that he either approved or disapproved of its program.

Youngdahl was a staunch advocate of Protestant unity and believed that the Church would have to move toward unification if it were to become an effective force in the world. In a Reformation address he said:

"The Church caught again the spirit of the Reformation during the recent holocaust of war. We must not allow the flame to be dimmed again, as we realize the church was a tower of strength in the defense of human rights. We must catch the spirit of unity. Religion must become the great unifying force among men — it offers divine power, one moral law, one family of mankind. There should be no impractical partitioning of the Christian community. We need to remind ourselves that in the beginning the Christian faith was above all a fellowship, and fellowship is central in the teaching of the Gospel. The weaknesses of division do not allow for the perfect attainment of fellowship. The challenge given to the Protestant Church of America is to help lead the way towards the achievement of unity of action and purpose. The job is simply too big to permit division and competition."

This, then, is the Christian faith that Youngdahl carried with him into politics. The subsequent account of his years in the Governor's office will describe his attempts to apply his Christian principles to the complex problems of government.

CHAPTER FIVE

The Judge Turns Politician

In 1946, attention was focused on the contest for United States Senator, rather than the governorship. The Republicans were gunning for isolationist Hendrik Shipstead, who had been Senator since 1922 largely on the strength of his popularity with Scandinavian and church-going people. Some Republicans thought Stassen was the only one who could defeat Shipstead, but Stassen had presidential ambitions. It was decided that Edward Thye, who had succeeded to the office of Governor when Stassen resigned to join the Navy in 1943 and had won re-election handily in 1944, should be the Stassen machine's candidate for the Senate. This left the gubernatorial candidacy vacant, and the Stassen group turned to Youngdahl.

It was not the first time he had been approached about filing for Governor. Some Republicans had urged him to run in 1938, but he had rejected their overtures because of his conviction that his young family needed more of his time than he could give it if he became Governor. He had been approached again in 1942 and asked to run for Lieutenant-Governor on the Stassen ticket; but he had chosen to run for the Minnesota Supreme Court instead.

Bernhard LeVander, later to become chairman of the State Central Committee, was chosen to contact Youngdahl. The conversation occurred in the judicial chambers the Monday after Lincoln's birthday, just before Youngdahl was to go into the court. LeVander told him that a group of men in the party had become interested in proposing his name for the Governorship and stood ready to provide him with full backing.

Youngdahl Decides to File for Governor

Youngdahl's answer came in a roundabout way. "Oscar died last night." He was referring to his brother, who had been a Congressman. Then, after LeVander had expressed his surprise and had offered his condolences (the news of the Congressman's death had not yet been announced publicly), Youngdahl continued, "His death will affect the answer I give you. I had decided to stay out of competitive politics as long as Oscar was in Congress because matters would be too complicated with two Youngdahls in the picture." Youngdahl agreed to meet with G.O.P. leaders in the Stassen group, and the conversation ended. Ten days later, after conferring with Stassen, Youngdahl filed as a candidate for Governor, his policy statement making it clear that he was entering the campaign without any commitments to anyone.

LeVander has revealed the reasons for Youngdahl's being selected as the gubernatorial candidate. In the following order they were: his record of outstanding public service on the bench, in community organizations and through many contacts made as a widely-sought public speaker; his familiar, Scandinavian name, an asset in Minnesota; his remarkable record for winning large majorities in areas of the state where the Republicans had not been too successful; his reputation for integrity; and his liberal political views. Youngdahl had not been active in the Republican party up to this time. This was not unusual, since the judicial offices were non-partisan. This did not counter-balance the factors in his favor. To understand the true significance of his qualifications, it is necessary to describe the political background in Minnesota. To do this properly, a brief historical sketch of Minnesota politics will be necessary, because Minnesota political history has not been primarily a story of the struggle of Democrats against Republicans. Rather, it should be considered in terms of the manner in which agrarian protest politics has shaped the present complexion of both parties.

The Republican Party and the Scandinavians

The appearance of the Republican Party as the reforming element in American politics, the arrival of early Scandinavian immigrants to Minnesota and the admission of Minnesota to the Union came at approximately the same time. With the influx of new pioneers from the east and from Europe (especially Germany and Scandinavian countries) the Minnesota territory so prospered and grew during the 1850s that it was admitted into the Union in 1858.

The first mass meeting of the Republican Party in Minnesota was held at St. Anthony, March 29, 1855. A convention assembled in St. Paul, July 25, 1855, and prepared a platform which denounced repeal of the Missouri Compromise, protested the extension of slavery, demanded repeal of the Fugitive Slave Law, favored river and harbor improvements and called for the prohibition of the manufacture and sale of liquor. It was a party of reform. In championing the cause of abolition, it attracted the aura of a crusade around it.

The Republican Party was congenial to the Scandinavians, not because it was conservative but because it was a party of reform, supporting moral issues in which the Scandinavians believed, chiefly abolition and temperance. That the subsequent Scandinavian population of Minnesota has been predominantly Republican is only a partial truth, but a truth that needs to be emphasized. Previous to the advent of the Farmer-Labor Party in Minnesota, Scandinavians usually voted Republican. A Scandinavian Democrat was very rare and looked upon with suspicion. The general opinion that Scandinavians believed Republicanism and Lutheranism should go hand in hand was not entirely without foundation.

Arthur Naftalin refers to another factor which kept Scandinavians from being Democrats in Minnesota: "This is the generally assumed domination of the Democratic Party in Minnesota by people of the Roman Catholic faith." He explains that this prevented a thorough fusion of the Democrats with agrarian political movements, which were dominated by Scandinavian Lutherans. The Democratic Party has two strongholds — St. Paul and the Iron Range Cities. There is a discernible correlation between the Catholic population and Democratic victories in those areas.

However, the Republican Party did not retain the whole-hearted loyalty of the Scandinavians. After the Civil War it became the party of Big Business, dominated by eastern financial and industrial interests. Minnesota farmers discovered that they could not rely on the Republican Party for the redress of their problems. They were frustrated by lack of representation, just at a time when the post-Civil War revolution in agriculture brought them prolonged economic distress.

The Midwest Problem

The changed economic conditions, occasioned by the opening of the Midwest to immigrants, brought a set of completely new political problems to that area and eventuated in the rise of agrarian protest movements, the triumph of the Farmer-Labor Party during the depression and a "liberalization" of Minnesota's Republican Party in the 1940's.

The Homestead Act of 1862 opened the fertile plains to hordes of settlers who streamed west to stake their land claims. New methods of agriculture greatly increased production. By 1900 the Midwest farmers had not only enough produce to feed the nation but to export millions of tons as well. They had become businessmen, selling in a free competitive market and facing risks peculiar to farming because of its subjection to climatic conditions.

The farmer was caught in the prolonged distress that accompanied the transition from a simple frontier economy to a complex, inter-dependent society. Most of the agricultural land in Minnesota was used to grow wheat, and the farmer's slowness in turning to diversified farming was a basic cause of his distress.

However, the farmer blamed the railroad barons, the bankers and the terminal grain elevator owners. Wall Street was the term symbolizing the enemy of agrarian interests. The farmer was dependent on the railroads for getting his crops to market, and the railroads were under the control of a few powerful men like James J. Hill, J. P. Morgan and the Harrimans. Since he sold his crops for cash to pay old debts and finance new crops, fluctuation in money values affected him swiftly and seriously; but he was not in control of currency policy, which was shaped by Eastern financial interests. Since the farmer had to borrow heavily in a credit system adapted to an industrial system controlled by Eastern interests, rather than an agricultural economy, he suffered. Tariff was a problem, too, since he sold in an unprotected market and bought supplies in one protected by tariffs whose schedules were set in favor of Eastern industrial interests. Therefore, he wanted more protection for the markets to which he sold and less for those from which he bought. The wheat farmers from Minnesota and the Dakotas suffered most from these problems. It is not strange that political agitation should be strongest in those states. (Note: An excellent analysis of the "midwest problems" is found in Russel B. Nye's **Midwestern Progressive Politics**, East Lansing, 1951)

Minnesota Protest Politics

When the farmer turned to political action for redress of his problems, he was frustrated. As has been noted, the Republican Party was dominated by Eastern interests. The Democrats had little influence in Midwest politics after the Civil War, because their party was regarded as the party of treason; this attitude was reflected in the remark of one Kansan, who said, "Hell is peopled by two kinds of folks, those who don't read the Bible and those who vote Democratic."

In the late sixties, there began a series of third party movements in the Midwest that furnished an outlet for the spirit of unrest and protest of the farmers — the Granger movement, the Anti-Monopoly and Greenback parties in the seventies; the Farmers' Alliance in the eighties and the People's Party and Populism in the nineties. Near the end of the century, the rise of organized labor in Minnesota and elsewhere added to the protest potential. The frontier had closed. Free land was gone. The worker had become dependent on the industrial system; he, too, looked for political action to redress his grievances.

The most important of these protest movements, as far as the history of Minnesota politics is concerned, was the Non-Partisan League. This movement, begun by Arthur C. Townley in North Dakota in 1915, gave the farmers a basic education in politics, the fundamentals of economic policy and the value of organization in gaining redress of their troubles. It laid a solid foundation for the Farmer-Labor Party, which dominated Minnesota politics from 1930 to 1938.

Since the League's program echoed prevailing criticisms of the business practices that had plagued the farmers for decades, it quickly won support from Minnesota farmers. By June, 1917, it had 50,000 members in Minnesota. The platform called for state-owned terminal elevators, flour mills, packing houses and storage plants; for state inspection of grain-grading practices; for exemption of farm improvements from taxation; for state hail insurance; and for rural credit banks.

Townley's original intention was not to establish a third party but rather to canvass a bloc of votes that could be shifted to candidates of either party who were favorable to the farmers' cause. However, the movement gradually developed into a full-fledged political party. In 1918, the League formed a coalition with the Minnesota State Federation of Labor, and in 1924 the League disbanded to make room for the Farmer-Labor Federation. The latter group's slate of candidates lost the 1924 election, because of charges that the Communists had infiltrated the movement, fear of the party's radicalism (it had advocated government ownership of basic industries) and the traditional Republican dominance of the state.

Because of the charges of Communist infiltration, the Federation dissolved and was replaced by the Farmer-Labor Association in 1925. Its constitution excluded Communists from membership but reaffirmed the socialistic doctrines of the Non-Partisan League and was organized in such a manner as to keep the most militant and politically-conscious members in control of the party. Not only individuals but economic organizations, such as unions and cooperatives, could belong upon payment of a 2% per capita tax. The biennial convention was empowered to endorse candidates for state offices and United States Senator, draft the platform, amend the constitution and appoint the executive committee; thus it controlled the party effectively.

Floyd B. Olson and the Farmer-Labor Party

It was the leadership of Floyd B. Olson that transformed this Association from an educational force to a potent political machine that won victories at the polls in four successive elections. The Farmer-Labor Party won the 1930 election with Olson as its candidate and thus the story of protest politics in Minnesota arrived at its climax.

The party was in power during a time of turbulent economic crisis, which stirred the people to a radical mood. Olson's dominance of the party, whose extremists demanded radical political revision, was won through masterful and realistic acumen. Emergency measures were necessary to relieve the poverty brought on by the depression. Olson carefully gauged public opinion to determine to what extent it would be possible to put the Farmer-Labor program into effect. He had to restrain extremists who wanted to launch the new order. The party's program, while the party was in office, did not depart markedly from the traditional pattern of Midwest protest in that it sought to relieve specific grievances of the people by specific measures. If these measures happened to call for a greater degree of governmental intervention in the economic order, it was not as much that the party was seeking to install a new system as it was a matter of finding a new means of meeting the crisis.

As the depression became more severe, Olson's strategy called for a gradual shift to the left. Desirous of extending the functions of government for the benefit of the under-privileged, he made speeches that were designed to accustom the people to the idea of governmental intervention. He frequently spoke of the curative function of government, lay-ing special emphasis on taxation power, which he believed could adjust the haphazard distribution of wealth resulting from the capitalistic system and provide social services for the underprivileged. He conceded that this was strong medicine but presented it as the only alternative to the complete socializa-tion of wealth. In a speech at Red Wing he developed his view of government: "The old pioneer idea of government as confined to police power has passed off the stage. We have now reached the socialized state. Just how far it shall extend its functions and services is no longer a matter of theory but a problem of practice and expediency. The present economic system has shown its inability to provide employment and even food and shelter for millions of Americans. Only Gov-ernment can cope with the situation." (Note: George H. Mayer, **The Political Career of Floyd B. Olson,** Minneapolis, 1951, p. 108)

Olson and his party were at the height of their power in 1933. Despite a hostile Senate and a lukewarm House, the Governor was successful in getting a state income tax, relief bills, labor bills prohibiting · yellow-dog contracts, limiting women on industrial jobs to a fifty-four-hour week and out-lawing the use of the injunction in labor disputes; important conservation legislation; stronger securities legislation; and a start on old-age pensions. At a special legislative session later in the year, Olson was successful in getting an extra appro-priation of $5,000,000 for relief.

Under Olson's regime, labor made significant strides. As a result of a series of strikes, the unions gained the right to organize, the right of collective bargaining, and wage increases. Olson's sympathies were on the side of labor, and that alone had a bearing on the outcome of labor disputes. He helped to bring about a public attitude favorable to the concept that organized labor, as well as management, deserved legal protection of its rights.

The effectiveness of the Farmer-Labor Party was drastically impaired by its failure to win control of the Minnesota legislature. Even when it was electing state officers by sizable pluralities, it could never gain mastery of the Legislature. Arthur Naftalin, associate professor of political science and administrative assistant to Gov. Orville Freeman, attributes the party's failure to control the Legislature to the process of electing legislators without party designation. Since the legislative candidate is not dependent on any party for his election, the winning party cannot control the individual legislators. Intended to abate the influence of partisanship in state government and put government on a more efficient business basis, this provision in the constitution has merely transferred partisanship from the polls to the hotel room and opened the door to all kinds of political jockeying farther removed than ever from the control of the voters. (Note: Arthur Naftalin, "The Failure of the Farmer-Labor Party to Capture Control of the Minnesota Legislature," **American Political Science Review,** Vol. 38, No. 1, Feb., 1944)

After Olson's death on August 2, 1936, the Farmer-Labor regime was marked by a growing division within the party between factions seeking to gain control of the patronage-dispensing machinery. Nevertheless the party left a permanent legacy of progressivism in state politics. The people had become accustomed during the thirties to the idea of the state assuming responsibility for the economic and social welfare of its citizens. When the Republicans returned to power, they had to contend with this change of attitude.

The Stassen Regime

The Republican Party regained control in 1938 on the

heels of an ambitious thirty-year-old lawyer, Harold Stassen, who acquired his early political training in campus politics at the University of Minnesota. He was elected to his first political office as Dakota County Attorney in 1930, an office he held until he was elected Governor. He organized the Young Republican League, and was its first chairman, while still in college.

The Young Republicans wrested power from the old guard, and Stassen announced himself as a candidate for Governor in 1938. He easily overcame the conservative candidate in the primary. In his campaign against Elmer Benson, the Farmer-Labor candidate, Stassen pledged himself to a clean-up of state politics and the scandals in the state administration; reduction of operating costs and at the same time more social security, extension of old age assistance, increased pensions for the blind and better relief standards, tax revision on the basis of ability to pay and a square deal for the worker. He did not promise a return to "the good old days," but advocated a new "Republican Liberalism." He was elected, at the age of 31, by the largest majority (291,000) ever amassed by a gubernatorial candidate.

What was this new liberalism? In an article written for the **Christian Science Monitor,** Stassen set forth his credo. In it he said: "We feel that the objective of government must be to make the greatest possible contribution to the welfare, happiness and progress of its people in every station in life: that this can be done best by maintaining the individual liberties of its citizens; by building confidence of the people in government. Democratic government should be an aid to individual initiative, not a substitute for it. We do not feel that we can answer the problems of social and economic maladjustment by shrugging our shoulders and saying, let the government do it."

Further insight into the philosophy behind Stassen's liberalism is gained from his answer to a question concerning the difference between his program and the New Deal: "I think the difference is a matter of emphasis. Individual opportunity and social security are the two great considerations of a people's government. The New Deal sought security above all else. I think now a new balance must be worked out between security and opportunity. Opportunity and the individual drive to acquire are the motive power of a democracy. Security is the safety device. I think that a Republican administration should seek to maintain the safety devices, but should make certain that the motive power is encouraged. A Republican tax program, for instance, should call for a re-adjustment of any tax which is repressive to business. The idea that taxation is a proper weapon to be used against business is a harmful fallacy. . . . Taxes must be contrived to encourage business to expand rather than to threaten its very existence." (Note: Harold Stassen, "Democracy in the Land of Lakes," **Christian Science Monitor**, March 23, 1940, p. 1.) In theory, at least, Stassen was securely within the Republican tradition.

Those who defend Stassen and his liberalism point to his record of achievement while in office. He cleaned up state politics. He brought about a re-organization of state government. A system of financial control, with power centered in a state business manager directly responsible to the Governor, was created. Open competitive buying brought a great reduction in operating costs. A civil service system was created by the legislature, and padded payrolls were reduced, resulting in a saving of $2,500,000 a year. Stassen also wrote and brought about the passage of the Minnesota Labor Law. This law defines mass picketing and lockouts while a contract is still in force as unfair labor practices. Its heart is a provision requiring a "cooling-off period" of ten days, during which the disputants are brought together by the state labor conciliator for direct negotiations. In case of disputes involving national security, a thirty-day moratorium is required; during this time a fact-finding board of three, representing industry, labor and the public, attempts to work out a solution. During the next seven years the amount of strikes was reduced by 70%. Nearly 1,200 labor disputes were settled without an hour of work stoppage.

In four years the state's indebtedness was reduced to $39,445,070; real and personal property taxes were reduced

46%; a bill controlling loan sharks was passed; programs were launched for the purpose of finding work for the unemployed, for the benefit of youth, and for the expansion and stimulation of the state's tourist trade.

Critics of the Stassen administration point to facts which prove, at least to their satisfaction, that Stassen was a "fake liberal." He put a homestead lien on the property of people who accepted old-age assistance, reduced taxes on banks by 50%, opposed federal aid for housing and slum clearance, gave tax reductions of $9,000,000 a year to iron ore mining companies, cut relief contributions, and reduced valuation on private utility lines from 40% to 5% of full value. The Minnesota labor law reduced the power of unions. The Stassen campaign committee received $50,000 for the 1938 campaign from mining companies. Between the time the civil service law went into effect and the period when its provisions as to appointees fully applied, Stassen fired 10,000 state employees and replaced them with his own appointees, who were frozen into service by the law. Such was the evidence that made some people skeptical about the "liberalism" of the Stassen administration. (Note: A. I. Harris, "Harold Stassen, Fake Liberal," **New Republic,** June 5, 1944, p. 756)

Nevertheless it was true that the liberal wing of the Minnesota G.O.P. was in control of the state government. Stassen was "as near to being a political boss as Minnesota will stand." He rarely associated with old guard leaders but gathered around him instead a group of young leaders who, with a strong intra-party organization throughout the state, dominated state politics. Stassen was able to pick his own successor, Edward Thye, a farmer from Northfield of Norwegian descent, when he resigned to enter the Navy. A cleavage developed between the old guard, which dominated the legislature, and the Stassen machine, which backed Thye and Youngdahl. The latter inherited this intra-party tension and the problems that trailed along with it.

Characteristics of Minnesota Politics

The peculiar characteristics of Youngdahl's political environment now stand out more clearly. The one which comes most quickly into focus is the strong tradition of progressivism in the state, which grew out of the farmers' reform movements and came to a climax in the Farmer-Labor Party administration. Even though the people of Minnesota have been cautious about radical changes in the American system, they have grown accustomed to the idea of the state doing something about social and economic problems. This innate progressivism tends to be dormant in times of prosperity, as in the period following World War II, but Minnesota politicians are not insensitive to its presence. The threat of drastic action to regulate the economy lurks beneath the surface, even though there is no need for action at the present.

The Republican Party has not gone untouched by this progressive tradition. Although it is still the party of the conservatives in the state, and although Stassen could scarcely qualify as an unambiguous progressive, there is an imposing faction of younger men who have pronounced liberal leanings, in the sense that they believe that human welfare is an important consideration in government. They may be chary of too much governmental control of the economy, but they are insistent that business and industry assume social responsibility and probably would be willing to use the processes of government to enforce this responsibility. The Young Republican Club has been the training ground for the G.O.P. liberals in the state, and the Stassen machine gave them the quintessence of political power in Minnesota. The conservative faction of the party was not inanimate, however, and such veterans as Roy C. Dunn, Claude Allen, Stafford King, J. A. A. Burnquist and Mike Holm were not always eager to follow Youngdahl's lead.

The second characteristic of Minnesota politics is that a weak party system prevails. This is due in part to the spirit of independence that characterizes Minnesota voters and politicians. Arthur Naftalin estimates that one-third of the voters are independents, and that in 1944 and 1946 not more than 3,000 to 4,000 persons in the entire state participated in the official caucuses of both major parties. (Note: Arthur Naftalin, **A History of the Farmer-Labor Party in Minnesota,** unpublished Ph.D. thesis, University of Minnesota, 1948, p. 73) Malcolm Moos and E. W. Kenworthy observed in 1946 that "Minnesota voters have always been rather adaptable in their party loyalties and are consequently somewhat tolerant of fence-jumping in their candidates"—as an explanation of the popular support given to independent-minded Hendrik Shipstead even though he deserted the Farmer-Labor Party to join the Republicans in 1943 when his old party fused with the Democrats. (Note: Malcolm Moos and E. W. Kenworthy, "Dr. Shipstead Comes to Judgment," **Harper's,** Vol. 192, July 1946, p. 22) The fact that Minnesota delivered for Truman and Hubert Humphrey in 1948, while electing Republicans to state offices, is indicative of the independence of Minnesota voters. Despite the fusion of the Farmer-Labor Party with the Democrats in 1943, the Republican Party kept its position of dominance in state politics, even though voters strongly backed Democratic candidates for national offices.

The weak party system is due also to two legalities. The election laws permit a man to file for an office in the primary under a party label if he voted for a majority of the party's slate in the previous election. This does much to destroy party discipline, since candidates not endorsed by the party can run for office. Furthermore, it is possible in Minnesota for a Democrat to vote for Republican candidates in the primary and vice versa. This has often led to a certain amount of jockeying. Party strategy may call for a wholesale vote for a weak candidate of the other party, who could then be defeated easily in the general election.

Most destructive of all to responsible party government is the election of legislators on a non-partisan basis. Adopted by the reform-conscious legislators in the 1913 session in revulsion against the low standards of morality in partisan politics around the turn of the century, this reform was meant to improve Minnesota's government. Ironically, in recent years it has been the chief bulwark in the way of reform-minded governors with progressive programs. It has greatly weakened political parties in the state. Reducing the number of offices to be filled by party candidates has destroyed local party organization, because citizens have no real incentive to be active in the party if the party cannot offer them political offices. Furthermore, candidates for the legislature are left to find their own means of support. This does not mean that they are as independent as the public would like to think. It only means that it becomes next to impossible to determine the nature of the commitments made by, or the type of support given to, the candidate. The result is the increase of the influence of special interest groups over legislators and the almost complete elimination of any party discipline over them during a session. Party government, at best difficult in American politics, is rendered even weaker in Minnesota by this legality.

Minnesota politics is also unusual in that the Scandinavian population has a prominent role. At first it was difficult for the immigrants to become politically vocal. The major parties, dominated by Yankee settlers, more or less ignored the immigrants and their problems; so the Scandinavians turned to the protest movements as their vehicle of power. Arthur Naftalin alludes to the dominant role they played in the various agrarian movements in his history of the Farmer-Labor Party: "It is significant to note that, in its first entry into Minnesota politics, the Populist Party . . . drew its strength chiefly from the Republican Party, and principally from the Scandinavian nationalities. Since the 1890's and particularly during the period of the Farmer-Labor Party's ascendancy, the Scandinavian nationalities have played a predominant role in Minnesota protest politics." The major parties began in the closing decades of the nineteenth century to place Scandinavians on the ballots as their candidates. Beginning with Knute Nelson in the 1890's, John Lind (Democrat) in 1896, and John A. Johnson in the early decades of the 1900's — all of whom became governors — there has been a recognition of the political asset of a Scandinavian name. Since Theodore Christianson's election in 1924, every governor except Harold

Stassen has come from Scandinavian parentage and has had a Scandinavian name — Floyd B. Olson, Elmer Benson, Edward Thye, Luther Youngdahl and C. Elmer Anderson. (Note: A History of the Farmer-Labor Party in Minnesota, p. 18)

The Scandinavians have been independent individualists rather than loyal party members, and it has not been easy for party bosses to deliver their votes. Their political philosophy tends to be liberal, as is evident in their support of protest movements, Theodore Roosevelt's Bull Moose Party in 1912 and the New Deal in the thirties and forties.

Youngdahl's 1946 Campaign

Against this political background, Youngdahl's assets as a candidate assume their proper significance. He had not been active in the Republican Party during his judicial career, since the judicial offices were non-partisan. To compensate for his lack of faithful service in the ranks of the party, he had behind him an impressive record of public service. The fact that he was an independent enhanced, rather than decreased, his value in a state where the party system is weak and the people approve of independence. His nomination also illustrates the fact that parties in Minnesota must often recruit their candidates from outside the party organization.

The dominance of the Scandinavian population in Minnesota politics also helps to explain Youngdahl's vote-getting ability. It was not just his name that was political capital, but his personality as well. A man who always "takes a good picture," he is an excellent example of the Nordic type of personality that has been idealized in Minnesota cultural traditions. He is a physical specimen reminiscent of the legendary "big Swede" of pioneer days whose feats are glorified in the mythical Paul Bunyan stories. Standing over six feet in height and weighing over 200 pounds, he possesses what seems to be an inexhaustible supply of energy. Silver-haired, with a ruddy complexion and blue eyes, and a hearty disposition, his physical attributes distinguish him as the kind of man no one could mistake for anything but a Swede.

Although deeply religious, Youngdahl impressed people as being not at all "stuffy." His speeches sparkled with humor and he was not hesitant about demonstrating his human side by leading a community sing or taking part in a home town talent show. His love of outdoor life, of hunting, fishing, hiking and golfing, and his belief in keeping physically fit, are typical of the Scandinavian people. On the platform and in social gatherings, he reveals a forceful, enthusiastic quality common to members of his family. His outgoing personality is combined with a genuine liking for people which enabled him to dominate a social gathering without domineering it. The impact of his personality prompted one reporter to describe him as "an awfully nice man, a strong, shining kind of man, not only because of his huge health but his delicate mental instrument. Remember he can make scholarly distinctions as to what justice is; he knows the difference not only between good and bad but between what is good and slightly less good. And this takes brains."

That the Republican party leaders should find his reputation for integrity to be a political asset is not surprising. A political party needs that type of candidate to display before the public eye, even if he is only a figurehead. Youngdahl was especially valuable, since he stood for the kind of honesty, sobriety, and humanity so much admired among Minnesota church people.

Due to his wide reputation as a speaker, Youngdahl's pronounced humanitarian views were well known throughout Minnesota. Against the background of the state's traditional progressive outlook in political matters, this trait was distinctly to his advantage.

Youngdahl campaigned with characteristic vigor to win the Republican nomination. He visited over 150 towns and villages in the state, making speeches and personal contacts wherever he went. His prodigious energy made him capable of a rugged pace.

Not only in this campaign but throughout his administration, he carried on a vigorous speaking schedule. He was willing to speak at any and all occasions, sometimes crowding several engagements into a single night, which necessitated his driving a good portion of the night in order to get back to his desk in time for other work the next day. He travelled as much as 5,000 miles a month, even during the periods between campaigns. A note of his speaking engagements, reported in the press, revealed that ranking first on his calendar were those addresses which he presented before church groups. He was much in demand at high school and college commencements, service clubs, Parent-Teachers' Association, unions, professional organizations, farmers' groups, fairs, civic celebrations and youth gatherings.

Youngdahl's willingness to give so many speeches may have been prompted in part by an awareness of his forcefulness on the platform. An illustration of his effectiveness was a speech he gave before the student body at Gustavus Adolphus College in May, 1951. Even though a program lasting an hour and a half preceded his address, he held the interest of the students for more than an hour. His platform presence commanded attention. He used a powerful delivery, frequently punctuated with effective gestures. A listener could not refrain from being convinced that he was very much in earnest about his convictions and his program. He was at ease before his audience and frequently injected humor and apt illustrations into his talk. His talks were a compounding of pertinent facts, moral exhortation and warm human interest material. Although his oratory was not flamboyant, he was a good showman, quick to take advantage of a situation to capture the attention of his audience.

Youngdahl campaigned extensively, because he believed that the personal contacts he made with people all over the state were the most significant of his campaign methods. "You can't be a strong leader unless you are close to the people," he has often told his friends; and he tried to keep close to them during his term in office, as well as during campaigns. He believed that the government belonged to the people and that the governor should report its activities to the voters by talking to them around a tractor, in the fields and at the work benches.

Herbert Nelson often accompanied him on trips to help him make contacts. On one of their expeditions, they stopped in a Sauk Center garage. Nelson was absorbed in political talk with the manager. When there was a lull in the conversation, he discovered that Youngdahl had disappeared and went to find him. He located him in the back of the repair shop bending down by a car. A closer look revealed a mechanic under the car. Youngdahl was lining up another vote. Mechanics had votes, just like managers.

Nelson claims that he never heard Youngdahl promise to fulfill special favors. His answer was usually the same: "I must be the governor of all the people. If what you ask is going to benefit only you, I shall not fight for it."

In his early association with Youngdahl on campaigns, he noticed that his friend always recorded the names of people who talked to him at any length. He asked Youngdahl about it and learned that he usually dropped them a line later. After he became Governor, he kept up this practice. People he had met would be surprised with his letters of congratulations or sympathy, as the occasion warranted. Such contacts enabled him to keep in touch with the people and gave him an insight into their thoughts. In following this practice Youngdahl was taking advantage of one of the practical realities of state politics, the fact that the citizens expect their governor to interpret their vague desires and formulate them into a program.

Youngdahl's first campaign was not particularly spectacular. He made a point of avoiding controversy over personalities and parties, which marked the campaign for United States Senator that year. In fact, his campaign was over-shadowed by the race between Shipstead and Thye. His platform followed the program of his party. When the primary election returns were in, Youngdahl had won with a plurality of 127,455 over his nearest opponent, Hjalmer Peterson.

His campaign for election against his D.F.L. opponent, Harold H. Barker, laid stress on good government, youth conservation, law enforcement, and tolerance and understanding in human relations; but it was no crusade. He stirred no controversy over such issues as the slot machine racket. He aroused no fears, or hopes, of a reform administration. When the returns had been counted he had garnered 519,067 votes to Barker's 349,565.

CHAPTER SIX

The Governor and
The One-Armed Bandits

Before the end of the 1947 session of the Minnesota Legislature Luther Youngdahl had gained a national reputation in politics, mainly attributable to his law enforcement campaign. He challenged the "one-armed bandits," the slot-machine racket, to a knock-down fight and thus touched off one of the most violent disputes Minnesota has ever had.

Youngdahl's inaugural address on January 8, 1947, gave portent of things to come. The message had a humanitarian emphasis that was to be characteristic of his administration. Its emphasis on human welfare is evident in such statements as these: "Money that is carefully appropriated for our schools, for certain essential activities in home building, for public health, for the care of the mentally sick, for dependent children, for the blind and for the recreation and guidance of our youth, is not an expenditure in the real sense of the word. It is an investment in the character, stability and happiness of our people. . . . We have advanced far in penetrating the frontiers of science. The frontier of the next few decades which we must explore is that of the field of human relations. There is no alternative if the world is to survive."

The address set forth four objectives which he wanted the Legislature to utilize as guides: building up human resources, strengthening economic resources, improving governmental efficiency and providing new revenue. The humanitarian emphasis is evident, both in the way he interpreted the program of the state in terms of human need and the amount of space he gave to his first objective. For example, in discussing housing, he said, "This is not simply a problem of lumber and bricks, but is directly related to our first main objective, the conservation of human resources. Worry, broken homes, juvenile delinquency; these are but a few of the evils which follow in the train of the housing shortage." The problem of delinquent youth he treated not primarily as a matter of protecting society against young criminals, but as a matter of the conservation of the greatest of the state's resources, the youth. Law enforcement was stressed, because lack of respect for law has a detrimental effect upon children.

In the closing words of his message, the Governor made it plain how he intended to function. He welcomed the opportunity of talking to legislators about problems concerning the welfare of the state and promised to recognize the separation of authority between the legislative and executive branches, expressing his hope that there would be cooperation between them. Then he said, "Although I believe in the two-party system of government, the governor is elected to serve all the people. It has been well said that politics is the machinery by which society makes its moral decisions. I believe strongly in that philosophy of politics. I will endeavor to serve you without reference to blocs or pressure groups and without regard to political consequences; I shall attempt to follow my own convictions on any matter that comes before me. I assure you that I am free to do just that." He told a story of a Coast Guard captain who commanded a rescue squad faced with the responsibility of rescuing the crew of a ship that had floundered onto the rocks in a raging storm. One of the inexperienced members of the squad said, "Captain, with that tide against us and the terrific gale, we will be able to get out there all right, but we will never be able to get back." To this the captain replied, "Prepare the boat. We have to go out, but we don't have to come back." Few Minnesotans today doubt that Luther Youngdahl meant what he said when he ended his address with the words, "So it is with us, we must go out; we don't have to come back." At the time few people, probably not even the Governor himself, were aware of the political dynamite hidden in his program and his intent to carry it out regardless of consequences to personal or party success.

G.O.P. party leaders were taken aback by his frontal attack on gambling and his openly-stated intention of enforcing the laws against it. One of them, who had helped draft the speech, claimed that Youngdahl had inserted the recommendations entirely on his own, without consulting party leaders. They had not been in the original draft.

Youngdahl lost no time in showing that he meant business about law enforcement. He declared he would use his full powers to oust sheriffs and prosecuting attorneys who did not enforce the laws to the letter, and he began to exert pressure on the legislators to pass the "anti-slot-machine bill," as it was labelled. In February he appointed a citizens' law enforcement committee, headed by Bradshaw Mintener, vice-president and general counsel of Pillsbury Mills. The purpose of the committee was to "keep law enforcement on a high plane, advise the governor with respect to all matters pertaining to law enforcement, study bills and arouse public support for the program."

As soon as people directly affected had caught their breath, outraged cries of disapproval went up, and the opposition began to form its battle lines. It should be remembered that Youngdahl made law enforcement an issue almost four years before the famous Kefauver Committee had dramatized it on television, abruptly arousing nationwide public ire against gambling syndicates. In Minnesota, during 1946-47, five thousand individuals or firms paid the special federal tax of $100 on slot machines. Churches and clubs regularly conducted raffles and bingo and other gambling games, although gambling was illegal. Youngdahl was going against popular opinion and practice.

Most vocal in their opposition were resort owners and country clubs, who claimed these restrictions would seriously damage their businesses. The tourist trade brought an estimated $200,000,000 to the state annually, and they believed that keeping the state "wide open" helped make Minnesota more attractive as a vacation spot.

Others complained that "the blue-nose governor" was trying to reform the morals of the state according to his own strict Lutheran beliefs and would succeed only in making the state appear prudish.

The American Legion post at Faribault expressed its doubt that it could finance the state convention the following summer without the help of income from the slot machines in their club-house. Roy T. Anderson, an American Legion spokesman, voiced an argument heard among law enforcement officers and other opponents, "I certainly am not supporting gambling, but enforcement should be at the local level."

Behind the opposition lurked the shadowy figures of the racketeers who owned the machines and whose "take" was about $4,000,000 annually, according to the Governor's estimates. Dr. George Mecklenberg, pastor of Minneapolis' Wesley Methodist Church and active supporter of Youngdahl during the legislative battle, took occasion to refer to a five-million-dollar underworld syndicate that was seeking to defeat Youngdahl's program. Sen. Harry Wahlstrand of Willmar recalled that, during the legislative battle over the bill, there was an influx of what he called "underworld characters from Chicago," presumably imported to wield their influence against the passage of the bill.

When the bill came up in committee, the gambling interests brought 600 of their supporters from all parts of the state to pack the public hearing. A campaign of ridicule was launched against the Governor. People who had supported him during his campaign were not too pleased with the unexpected turn of events. G.O.P. state chairman, Bernhard LeVander, wrote a note to Youngdahl in which he told him that many people thought he was attacking the problem too zealously and stressing the anti-slot machine bill out of all proportion to the rest of his excellent program. LeVander urged him to push for local enforcement instead.

To win the support of the legislators, Youngdahl attempted to exert his personal persuasion on them. He began by calling in the top leaders and lecturing them about the course he thought they should follow but he abandoned that approach and started scheduling a series of dinners at which he talked over legislative matters with a dozen or fifteen of the members at a time. By this method he formed his own bloc of legislators who were sympathetic to his program. Senators Harry Wahlstrand and A. L. Almen carried a great share of the burden of the law enforcement battle.

In winning the support of one key senator in the opposition party, Youngdahl displayed a shrewd sense of politics. Like many state senators, this man was a lawyer and his firm had clients who had an interest in legislation. In this case the clients were brewers. Unlike some state legislators, this man had earned a reputation for integrity as he carried out his difficult dual role as a representative of the people and the lawyer of a powerful company.

Youngdahl had a conference with the senator one day during the battle over the slot machines. "Why don't you go to those brewers? There's no good reason for them to undermine the reputation of their companies by being mixed up in defending this law-breaking gambling business. If they are wise, they'll stop lobbying against the bill."

The senator promised. His arguments were heeded. The brewers ceased pressuring the legislators amenable to them.

By these methods, Youngdahl gradually formed a bloc of legislators who supported his program.

When it was apparent that the Legislature was walking gingerly and hedging in the face of violent opposition, Youngdahl took his appeal directly to the people. Twice a week, over seventeen radio stations, he set forth his cause to the voters. He warned them that a small minority was jeopardizing his law enforcement program. In one of his speeches he expressed his opinion that the law enforcement program should alarm only those who seek to profit through the evasion of laws. "Organized vice and corruption can exist only where officials are lax in the performance of their responsibilities and when the public is apathetic in its duty," he said.

A week later he called attention to the disclosure by Richard Golling, public examiner, of connivance between public officials and slot machine owners. In the village of Savage, slot machines had been installed in the municipal liquor store. In Benton County the sheriff admitted he knew that officials had arranged with slot machine owners for machines to be installed in the county on a fee basis and had played them himself. Youngdahl proceeded to alert his listeners to "a most persistent effort to prevent enactment of the anti-slot machine bill" and to urge the people to counteract it. He said, "If the people who want to see this racket driven from the state are going to see their wishes fulfilled, they must make it clear to their legislators that they want the bill passed."

The people responded. Letters from all types of persons began to pour into Youngdahl's office and flooded the desks of the legislators, some of whom declared it was the largest avalanche of mail they had ever received. Most of it favored the Governor's program. The clinching argument, clearly revealing the sentiment of the people, was the result of a poll taken by **The Minneapolis Tribune,** which found that 70% approved, 23% disapproved and 7% were undecided about the anti-slot machine bill.

The churches of the state were active in rallying public support. The St. Paul Council of Churches chose a committee to call on key legislators and made a concerted effort, by letters to the pastors in the city, to get the people to write to their legislators. Nearly all the denominational bodies in the state backed the cause by official resolutions or letter-writing campaigns. Alton M. Motter, Executive Secretary of the St. Paul Council of Churches, recalls that Congregational, Presbyterian, Augustana Lutheran, Evangelical Lutheran and Methodist church groups went on record in favor of the bill. The St. Paul Council petitioned the Minnesota Council of Churches to organize a social action committee that would rally the pastors and people of the state to support the bill. This was accomplished, and the move marked the beginning of the organized political action program of the Council. The Brotherhood of the Svea Lutheran Church of Svea, Minnesota, passed a resolution which was sent to legislative leaders: "We deplore the laxity in law enforcement pertaining to drinking and gambling in the past, and we pledge Youngdahl our individual support." The St. Paul Presbytery of the Presbyterian Church adopted a resolution expressing unbounded enthusiasm for the Governor's program, particularly for his stand on law enforcement and his opposition to legalized or tolerated gambling.

There were ministers present at the first public hearing on the bill. The Rev. Howard Wiley, Executive Secretary of the Minneapolis Federation of Churches, testified, "You are going to see a lot more church people taking an interest in legislative affairs," in a statement supporting the bill. The Methodist ministers of the Minneapolis District endorsed the campaign and pledged not only their support but "the support of thousands of Methodist people throughout this area, irrespective of political connections."

The Minneapolis Tribune printed an article by its veteran political reporter, Mike Halloran, in which he referred to the "green lettuce" hanging out of legislators' pockets. The reference to the "pay-off" was too obvious and disconcerting to legislative leaders. "This is more than we can take," one of them said. Youngdahl praised the article as one of the key blows against the opposition to the bill.

The pressure of public opinion was becoming too oppressive to resist any longer. On April 9 the bill was passed by the House by a vote of 98-9 and was sent to the Senate. Up to the last minute, attempts were made in the Senate to kill it by crippling amendments. Two amendments designed to permit private clubs to have slot machines and to prevent revocation of licenses until after convictions of offenders, were defeated by the efforts of Wahlstrand and Almen. Sen. Donald Wright proposed an amendment that would have required the bill to be sent back to the House, but Wahlstrand stood up and warned the Senators that this would kill the bill for the session.

The bill was finally voted on and passed by a vote of 58-0 and sent to the Governor for his signature.

In its final form the law defined gambling devices to mean slot machines, roulette wheels, punch boards, numbers jars, and pinball machines which return coins or tokens redeemable in cash or goods. Bingo games when played to raise money for churches or charities were not prohibited. It also provided that the intentional possession or keeping of any gambling devices upon any premises licensed for carrying on any business, trade or commercial enterprise is cause for revocation of such licenses.

Law Enforcement is Demanded

Youngdahl did not let the matter rest with the passage of legislation. In June, 1947, he called together the local law enforcement officers for a conference to acquaint them with the new provisions of the laws passed by the 1947 Legislature and to discuss policies and interpretations with the intention of developing a uniform enforcement program. It was an unprecedented move in the history of the state. Jay Vessels wrote, "Certainly most of the veteran sheriffs and county attorneys were definitely hostile at being summoned to St. Paul to learn how to be policemen. It was another 'make or break' crisis, (but) Youngdahl's audacity and sincerity pulled him through."

That parley turned out to be one of the more dramatic incidents in Youngdahl's administration, as reporters' accounts of it bear out:

"Governor Youngdahl is ready to risk his political hide if any one or ten or fifty of the eighty-seven sheriffs and attorneys are scared they'll lose their political hides for enforcing the gambling laws. The governor made that plain today after he had told those 174 local officials, Wednesday, that all gambling laws must be enforced and that it was up to them to do the job.

" 'The time has come when the public officials have got

to quit worrying about the next election. If the public feels it doesn't want laws enforced, then it must ask the legislature to repeal them. They are going to be enforced as long as they are on the statute books and I am Governor. I refuse to assume an easy policy with respect to them. I refuse to lay off because I may lose votes,' the Governor told the officers.

"At the beginning of the afternoon session, Youngdahl faced a revolt. The forenoon session had been dull, far from enlightening. As the boys sat around wielding their knives and forks at their noon repasts a lot of them worked up quite a fury. 'What about it? Why have we got to take the heat for this guy's notions?' some of them asked.

"In the afternoon Sheriffs George Matson of Redwood Falls and Sam Owen of Duluth put some questions to Bradshaw Mintener, chairman of the Governor's law enforcement committee, who sent for the Governor post-haste. The Governor appeared a few minutes later. He looked pretty grim. His jaw was set.

"Matson asked, 'Practically every organization in the state is raffling off cars. Do you mean you want us to stop them all?'

"Youngdahl answered, 'If it is a lottery it must be stopped. I have never thought it was right to have those things upon the streets. If the people want them, let them say so through their legislators.'

"Tom Reed asked, 'Suppose there is a little church out in the rural area, holding a raffle for some widow and her five kids, and we don't have any advance knowledge of it. Are we supposed to go out there and arrest the officers of the church?'

"Youngdahl: 'I can't understand why the sheriff shouldn't have knowledge of what is going on in his county. Of course, I expect you to adopt a reasonable attitude to gain public support for law enforcement.'

"George Erickson asked, 'All county fairs have carnivals. And I never saw a carnival that didn't have gambling devices. What are we supposed to do about them? And about these church matters. If we are making a policy here, then these church groups have got to be notified. How is that going to be done?'

"Youngdahl: 'I think the matter of notification is an individual one. It is, of course, a good idea to announce the policy. But the important thing is that the policy is uniform.'

"Matson asked, 'Ask the Governor what he would do if he gets a complaint from someone that the American Legion is raffling off a car somewhere in the state.'

"Youngdahl: 'When I became Governor I said I wanted the laws uniformly applied, and that is what I mean. There is no law which says that a gambling device in one place is not a gambling device in another place.'

"Reed asked, 'As a jurist, Governor, what chance do you think I have of getting a conviction if the Legion is raffling off a car? Why, there'll be three or four Legionnaires on the jury!'

"Youngdahl: 'Are you going to stop prosecuting because you can't get convictions? Should we throw our whole law enforcement program out the window?'

"Bert Hanson spoke up, 'Where I come from, if we close up a Lutheran raffle there will be eleven Lutherans on the jury.'

"Youngdahl: 'I am not in the business of removing county officers. I am going to be very cautious and act only when every other means has been exhausted. My policy will be one of friendly cooperation with the officers. (But) a gambling device is a gambling device, whether it applies to one organization or another. No person is exempt from the penalties for violation.'"

"After adjournment," Mike Halloran wrote, "Youngdahl stood on exactly the same spot he stood on in the house chamber less than six months ago on his inaugural day when he received the congratulations of the legislators and others. And on Wednesday he was surrounded by scores of sheriffs and county attorneys, some of whom were ready to revolt against him two hours before. They thanked him for telling them straight from the shoulder what the policy should be and they eagerly told him they would pitch in and do their jobs in carrying it out. It certainly was a triumphant finish for him, and I am taking the word of an enforcement officer in one of the largest counties in the state in saying that." (Note: The account of this meeting is taken from articles by Wallace Mitchell in **The Minneapolis Star,** June 26, 1947, and by Mike Halloran in **The Minneapolis Tribune,** June 26, 1947)

The incident caused the **Des Moines Register** to editorialize, "Youngdahl has a trait puzzling to professional politicians — he means what he says. . . . The Minnesota record proves that old-fashioned civic morality can still be sold to the public."

Public Reaction to the Program

Once the law was passed and Youngdahl had won the support of local officials, the slot machines and other gambling games disappeared rapidly. In response to warnings posted by mayors and sheriffs and published in county newspapers, business places disposed of their machines without further demonstration, except for grumbling and caustic comments. Signs appeared on walls along which slot machines had once stood in taverns and clubs — "Youngdahl was here." Proprietors sadly draped funeral wreaths over dice tables. A satirical lyric in tribute to unemployed dice girls, performed by Darrell Fischer and His Log Jammers at Breezy Point Lodge on Pelican Lake, became very popular for a while. It went like this:

"I feel so sorry for Daisy, the dice maid,
    Down at the corner saloon;
    She'd shake with anybody
    Who came in the door;
    She'd shake them on the table
    Or throw them on the floor.
    Then Youngdahl got elected
    And it sure played hob,
    For now our Daisy is out of a job.
    That's why I sorrow for Daisy, the dice maid,
    She don't shake dice any more."

(Note: Rufus Jarman, "The Governor and the Gamblers,"

Saturday Evening Post, Vol. 220, No. 24, (Dec. 13, 1947) p. 22)
The law enforcement program was generally effective throughout Luther Youngdahl's administration.

It was not that all the people liked it. A poll showed that
44% of the people surveyed six months later thought the policy
was too strict, as compared with 48% who thought the program was all right. One beer tavern operator expressed the
bitterness of many people by saying to a canvasser seeking
contributions to the Boy Scouts, "My business manager,
Youngdahl, is managing my business to hell. I'll donate nothing until he is out of the capitol." Along the shores of the
sky blue waters, resort owners were deploring the loss of
revenue during the summer after the law was passed, and
blaming the situation on the Governor's program. For example, Bar Harbor, a resort on Gull Lake, suffered a loss of
$15,000 during the 1947 tourist season. In the "before Young-
dahl" days, the resort had drawn capacity crowds that spent
an average of $3 a person. In 1947 the average crowd was 300
and spent an average of fifty cents.

On one of his trips Youngdahl stopped in a restaurant.
During the meal two women in another booth kept looking
his way and whispering. When he had finished and went to
pay his bill, one of them staggered over to him. "That's him
all right," she said, over her shoulder to her companion. Hands
on hips, she thrust her chin up at him and said, "I'd like to
cut your head off." The Governor replied, "Well, you'd have
to start early in the morning. I have a thick neck. Why do
you feel this way about me?"

" 'I owned a tavern down the road," she said, "and slot
machines provided me my margin of profit. Now I have to
close. You are ruining my business!"

Some were grateful for what he had done, such as the
proprietor of another restaurant in which the Governor had
dinner one day. When Youngdahl went to pay his bill, the
owner said the meal was on the house. "How come?" the
Governor exclaimed.

"You see, Governor, it's like this. I was going to fight you
on this slot machine business. I used to get a lot of income

from kids who came in to play the machines. But they would run up charge accounts for malted milks, candy and hamburgers. Now that they can't play the slots they pay their bills. You were right. I am glad for this chance to show my appreciation."

At the Aitkin County Fair in August, 1948, a teen-ager asked Youngdahl for his autograph. As he signed a slip of paper, the boy said, "You saved me $200 this year, Governor." The Governor looked at him in surprise, wondering how a boy looking no older than fifteen could say a thing like that. The lad continued, "I haven't been able to play the slot machines." Such experiences helped to offset others more bitter, such as the time he was booed by the crowds lined along the streets to watch a Minneapolis Aquatennial parade, or when the papers reported that he had been called a "blue-nosed prig."

The rest of Youngdahl's law enforcement proposals did not fare so well. The Legislature defeated the power-of-arrest bill, not only in 1947 but at every session while he was in office. The bill called for granting power of arrest to liquor control commission inspectors. Youngdahl publicly accused legislators of yielding to the liquor lobby. While there were undoubtedly some who voted against it for selfish reasons, there were others who opposed it on principle — they were against shifting the burden of law enforcement from local to state officers. One of the latter was Gerald Mullin, for whom Youngdahl had the highest respect. He wrote in a letter: "I feared that the shift of court police powers to the state, while they might be successfully employed under a man such as Governor Youngdahl, in the hands of unscrupulous individuals might create greater adverse effects than benefits, and from the long-term view it is better to create interest (in law enforcement) on a local level." Despite active lobbying for its passage by church leaders and the Governor's vigorous efforts on its behalf, the bill was defeated by a narrow margin.

In 1949 the Legislature passed a bill, proposed by Youngdahl, which established uniform closing hours for all taverns and liquor stores in the state. Beyond this the Legislature did not go, although Youngdahl had proposed such measures as a bill prohibiting the transmission of betting information over public communications systems.

How justified was Youngdahl in making such an issue of law enforcement? It is not difficult to see why G.O.P. party leaders were critical of his program at first. They feared he would engender so much hostility that legislators would refuse to cooperate on other more important aspects of his program. It seemed to them that he emphasized the issue all out of proportion to its importance. Four years later, the sinister influence of racketeers in government was to have the spotlight of national publicity play upon it, but in 1947 it was not yet a widespread concern. It may have appeared that Youngdahl had a very narrow conception of what the moral issues in politics were — limiting them to gambling, liquor problems and similar vices but not including such issues as tax policy, social welfare, conservation or governmental reform. It was, and is, common for church people to think in such limited terms about the moral issues in politics. It is within such a context that the opposition of conscientious political leaders developed, opposition based on the fear that Youngdahl's emphasis on law enforcement proved he had a narrow conception of what moral issues in politics were.

Youngdahl argued that all forms of gambling had been illegal in Minnesota for years, but the laws were not enforced. Having laws and not enforcing them tears down respect for all law, which promotes crime and undermines the moral strength of a nation; thus foreign nations, especially Russia, are encouraged to believe that democracy in the United States is in a state of deterioration. It encourages our youth to disregard laws and leads to their delinquency. If we are going to be concerned with youth, law enforcement should be the starting point. He felt that a wholesome respect for law had to be the foundation upon which his program of constructive measures for human betterment must rest. In his first inaugural address he said, "To implement our constructive program for the strengthening of those great human resources which are found in the youth of our state, it is my intention to do everything in my power to enforce the laws of this state fairly, fearlessly and effectively."

Observers who were inclined to be cynical said that Youngdahl knew a good political move when he saw it and that, in this case, he recognized that to be "against sin" in a state like Minnesota was a highly expedient tactic, since it would be popular among the strict Scandinavian Lutherans. Youngdahl's supporters answer this by the comment that Youngdahl really did not have any guarantee in the beginning that he would get the support of the people and by the reminder that his critics were the first to argue that his inflexible attitude toward law enforcement would be his political suicide.

At any rate, Youngdahl emerged from this dramatic fight with a reputation for being a man of integrity, with increased authority to carry on his program for human betterment. His fight for law enforcement won him the support of church members by arousing them to a new interest in politics. After his resignation **The Minneapolis Tribune** ran the results of a public opinion poll, which revealed that 64% of the people believed that Youngdahl's anti-gambling drive was the achievement for which he would be the most remembered.

CHAPTER SEVEN

Labor Conciliator

A politician's mettle is tested by problems arising from the struggle of labor to achieve power and prosperity. Labor problems involve human welfare and business prosperity, and reflect class tensions of long standing in American society. As a result, protagonists of one group or the other promptly evaluate a politician on the basis of what he says and does about labor problems. He is apt to be labeled the "friend" of labor or the "reactionary" defender of vested interests. People become emotional in their judgments on this issue, and it is impossible to please everyone.

Youngdahl did not escape this test. As though the law enforcement battle had not sufficiently complicated his first term in office, he had to contend with labor trouble. Two major strikes receiving national attention broke out, and controversy over two bills passed by the 1947 Legislature flared up. It will have to be determined, on the basis of his record, whether he was the friend of labor or the defender of business interests or a skillful tactician cleverly weaving his way through the political maze.

155

Labor Legislation

In the area of labor legislation, Youngdahl proposed no basic changes. He expressed his hearty approval of the Minnesota Labor Relations Act of 1939. He had great faith in the method of peaceful conciliation, acquired while mediating controversies as a judge. He believed the Minnesota law provided the opportunity for the human element to be the prime consideration in the settlement of disputes. His views on the subject were stated in a speech at the annual Governors' Conference at Salt Lake City, in July, 1947. He said, "Containing few restrictions, our Minnesota law has provided a unique opportunity to test the human element in adjusting labor disputes. Men can't stay bitter and unyielding forever if they sit down together and honestly try to examine their differences. I have seen workers and employers come in utterly hostile and go out shaking hands and laughing. I have had both sides come to me and thank me for getting such a fine settlement for them when all I did was break down the wall of suspicion between them and get them to look upon each other as fellow men and, that done, let them talk themselves into agreement. . . . The public is given a real voice in determining whether there is to be a strike in vital industries — people are informed in advance through the filing of a strike notice. Housewives ask the milkman why he proposes to strike. Business men ask the employer what his trouble is. Each is called upon to justify his position." (The Minneapolis Star, July 15, 1947.)

Youngdahl disapproved of the Taft-Hartley Law, because he believed its restrictions on labor were too extreme. On the other hand, he was aware of the new power of the labor movement and that a monopoly of the labor supply held by the unions could create injustice, with the result that temptations to misuse power were as present in the union hall as in the board of directors' meeting. He expressed these views frankly to a meeting of business agents of the Twin Cities A. F. of L. unions. (The Minneapolis Tribune, Dec. 27, 1947.)

The 1947 Legislature passed a number of laws dealing

with labor relations. The two most important acts covered the banning of secondary boycotts and the authorization to sue unions for damages arising from labor disputes.

The anti-secondary boycott bill was opposed by labor unions, because it deprived them of a means of coming to the assistance of a striking union, whereas there were no commensurate restrictions to prevent one business from helping another during a strike. Through its interlocking corporations, industry could continue producing; and the unions were powerless to remedy the situation when deprived of the secondary boycott. The unions fought against passage of the union sue-ability bill, because it renders unions liable to suit for such causes as loss of income by the employer during a strike. (These reasons were given by Robert Gannon in an interview on June 11, 1953. Mr. Gannon is Minnesota C.I.O. research secretary.)

Youngdahl signed both bills. His delay in signing the anti-secondary boycott bill created rumors that he was dickering for the passage of other legislation close to his heart, such as the anti-slot machine and school aid bills. It was also rumored that he accepted the secondary boycott bill in return for a promise that fair employment practices legislation would at least be pried loose from the labor committee and allowed to go to the House floor for debate. Youngdahl resented these interpretations of his actions and was reported to have exclaimed, upon hearing them, "I made no deals! I deal with each measure on its merits. The outcome of the F.E.P.C. bill bears me out." (**Minneapolis Tribune,** Apr. 13, 1947.) The fact remains that in January he had expressed hostility towards the bill outlawing the secondary boycott and then later passed it. This action brought criticism from labor officials. On the other hand, he successfully opposed the attempts of some legislators to pass bills outlawing the closed shop.

In an address given at the Chicago Sunday Evening Club, Youngdahl maintained that it was a matter of principle with him to deal with legislation on its merits. "They passed a law providing for thirty liquor licenses for a community of 20,000 people, instead of fifteen licenses. And I was threatened that if I did not sign that bill they would not support some of this other constructive legislation, like mental health, youth conservation and education. I said, 'Each piece of legislation has got to stand on its merits. We're not making any trades at this desk, brother. You've got to talk to us on the merits of this legislation.' And I vetoed the bill. It didn't make sense for them to say to me that you couldn't enforce a law with fifteen liquor licenses; you had to have thirty liquor licenses in order to enforce the law in that community. You'll scratch my back and I'll scratch yours. You go for this hodge-podge piece of special legislation and then I'll go for that one in your community. That does not make for good legislation."

The Telephone Workers' Strike

During his first six months as Governor, Youngdahl settled or headed off four major strikes and several smaller ones. The most important labor controversy was the telephone workers' strike, in the spring of 1947, in which he served as mediator in the negotiations leading to its settlement.

Taking part in a nation-wide walkout of telephone workers, the Northwestern Union of Telephone Workers representing 16,000 workers in five Midwestern states went on strike April 7, 1947, to enforce their demands for a $12-a-week wage increase, union shop, protection against layoffs and an improved old-age security plan.

On April tenth, Youngdahl was asked to take part in the negotiations; so he called a conference, for April 24th, of union and company officials. During the four days of conferences that followed, Youngdahl won the respect of the disputants. Henry Mayer, counsel for the unions, announced in an interview, "Regardless of the outcome of this proposal (a company offer of a $2.50-a-week wage increase) the union feels a tremendous debt of gratitude to the Governor. He is the only public official thus far who has succeeded in obtaining a money offer from the company." Kraemer, the company's representative, stated, "I agree that the Governor is to be highly commended. He has been very fair, and he has been tireless in his efforts to bring about a settlement." (The Minneapolis Tribune, April 28, 1947.)

The strike was settled on May 6, after thirteen hours of continuous conversations. "The Governor wore down their resistance," commented the Governor's secretary, who was an eye-witness to the proceedings. "He insisted that this meeting should not break off until the strike was settled. At one point in the proceedings, the company officials announced their intentions of returning to Omaha and prepared to leave. By this time Youngdahl's patience was worn thin by their stubbornness. He got angry. He walked over and, towering over them, gave them a severe tongue-lashing in the presence of the union officials. He threatened to make public their unwillingness to settle the dispute and mixed in for good measure a strong portion of moral exhortation. The officials settled back in their chairs and negotiations were resumed." (Paul Albrecht in an interview, June 11, 1953.) Shortly after midnight the parties had agreed on wage increases of from $3.50 to $4.00 a week. The union withdrew its other demands, convinced that Youngdahl had done the very best he could do for them.

Youngdahl liked and believed in his role as a mediator. His success in this strike strengthened his faith in this method of settling disputes. In a radio speech, shortly after the strike was settled, he reported: "As the discussions proceeded, both sides warmed up and gradually began to take on a more conciliatory attitude. It showed, as the conciliation process under our Minnesota law has often shown, that when the wall of suspicion that rears itself between two parties in a labor dispute can be broken down and the parties brought together around a conference table in a spirit of tolerance and understanding the worst disputes can be adjusted." (Minneapolis Tribune, May 8, 1947.)

He was made an honorary member of the Communications Workers of America a year later in recognition of his "coura geous stand" in negotiating the strike.

The Packing-House Workers' Strike

The sailing was more turbulent in the packing-house workers' strike, which began on March 16, 1948, to enforce demands for a twenty-nine-cent wage increase. Before it was settled, violence broke out, the unions accused Youngdahl of being a strike-breaker, and Col. McCormick's **Chicago Tribune** called for his impeachment for not calling out the National Guard soon enough.

The strikers belonged to the United Packing House Workers of America, C.I.O., which had a total membership of 100,000. Approximately half of the 100 meat-packing plants affected by the strike were operated by the "Big Five" — Swift, Armour, Wilson, Cudahy and Morrill, all of which had large plants in Minnesota. The union was not in a very strong position. Organized in 1943, it was not wealthy. It was torn by an inner dissension involving its right-wing, a few Communists, its "go-slow" faction and the "hot-heads." Its position was weakened, too, by the way meat was kept moving to the butcher shops, and the resultant apathy of the public towards the strike. Defending the packing house workers' action, Ralph Helstein pointed out that two-thirds of the workers were getting less than $1.10 an hour, which is 13 cents less than the average hourly earnings reported by the U. S. Bureau of Labor Statistics. The demand for a 29-cent increase was based on a city worker's family budget prepared by the Department of Labor, which called for $1.65 an hour for a family of four. ("The Packing House Workers' Case," **New Republic,** Vol. 118, No. 7, Mar. 29, 1948.)

The union rejected the companies' offer of a nine-cent increase, which had been accepted by the A. F. of L. meat cutters and butchers; and the employers rejected the proposals of the unions to arbitrate the dispute. A board of inquiry began hearings on March 17 and reported on April 8 that a compromise between the wage increases suggested by the parties in the dispute would be adequate, but made no specific recommendations. The Federal Mediation and Conciliation Service continued its efforts to bring the disputants together.

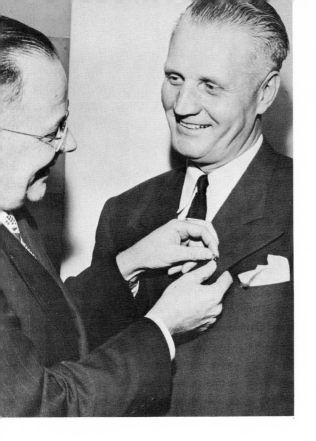

Presentation of Jeweled Hi-Y Pin given by the National Y.M.C.A. in recognition of his outstanding service to youth

Boy Governor Gene Booker addressing the Boy Legislature conducted by the Y.M.C.A. Seated next to him is Gov. Youngdahl

The Governor talking to Boy Scouts and Cub Scouts

Planning a trip to the Scandinavian countries

Early in the dispute Youngdahl had invited the parties to meet with him at the state capitol, but the companies had ignored the invitation. They insisted that the Governor had no jurisdiction, since the dispute was national in scope and under the authority of the Taft-Hartley law; yet they urged the Governor to call out the Minnesota National Guard unit. He was not directly involved until violence broke out in South St. Paul during the first week in May.

On the morning of May 13, more than 200 strikers barred the entrance of the Swift packing plant in South St. Paul. Since this was illegal picketing, the local court issued a temporary injunction ordering them to stop; but it had no effect. The sheriff and the police at his disposal attempted to force a path through the pickets but were hurled back. The court issued a contempt citation and the sheriff informed Youngdahl of his inability to enforce the court order.

Youngdahl went on the radio that evening to explain that he intended to enforce the law and to issue an appeal to the strikers to abide by it. His high regard for the law and his insistence that it be enforced are evident in these words from that statement: "It has been my position all along that all the laws pertaining to this labor trouble should be uniformly enforced, the same as any other law. There can be no justification for excepting any group or individual from compliance with the law or permitting any group to flout the law."

The same evening two hundred men entered the Cudahy plant, smashed some machinery, set free about 100 hogs, ripped telephones from their connections, beat up some of the 65 non-striking maintenance men and abducted some of them as hostages, and freed them soon afterwards. Youngdahl no longer delayed in summoning the National Guard. By eight o'clock in the morning of May 14, the Guard was on the march and the strikers were dispersed.

Youngdahl was severely criticized for not calling out the National Guard sooner. The companies blamed him for being too friendly with labor, and other critics thought he showed too much hesitancy when the union resorted to mass picketing. Youngdahl defended his restraint by pointing out that it was the duty of the sheriffs, in the counties directly affected, to take action first. Earlier he had refused to call out the Guard to police the strike-bound plants, because the Constitution does not countenance the use of militia until the outbreak of disorder calls for it.

On May 15 the strikers descended on the capitol to ask removal of the Guard. An eye-witness account of the incident was given by Wallace Mitchell in the **Minneapolis Tribune.**

"A crowd of South St. Paul packing house strikers filled Gov. Youngdahl's capitol reception room Saturday from wall to wall. They were sullen. They had stood under the bright sun on the capitol steps for an hour while a 24-man committee carried their requests to the Governor. They asked that the Guardsmen be removed from South St. Paul and that the Governor close down the packing plants.

"Quietly they entered the capitol when the guardsmen were notified that the Governor would talk to them. A few of the men and women were carrying babies. Their faces showed concern. Before they all got into the room, Youngdahl and the committee came out of his private office. The Governor stepped upon a platform and chatted with those in the front row. He looked at the purple and white ribbons they wore.

" 'I hope we can get them all in here,' he commented as he looked over the crowd. 'Maybe we should sing a song while we're waiting.'

"A man at his side, with a note of sarcasm in his voice, said, 'Maybe we should sing God Bless America.'

"The Governor's good humor did not disappear, but he grew serious instantly. 'Now you don't want to be feeling sarcastic, you know,' he said. 'No matter what our troubles are here in Minnesota and America, we're better off than anyone else in the world. We've got a lot to protect. Our country is still the best in the world.' By this time the man obviously was ill at ease as the Governor continued speaking to him quietly. 'We can't afford to be sarcastic. We've got the right to work these things out in a democratic manner, and you don't want to lose faith in our way. It's the best way.'

"By that time the room was filled, and the strikers spilled out into the hall. 'I have had plenty of butterflies in my stomach these nine weeks you've been out,' he began. 'I'm sympathetic with the fact that you are not working, that you need relief and help.'

"He told them that he had been under heavy pressure for weeks to call out the National Guard but had been hoping against hope it would not be necessary. 'I'm not happy that I've had to call them out either. I went on the radio the other night — did anyone hear me?' There was a chorus of affirmative answers. 'I pleaded that there be no incident so I wouldn't have to call out the Guard. I said it would be done only as a last resort. Right after I was on the air, pleading that nothing happen, somebody — I don't know who — was making plans to enter that plant with resulting injury to people and property. As long as I am Governor I am not going to let that happen. That's not the kind of Governor you people would have in here either. Guardsmen will not be used to break a strike or break any union. Their use is only to prevent anarchy and violence. You have not got the public with you in connection with violence. We will continue to try to settle the strike. And I ask you not to do anything that will hurt this cause. Keep your shirts on. The Guard is there for only one purpose — to prevent violence.'

"As the Governor concluded, Jean Paddock, who works in the Swift & Co. plant, spoke up from the front row. 'Use the military to shut the plants and then there won't be any violence,' she said loudly. There was a burst of applause and cheers. 'Put some pressure on the packers to remove the charges against some of our people too!'

"As the Governor listened, Miss Paddock said that the Cudahy violence resulted because the company brought 40 men into the plant in a boxcar. When she finished the strikers moved out, and Youngdahl returned to his office. In a press conference following the meeting he said he would study the question of plant shutdowns." (**The Minneapolis Tribune,** May 16, 1948.)

The day after the strikers had called on him, Youngdahl

flew to Chicago to see what he might contribute to the settlement of the strike. Not only was he concerned about the hardships caused to the disputants by the strike, but also about the boys in the National Guard, many of whom were young enough to be seniors in high school. His phone was deluged with calls from mothers anxious about their sons and urging him to do something to end the dispute. Youngdahl had not been invited to step in. Paul Albrecht believed the companies feared his prestige and influence with the people and therefore did not want him as a mediator. He thought that Youngdahl's trip to Chicago had an effect on the outcome, even though he did not take a direct part in the negotiation of the strike. The strike was settled soon after, when the union accepted the nine-cent wage increase offer made by the companies, with the companies accepting the recommendation that disputes over the re-instatement of strikers charged with unlawful acts be arbitrated. Youngdahl, looking back on the strike, regarded it is his most trying controversy while a Governor. "I came out of that experience feeling the trouble was on both sides," he wrote recently. "There were racketeer and wrong elements in the labor group and there was too much of an inhuman attitude toward labor, in my opinion, on the part of some of the management groups. I was blamed by the labor groups for being a strike breaker and blamed by the management groups for being too friendly with labor." Then he added wryly, "I figured I must have been pretty nearly right when I was blamed by both sides. At any rate, I acted in accordance with the dictates of my conscience." (Letter of Dec. 20, 1954.)

The Minneapolis School Strike

Youngdahl's skill as a conciliator was taxed by another difficult labor dispute that flared up during his third term. On January 23, 1951, the janitors in the Minneapolis public school system went on strike, after negotiations with the school board were disrupted. The janitors were members of the Public Service Employees' Union. They were joined shortly by the teachers belonging to the American Federation of Teachers and the members of the American Federation of State, County and Municipal Workers. Ninety-three public schools — affecting 63,000 children, 5,000 adult pupils, 2,200 teachers and 900 clerical and maintenance employees—were closed by the strike.

The grievances of the strikers centered around the unwillingness of the school board to sit down and discuss salary increases. The unions did not believe that the $4-a-month increases given for the school year were sufficient. They had tried to negotiate with the board for four months and, being unsuccessful, finally decided to strike. The school board, having raised the salaries for a total of $979,000, maintained that they could not afford further increases. The unions argued that the Board had refused to levy the full 8.5 mills allowed by action of the 1949 legislature. The Board countered by saying they would not resort to deficit financing to pay for further increases. The teachers were getting salaries ranging from $2,600 to a maximum of $4,800. Janitors were being paid $197.50 to $345.00 a month, with about one-half of them getting $267.50.

The school board tried to get the courts to issue an injunction against the strikers, but Judge John A. Weeks ruled that the janitors had a right to strike. On February 2, the Supreme Court ruled unanimously to uphold the janitors' right to strike on the grounds that the state's anti-injunction law allowed its use only when the public safety was jeopardized.

As the strike continued, the parties concerned concentrated their hopes on the Governor for a settlement of the dispute. Soon after the strike began, the unions appealed to the Governor to persuade the school board to open negotiations with them; so on January 26, Youngdahl urged Superintendent Putnam to meet with union representatives and State Labor Conciliator, Harry Hanson. Putnam agreed, but little progress was made. A group of parents organized themselves into the Minneapolis Citizens' Committee on Public Education. Impatient with the stalemate, the committee authorized its special fact-finding sub-committee to call on Youngdahl and ask him to intervene directly. After a long and fruitless session on February 11, Harry Hanson reported that agreement was no closer and expressed his belief that the only man who could straighten out the dispute was Youngdahl.

The Governor cancelled all engagements and called a meeting of all parties for the next day. He told them to be prepared to sit in session until a settlement was reached and to yield ground from their previous positions. He said that his desk was stacked with telegrams from parents demanding that the schools be opened at once.

After a grueling all-day session, in which the Governor refused to leave his office as he consulted first with one party and then the other, and then with both together, an agreement was reached. The Central Labor Union, representing the striking unions, accepted the compromise offer of the school board. The Governor persuaded the Board to agree to spend $300,000 more on salary increases by pledging his support to efforts to get the Legislature to increase state aid and raise the mill rate. An agreement was reached on the following offer:

1. A $100 annual increase for 2,200 teachers, an increase of $400 to 65% of the teachers earning maximum salaries and $200 increase for teachers with less than twelve years' experience — all of which were in addition to increases already granted.

2. Monthly raises of $22.50 for janitors, nurses and oral hygienists and $12.50 for women janitors, bus attendants, school clerks and cafeteria workers.

3. Appointment by the Governor of a fact-finding committee to survey the entire school situation by May 1 and assurance of joint action by all parties to get increased financial help for schools.

5. A schedule to make up for time lost by the strike, in order to allow for full pay.

The janitors' union voted to accept the compromise, but the teachers rejected it at their meeting. Their action antagonized not only the Governor but the Central Labor Union as well. The latter issued an ultimatum — either withdraw their pickets, or members of other unions would be instructed to cross picket lines. As soon as the Governor learned of their action, he recommended that the schools be re-opened without further delay. Obviously weary of the whole affair, he issued the following statement: "I am keenly and sadly surprised and disappointed that the teachers' union has seen fit to reject the offer of the school board and my sincere and urgent appeal, on behalf of the parents and children of Minneapolis, to open the schools. I believe the proposal was fair and reasonable and was as far as the school board could go without impairing its financial structure. In view of the action of the janitors and all other school employees in accepting the offer of the board and their willingness to go back to work and to protect the city's share of state aid, I have recommended to Mr. Putnam that the schools be opened at once. He is following the recommendation and the schools will be opened in the morning. For the sake of our children, I ask that all teachers return to work." (Minneapolis **Tribune,** Feb. 14, 1951.)

By 3 p.m. on February 13, the teachers had decided to go back to the classroom and to accept the settlement of the dispute. Some of them felt that the Governor had "railroaded the teachers into line" by issuing the peremptory statement, with the result that many grievances were left unsettled. At the same time, they had come to respect the Governor for the way he dealt with them. George Beacom, President of the Federation of Men Teachers, reported after one of the meetings with the Governor: "The Governor took time out to talk with classroom teachers as human beings, extending a certain amount of admonishment, yet lending a sympathetic ear in an exchange of opinions."

As a result of the school strike, one of the most controversial bills in the history of Minnesota labor legislation came before the Legislature, the No-Strike of Public Employees bill. It was passed by the Legislature; and in deciding what to do about it, Youngdahl displayed an uncharacteristic uncertainty and reluctance. The bill provided for adjustment of grievances by a panel of three people and authorizes employees to discuss conditions of re-employment. The penalty for striking is loss of the job. Considerable public sentiment in favor of the bill had been created by the strike. Youngdahl announced his support of an amendment that would provide for conciliation, for fact-finding procedures, and for prohibition of strikes during the conciliation and for sixty days thereafter. When efforts to attach such an amendment failed, he found himself in a tight spot politically. The legislators were determined to pass the No-Strike of Public Employees bill, and a veto would have jeopardized the rest of Youngdahl's program. The volume of mail from the people was preponderantly in support of the measure. When the Governor finally endorsed it, he made a statement disclaiming any reasons for signing except his appreciation of the meritorious features of the bill. He said, "After a rather exhaustive study I have reached the conclusion that public employees cannot be permitted to use the weapon of strike, for to do so may interfere with or destroy the orderly processes of government." Following a quotation from Franklin D. Roosevelt, whose views at this point coincided with his own, Youngdahl concluded, "It should be made clear that the law is not a panacea. It will not solve fundamental problems or grievances of public employees as to wages and working conditions. It will not relieve us of the responsibilities to adequately support our schools and provide justice to our public employees." (The Minneapolis Star, Apr. 26, 1951.)

CHAPTER EIGHT

Human Engineer

"The greatest need of our day is for human engineers who will take the products of science and use them with compassion and understanding, not to the hurt but the healing of men." (Second Inaugural Address of Gov. Luther W. Youngdahl.)

If a stranger had visited Minnesota in 1947, while the battle over the slot machines was at a high pitch, his curiosity would surely have been aroused by a Governor who could risk his political future over that type of an issue. He may have discovered, upon asking questions, that this man was a leading churchman, who had moral scruples about gambling and drinking. He perhaps might then have asked, "Doesn't your Governor have anything better to do than fight 'one-armed bandits?' Is this what his 'Christian' emphasis leads him to do? What is he doing for civil rights, for dependent children, the youth and the helpless aged, for the mentally-ill, for the working man and for minority groups?" Perhaps the Minnesota citizen would have been hard-pressed for a ready answer. In the early months of 1947, the law enforcement campaign had cast other considerations in a shadow. Everyone was discussing it, so it would be understandable that Mr. Minnesota Citizen would have forgotten that Youngdahl had stressed what he called "human goals" in his inaugural. He had placed human welfare first on his list of aims, elaborating at greater length on the subjects of compassion and understanding than on any of his other goals. The Minnesota citizen could not have known then, as in retrospect he would know now, that the humanitarian emphasis was to predominate during Youngdahl's administration.

Youngdahl succeeded in demonstrating what he meant by being a "human engineer," convincingly enough to win several awards bestowed on him in recognition of his humanitarian work. Among those honors was the rarely-given Brotherhood Week award which he received in 1951 from the National Conference of Christians and Jews for his work on behalf of mental health, youth conservation, displaced persons, integration of Negroes into the National Guard, the Crusade for Freedom and human relations agencies. He was also Big Brother of the Year recently. The Indian Council Fire made him an honorary member for his endeavors on behalf of the American Indians. He received the Human Endeavors in Public Service award given by the Minnesota chapter of the Jewish War Veterans of the United States. He was recognized by the National Conference of Catholic Charities as an outstanding humanitarian and was invited to speak at its 1949 conference.

Youngdahl's inaugural addresses and other speeches repeatedly set forth his "human goals" and were permeated with a humanitarian spirit. For example, in his second inaugural address he said:

"There must be a place in our scheme of things for those great intangible human values which cannot be represented on graphs and ledgers. Our values must stem from the Fatherhood of God and the Brotherhood of man. We must stop gauging our success by production of machines or dollars of income. We have got to understand that, important as it is to produce efficiency in the factory, it is more important to build character in its workers and to turn out a product that will strengthen our nation. No standard of living is high when jobs become drudgery and hours dreary; when rancor and bitterness exist between management and labor; when young men and women can't afford a family; when children in slums are walled off by brick from sod and sky; where there is not equality of educational opportunity for every boy and girl; where decent health conditions are not afforded to all of our people. No standard of living is high where we do not fulfill our obligation to the needy, the aged, the crippled, the blind; the dependent and neglected children; where we fail in our duty to the individuals sick of mind; when we deny equal rights to our people because of race, creed, color, or nationality."

Youth Conservation

Despite his concern for law enforcement, Youngdahl did not think of it as anything more than a means to the greater end of conserving the state's human resources, especially the youth. The anti-slot machine bill was not the most important statute he proposed to the 1947 Legislature. In his opinion, the Youth Conservation bill was more important — an opinion rooted in his interest in youth dating back to his experience on the bench, where he came into frequent contact with juvenile delinquency.

The bill he submitted to the Legislature was modelled after the Youth Authority Plan proposed by the American Law Institute and was similar to projects already in operation in four other states. As it was passed by the 1947 Legislature, the act created a Youth Conservation Commission of five members, which was to supplement local resources for dealing with youth problems. Its functions were: to be responsible for the care of and rehabilitation of all delinquent children and convicted offenders under 21 years of age whom the courts feel cannot be dealt with locally; to provide probation services to the counties which do not have a sufficient case load to justify a full-time probation officer; and to educate the many communities that need help in analyzing their delinquency problem and in identifying the major contributing factors and lacks that need attention if local services to youth are going to be improved. (Youth Conservation Commission, **Progress Report**, St. Paul, Minn., Dec., 1950, p. 13.)

The Commission accepts as its premises the following: the causes of delinquency and crime must be removed; the major responsibility for prevention and correction must remain within the community; and prevention and correction must not be divorced. (Ibid.) The Commission has complete control over the offender and over all steps in the treatment.

During the first 21 months of the plan's operation, over 35% of the 824 cases processed had been placed on probation without ever being sent to a correctional institution. Only 31 had violated the terms of their probation. (Ibid, pp. 17-18.) "Governor Youngdahl is given a great deal of credit for the fact that the 1947 Legislature passed the youth conservation bill," Sidney Shalett wrote in the **Saturday Evening Post.** "He never misses a chance to advance the program." (Sidney Shalett, "De We Have to Throw Our Kids in Jail?" Mimeographed reprint of an article in a December, 1950, issue of the magazine.)

To add impact to his program of youth conservation, the Governor appointed an advisory citizens' committee which planned a Governor's Conference on Youth. The conference was so successful that Youngdahl asked the 1949 Legislature to give the committee official status. This was granted, and late in 1949 the committee began to lay plans for the second Governor's Conference on Youth, which was held in St. Paul, March 23-24, 1950. Through its twelve panel discussions the conference sought to analyze the total needs of the child and the obligations of parents, the local community, and the state in meeting those needs. Resolutions of the conference covered such items as the importance of religious values, authorization of funds for a youth camp for delinquents, establishment of domestic relations courts, approval of probation and parole survey, and recreation. The delegates officially expressed special appreciation to Youngdahl for his "inspiring leadership and guidance." He gave the keynote address, "The Challenge of Youth Conservation in the New Half Century." (**Governor's Second State Conference on Youth.**" St. Paul, Minn., 1950, p. 116.)

Youngdahl proposed other measures to strengthen the youth

conservation program, the establishment of a reception center where diagnostic treatment could be handled, and a boys' forestry camp. The legislators cooperated by expanding and revising the powers of the Youth Conservation Commission and voted approval of the forestry camp, appropriating funds for it in 1951.

"The Crusade for Forgotten Souls"

The state's mental health program was the issue that dominated the 1948 election campaign and the 1949 legislative session.

Minnesota's care of the mentally ill followed the pattern familiar in other states until recently. Asylums were built not to cure mental patients but to confine people considered by society to be dangerous because of their unconventional actions. This custodial or "brick-and-mortar" solution was based on the logic that the patients were incurable and destined for life-long institutionalization, which made necessary the lowest possible expenditure — a policy that assumed that the patients were devoid of human feelings.

The state had an ever-increasing back-log of patients, because so little was being done to rehabilitate them. Regardless of the effect on the patient, he was assigned to chores on the hospital farm or in the office and expected to help keep expenses down by working for his "keep." The attendants were not given specialized training and were looked upon as guards rather than as psychiatric aides. There was a double-standard of food, one for the patients and one for the staff.

No hospital had even fifty per cent of the number of trained people it needed. No hospital had pathologists or dieticians. One hospital had one doctor or 700 patients when it should have had one for every 150. There were only 82 nurses, compared with 422 needed. Only half the required number of attendants could be provided. No hospital had equipment adequate for serving hot meals to patients. Whereas the minimum daily expenditure for one patient should have been from $3 to $5, it was only $1. Restraints were used on 655 patients. Instead of being cured, patients were too frequently deteriorating beyond all hope of recovery. (The Minneapolis Tribune, March 28, 1948. See also report of the Minnesota Unitarian Conference Committee on Institutions for the Mentally Ill, "A Summary of Conditions in Minnesota State Hospitals for the Mentally Ill," St. Paul, Minn., 1947.)

Youngdahl had become acquainted with the problem of the mentally ill when he was a municipal judge. All types of emotionally disturbed people had come before him, and he had tried to deal with their problems by having a psychiatric adviser. In his 1947 inaugural address, he had stated his concern for the problem but did not push for action on this aspect of his program. In fact, he was reported to have cut the mental hospital budget, blue-pencilling many items deemed essential by hospital officials.

Within a few weeks following his inauguration in 1947, the conditions in the state mental hospitals became a public issue. It all started with Engla Schey, an attendant in one of the hospitals, who had worked among and fought for the patients for years. In October, 1946, she attended the annual conference of the Minnesota Unitarian Association. During a discussion on the disclosure of cruelties inflicted upon prisoners in Nazi prison camps, she arose and told of the conditions existing in Minnesota's hospitals and urged the delegates to do something constructive about a situation within their sphere of influence. The delegates passed a resolution authorizing an investigation of state institutions.

With the able assistance of a trained social worker, Mrs. L. D. Steefel, the committee initiated the project on a sound basis by assembling a group of experts to help it gather and interpret data. This committee's work was unheralded until its chairman, Mr. Arthur Foote, Unitarian minister in St. Paul, ended a speech at a small meeting with an off-the-cuff remark asserting that the committee had discovered that doctors were signing commitment papers for patients they had never seen. There happened to be a reporter in the audience, and Mr. Foote's comments received unexpected publicity. The next morning he got a phone call from the Governor's office requesting that he come to see Youngdahl. Foote sensed that the Governor had been jolted by the adverse publicity, because he began the interview by upbraiding the minister. However, Foote was given an opportunity to state his case and, when Youngdahl asked for documentation, he was ready with a printed memo on the committee's work and findings.

Youngdahl studied the report with care, and from that time on he took over the crusade for mental health with his typical zeal. In March, 1947, a Governor's Advisory Council on Mental Health was formed. The group consisted of 47 members from the medical profession, the University's department of psychiatry and the Mayo Clinic as well as two laymen, Mr. Foote and Frank Rarig, head of St. Paul's Wilder Charities. This committee was assigned to make a preliminary survey of the conditions in all the hospitals.

Youngdahl described his incredulous reaction to the facts these committees put before him, as well as the conclusive evidence amassed during his own visits to the hospitals, in an address to the annual meeting of the Menninger Foundation of Topeka, Kansas:

"I met with these advisers, intellectually accepting the facts as they were presented and the conclusions of months of personal research, but emotionally I was not quite prepared to believe that these conditions could exist in my state; nothing prior to visiting the hospitals could prepare me for what I was to find.

"I have visited all the hospitals in Minnesota by now, most of them many times, but I vividly remember my first — row upon row of unattended human beings, figures created in the image of God whom we were desecrating by plunging them into this inferno which had the name 'hospital' on its gate.

"With my own eyes I saw nude men and women, thoroughly shackled to slats and benches, whole wards of men and women with bare feet on a stone floor, with many confined in strait-jackets. I looked and could hardly believe my eyes.

"And those that were not restrained, what of them? Sitting in crude benches, their eyes downcast, with the grim silence of the ward interrupted only by the strident voice of the attendant, 'Sit down, sit down.'

"I saw the boiled potatoes and cabbage served the patients. Neither could I eat the patients' food nor could I eat upstairs with the staff while knowing what the patients downstairs had before them." (Luther W. Youngdahl, "The Challenging New Frontier in Mental Health," pp. 11-12, Oct. 4, 1949, mimeographed copy of speech in the author's possession.)

Youngdahl, realizing that the manner in which the mentally ill were treated was a true measure of the state's concern for human values, determined to take up the banner on their behalf as the next step in his program of human welfare. His actions coincided with the rising crescendo of public outcries over hospital conditions throughout the country, which were exposed by the reports of investigators and dramatized by such books as The Snake Pit. Minnesota became the first state to adopt the new policy emphasizing the cure and rehabilitation of the patients. As in the case of his fight against gambling, Youngdahl displayed what one observer called "an unpolitician-like skill in anticipating what would interest people and capture their loyalty." (This was Bernhard LeVander's evaluation in an interview, May, 1953). Youngdahl's sense of timing was such that he intuitively recognized when public opinion was on the up-swing. This often gave him the advantage over his colleagues in the race for leadership.

By March, 1948, the Governor was ready to launch a campaign to win public support for his mental health program. The work of the advisory committee had been well-publicized, and popular interest had been aroused. In March, he appointed a non-partisan Citizen's Mental Health Committee of fifty members to supplement his own efforts to alert the public. As chairman he appointed Attorney Leslie Anderson, whose interest in the mental health program had been stimulated by personal contact with the misfortunes of patients committed to the hospital, while serving as counsel for them. Youngdahl's personal efforts on behalf of mental health were well-publicized in the press and on the radio. The Twin Cities press ran human interest articles on what one newspaper called

"Governor Youngdahl's Crusade for 'Forgotten Souls.'" He made radio addresses regularly and traveled to all parts of the state to give speeches in the effort to keep the issue constantly before the public. Directing the hospitals to abandon use of restraints was one of his first achievements. The dramatic news story of the bonfire at Anoka State Hospital, where he personally set fire to a huge pile of strait-jackets, straps and manacles, was widely featured as a symbol of the state's new intentions.

The citizens' committee proved its effectiveness as a link between the public and the administration by bringing about a greater concern for the mentally ill in administrative and official quarters and by carrying on an active publicity campaign. Youngdahl told the Menninger Foundation audience what occurred as a result of the spirited campaign.

"Then a remarkable thing happened. The people spontaneously rose to the challenge. There was not enough room on the original state-wide committee for all who wished to participate. The committee became a movement, including legislators, civic leaders, plain citizens, many relatives of mental patients and institutional personnel — from superintendents to the employees' union. There were no dues or regulations. Each member was a committee of one, dedicated to bringing about a new era in the conservation of human resources. In most key counties of the state, supporters of the program banded together in local and county citizens' committees. Such was the interest in the drive that shortly after its inauguration, and months prior to the legislative session, poll after poll showed that the overwhelming majority of voters were for the program; one actually showed that a majority of citizens regarded mental illness as a sickness from which people recovered."

Despite Youngdahl's involvement in the mental health crusade, there was speculation in the winter of 1948 concerning his political plans. Rumors were circulating that Thye would resign if Stassen failed to land the presidential nomination, so that Youngdahl could appoint Stassen to the vacancy in the Senate. Mike Halloran mentioned these rumors and reported that Youngdahl almost erupted through the roof of the automobile in which they were riding. " 'There can be no such a deal!' he shouted. 'To begin with, Stassen wouldn't suggest such a performance. I feel positive neither he nor Ed Thye would think of such a thing. Under no circumstances would I enter into such a deal.' " (The Minneapolis Star, December 15, 1947.) Another rumor had it that Youngdahl and Hubert Humphrey, then mayor of Minneapolis, had agreed that the Governor would run against Ball in the Republican primary, thus giving the mayor an unobstructed chance at the governorship as a Democrat-Farmer Labor candidate. This, too, Youngdahl denied, re-affirming his dedication to the program he had launched. The delay of both Youngdahl and Humphrey in filing for offices revived speculation in July and August concerning Youngdahl's plans — some observers saw the delay as a bit of political jockeying. The speculation ended finally with Youngdahl's filing for the governorship on August fourth.

Conservatives in the Republican party had prevailed upon Stafford King, State Auditor, to file for the governorship against Youngdahl. This move indicated that the conservative bloc in the party was not satisfied with Youngdahl's expensive program and proved to be a portent of its growing opposition to him.

Donald Dickey, Youngdahl's campaign manager, executed an unexpected political maneuver within a week after Youngdahl had filed his candidacy. He aligned all but two or three of the Republican county chairmen behind Youngdahl's candidacy by making personal phone calls to every chairman in the state. King and his supporters assailed the propriety, even the ethics, of the move, since it was party policy that party officials are supposed to remain neutral in the primary election and allow voters to choose their candidates without official party endorsement. LeVander, State Chairman of the G.O.P., reported that several of the chairmen were very reluctant to declare themselves but felt that they could hardly refuse a request that seemed to originate in the Governor's office. Dickey defended his move by explaining that he had asked the chairmen to support Youngdahl as individuals rather than as party officers, but this explanation failed to mollify the tempers of those who assailed it. At any rate, no serious damage to Youngdahl's candidacy was done. He won the primary handily, defeating King by 67,118 votes.

Youngdahl's campaign for re-election was dominated by his mental health proposals and with assurances to continue the program of human welfare, law enforcement and good government for which he had been working. Despite the fact that Minnesota voters delivered a majority for the Democratic national candidates, Truman and Humphrey, and the fact that Youngdahl had backed Dewey and Joseph Ball, their opponents, he was returned to office by a vote of 643,572 over Charles Halsted's 545,766.

Youngdahl's second inaugural address, delivered on January 6, 1949, was distinguished by the same emphasis upon human goals that characterized his initial one. His proposals were headed by his recommendation that Minnesota adopt a new approach to the problem of mental illness and provide the resources for the reforms. The program would replace the asylum with "the house of hope," a modern therapeutic center in which rehabilitation rather than custody would be the aim; it would also provide for research, training of personnel, clinics for non-hospital treatment, social work contacts with the home and community, post-hospital follow-up care of discharged patients and consultative services to courts, schools and welfare agencies. To implement this new approach, Youngdahl called for the following provisions:

1. Establishing a quota of trained psychiatric workers in line with the recommendations of the American Psychiatric Association, a training designed to qualify attendants as "psychiatric aides."

2. Establishing a single diet for patients and staff and the service of trained dieticians.

3. Providing occupational, recreational and other therapies designed to end deteriorating idleness of patients.

4. Providing better living conditions, clothing and other personal necessities.

5. Providing an adequate staff of chaplains.

6. Changing archaic content of laws concerning mental illness.

7. Transferring mental health program from the Department of Health to a special bureau under the Division of Public Institutions.

The 1949 Legislature faced many unusual problems, due to the inflated dollar, resulting in higher building costs, demands for higher salaries and larger social security grants. Highway construction deferred by the war had to be financed. Payment of the veterans' bonus had been authorized by the people in the November election.

Such popular interest in mental health had been aroused by the Governor and the Citizens' Committee on Mental Health that it was a foregone conclusion that the Legislature would take action on the new program. No achievement of the 1949 Legislature surpassed in importance its passage of the Mental Health Bill, inaugurating a new day in the care of the mentally ill. The bill was passed with bi-partisan support and signed by Youngdahl on March 20. The Act declared that the **official policy** of the State of Minnesota is to recognize mental illness as a sickness, not as a stigma upon a patient, and that appropriations are to be guided by the requirements for preventing, detecting and treating an illness. The Governor introduced a minimum appropriations request in his budget message, based on the minimum standards of the American Psychiatrists' Association, of $30,000,000 for the biennium.

The Legislature appropriated $28,000,000 ($13,000,000 more than in 1947) as well as an additional $17,000,000 to continue building programs initiated in previous years. This allotment raised the allowance for care from $1 to $3 per patient. The money provided for increases in personnel, a forty-hour week, reclassification of attendants as psychiatric aides, a single standard of food and improved clothing, a research and training program, two clinics plus as many out-patient clinics as increased personnel could handle, an increased staff for the central office, and the resources and authority for the Commissioner of Public Health to develop preventive and educational programs. The appropriations marked the end of the "brick-and-mortar" mental patient program and the beginning of a modernized mental therapy approach to the problem.

The Youngdahl administration lost no time projecting the new program into action. By November, 1949, less than fifty people were under restraints. Six months after the new program was approved, Carl Jackson, Director of the Division of Public Institutions, was able to announce that recruiting of personnel had far exceeded expectations. Every hospital had a psychologist, and all but one had a dietician. He expected to announce that over 800 new employees were added in the first year of operations — most of them in positions involving direct patient care. The number of employees in training programs increased by 367%. As a result, patients were getting more attention, recreation and freedom than had ever been possible. The single diet was an accomplished fact, and the quality of meals was improved. Training programs for psychiatric aides had begun, and the Mayo Clinic had made possible post-graduate training for doctors. The first of a series of clinics and rehabilitation centers had been established in the Fergus Falls area. Dr. Ralph Rossen, superintendent of the Hastings hospital, began his work as Minnesota's first Mental Health Commissioner on February 1, 1950. (Carl J. Jackson, "Minnesota's Mental Health Program Soars Ahead," January, 1950, mimeographed copies in the author's possession.)

The battle for the mental health program was won **before**, rather than during, the legislative session. The victory was a clear case of the effect of arousing the people to action. The role of the churches during this crusade was minor. Apart from the work of the Unitarian committee on mental health, there is no evidence that the Protestant churches made a concerted effort, either collectively or singly, to bring about passage of this legislation. There were post facto resolutions commending the Governor after the program had been launched. That individual church members took part in the work of the citizens' committee is a well-known fact. Furthermore, church auxiliaries cooperated very well by participating in the program of hospital visitation which the citizens' committees organized; and they must be given credit for helping to make that program a permanent feature. However, the churches were not anxious about the deplorable conditions in the hospitals and were not active pioneers in urging that the government do something to improve the situation.

Human Relations

Youngdahl did not "pussyfoot" when it came to advocating measures to check discriminatory practices against minority groups. He used unequivocal language in demanding passage of fair employment practices legislation. In his 1947 message to the Legislature, he said, "Every unfair discrimination a white man practices against a Negro in our community relationships; every nasty slur voiced by a Gentile against a Jew; every expression of contempt against a whole nation; every act of discourtesy or prejudice makes less possible the solution of mankind's gigantic problem. Essentially this is a matter of conscience and good will; living together cannot be accomplished legislatively, but to prevent injustice, legislation is necessary." Youngdahl advocated the passage of an F.E.P.C. bill which would provide for a commission to arbitrate appeals from members of minority groups who feel they have been victims of discrimination in competing for jobs and in retaining them. The measure had failed to win support in 1947, so Youngdahl campaigned vigorously for it during the 1949 session. In one radio address he accused opponents of F.E.P.C. of deliberately maneuvering to keep the bill from coming up on the floor. He described their tactics and deplored the bitterness with which a few legislators and pressure groups opposed it.

The Minnesota Employers' Association worked skillfully to prevent passage of the bill through the efforts of its executive secretary, Otto Christianson. The House Labor Committee spent a month in deliberations over this bill without reaching any conclusions. A lobbyist from the Minnesota Employers' Association was heard to remark, "We are sure blocking all those labor bills with this F.E.P.C. measure, and it won't pass either." (Minnesota State C.I.O. Council, **Did You Vote for This Last November? A Report on the Minnesota Legislature and Legislators, 1949 Session,** Minneapolis, 1949.) In the Senate Labor Committee the same stalling tactics were used. The final vote in the Senate was 34 to 29 against its passage; it was not a record vote (in which each man's vote on the measure is recorded) because its opponents managed to have the vote taken while the Senate sat as a "committee of the whole." This maneuver made it impossible for the people to discover who opposed it. Youngdahl's efforts in 1951 were no more successful, despite a hard-hitting section devoted to the subject in his inaugural address.

He was more effective in abolishing segregation in the Minnesota National Guard. In March, 1948, he asked Secretary Forrestal to sanction de-segregation in the State Militia upon recommendation of the Governor's Inter-racial Commission. A short time later, Minnesota's Attorney-General Burnquist ruled that the Governor could not abolish segregation, because federal laws prohibited it. In July, Youngdahl urged President Truman to order a change of national policy. Nothing resulted from these maneuvers except vague intimations that federal funds might be cut off from the Minnesota unit if segregation were abolished. The 1949 Legislature passed an innocuous bill urging action on the matter; so finally in September, 1949, Youngdahl took matters into his own hands and issued an executive order which opened the National Guard to Negroes on a non-segregated basis. The national government respected the order and when the Guard was called to the colors during the Korean war, the Minnesota unit was the only one left intact when it arrived at Camp Rucker, Georgia.

Youngdahl also insisted that employment practices in state departments be conducted on a non-discriminatory basis. Commenting on the Governor's efforts for equal rights, Clifford Rucker, executive director of the Inter-Racial Commission, credited him with being thoroughly and sincerely committed to the principle of equality. "He could hardly be motivated by a desire to win the Negro vote," he said, smiling, "since it consists of less than 1% of the state's entire vote." (In an interview, June 17, 1953.)

Youngdahl's Efforts on Behalf of Minnesota's Indians

Minnesota has an Indian population estimated in 1950 at 18,000. (Note: Information on the Indians taken largely from a publication of the Minnesota Legislative Research Committee, "Minnesota Indians," Publication No. 27, March, 1950.) Most of them live in rural areas in the northern Minnesota counties of Beltrami, Clearwater, Lake of the Woods, Koochiching, Cass and Cook. A few scattered groups and individuals are found in the southern part of the state and in cities. Lands on the reservations are generally unsuitable for farming, and the remaining forest reserves are of little value at the present time. In sections where the land is fertile, the Indians' holdings are so small as to make large scale farming impossible. Employment opportunities available in the areas surrounding the Indian lands are limited, both by the reluctance of non-Indians to hire Indians and the slow-moving economy of the counties in which they are located. The Indians show little interest in farming and are reluctant to leave their reservations to find employment and face hazards elsewhere. The occupations in which Indians most frequently are engaged include small forestry operations, commercial fishing (mainly on Red Lake), the tourist business and seasonal employment in agriculture and mining. Indians live at a low economic level and constitute a major welfare burden, costing Minnesota taxpayers upwards of $433,258.

The Minnesota Indian problem has its roots in the accepted theory that Indians should be confined to reservations (originally as a control measure) and that they were different from non-Indians and should be given different treatment. The result has been to isolate the Indian from the rest of society and to make him dependent upon government support. (These are generalities not always applicable to individual Indians).

The problem has two parts. The short-term problem involves the assumption of responsibility for determining that Indians receive proper treatment from a humanitarian viewpoint. The long-term problem is to fully assimilate the Indian into a new culture.

At one time the federal Indian Office was completely responsible for all aspects of the Indians' life. In 1934 the Indians were suddenly given self-government, after a generation of subjugation had destroyed tribal organization — which complicated the matter of law enforcement. In recent years the state of Minnesota has gradually become involved in responsibilities created by the Indians' condition. The Hoover Commission studied federal Indian policy and recommended that the administration of social welfare programs for Indians be progressively transferred to the states.

At present the Indian problem is still under the jurisdiction of the federal government, and yet Minnesota finds itself actively involved in Indian welfare programs and the cost of maintaining them. This can be illustrated in several ways. Indian lands in Minnesota are held in trust by the Federal government, and no taxes are collected on these holdings. Yet, Minnesota Indians receive local governmental services financed by property taxes they are not required to pay. This creates revenue problems for the counties involved, most of which have a small revenue as it is. Maintenance of law and order usually falls upon local and state authorities in Minnesota, even though legal jurisdiction does not belong to them but to federal and tribal authorities. Federal funds have been appropriated to help Minnesota educate Indian children in public schools, yet the increases in aid have not kept pace with increases in cost of education. Counties furnish substantial additional funds for medical care for indigent Indians. The state appropriates $10,000 annually for a public health nursing program among Indians. Welfare care, formerly provided entirely by the Federal government, has been shifted to the states and counties in which Indians reside.

Youngdahl was aware of the nature of the problems of this "unrepresented minority" and was involved several times in actions on their behalf. In 1947 he was confronted with an interesting dilemma involving the issues of liquor consumption by Indians, law enforcement and human rights—all of which were of much concern to Youngdahl. There is a federal law prohibiting the sale of liquor to Indians, first enacted in 1802. Indians consider the law to be discriminatory and therefore take little interest in its enforcement. Four federal government men are able to spend only a small portion of their time policing liquor sales to Indians, who are so widely scattered that it means scarcely any enforcement. Minnesota also had a law prohibiting the sale of liquor to Indians. In 1947 a bill proposing its repeal was recommended by legislative approval. As it finally passed, the bill resulted in an amendment making it illegal to sell liquor only to Indians who had "not adopted the language, customs and habits of civilization." (Note: Laws 1947, Chapter 87, Section 1.) Youngdahl signed the bill. The sale of liquor to Indians, previously possible quite generally, was made legal, too. The dilemma involved stems from the fact that local law enforcement officers have stated that their biggest problem among Indians arises from their consumption of liquor (which does not mean that every Indian drinks excessively, of course). Yet, to have a law prohibiting its sale to them is both unenforceable and discriminatory.

A crisis in the Indian situation loomed when the 1949 Congress seriously considered the recommendation of the Indian Office to close the Pipestone Indian School, which cared for and educated neglected and dependent Indian children. In February, a delegation of Minnesota legislators visited Washington and prevailed upon Congress to continue the appropriation for the school, and Congress allotted $200,000. Prompted by the crisis, Youngdahl urged that a legislative committee be appointed to study the problem and recommended the extension of financial aid to the Indian population and the resulting welfare burden. The Legislature took favorable action on both of his requests.

In February, 1950, Youngdahl called a 15-state conference to deal with Indian problems; and in June he called upon the governors of states with Indian populations to support the Indian Council, organized to deal with Indian problems on an inter-state level. He urged their endorsement of a federal-state program of action covering the following points: early and fair settlement of Indian treaties; utilization of the initiative of the Indians in accomplishing their rehabilitation; training Indians to live within our American culture rather than separated from it; encouragement of the preservation of the Indian's best customs; and provision of adequate federal aid pending an early end of federal wardship.

The Indian Council Fire, an organization devoted to the advancement of the Indian race, saluted his efforts with a citation. He was also invited to speak at the annual meeting of the Association on Indian Affairs in 1950.

Program for Displaced Persons

Minnesota became the first state to take definite steps to help displaced persons in Europe when, in November, 1947, Youngdahl appointed a ten-man commission to study the matter. He called upon the leadership of the churches to play a major role in the program. Headed by Dr. T. F. Gullixson, former President of Luther Theological Seminary of St. Paul, the commission comprised members representing the major religious groups in the state and the State Directors of Employment and Security, Social Welfare and the Commissioner of Agriculture. The commission sent 150,000 questionnaires to 3,000 clergymen. The replies revealed that Minnesota citizens were willing to welcome 2,066 families. Dr. Gullixson reported to the Governor in February, 1948, and he directed the commission to proceed with the resettlement program. Youngdahl continued his efforts on behalf of displaced persons a year later, when he called a parley to explore the matter of restrictions barring European doctors from practicing in Minnesota and appealed to the Minnesota Dentists' Association to cooperate in bringing D.P. dentists to Minnesota. By October 18, 1949, 2,528 displaced persons had been brought to Minnesota, almost half

(1,236) under the auspices of the National Catholic Welfare
.Conference. Youngdahl wrote a short personal letter of greet-
ing to each family as it arrived.

Youngdahl evaluated the program in his speech before the
National Conference of Catholic Charities. He regarded the
D.P. program as a "splendid opportunity to show how well
the voluntary agencies, with church affiliations, can meet the
humanitarian problem," and as an opportunity for Catholic,
Protestant and Jewish people to work together in a common
cause. In the speech, he made the following comment about
the role of voluntary welfare agencies: "Today we accept
the basic principle that government is obligated to give
a minimum amount of protection to those who are unable
to meet their own needs. But regardless of governmental
economic assistance to this segment of the population, there
will always be a need for the voluntary agency, which can give
best to the unfortunates the human love and warmth of spirit
so vital to the individual." (Proceedings of the Thirty-Fifth
Conference of Catholic Charities, p. 55.)

Other Welfare Legislation

"Education must now be given its full day in Court,"
Youngdahl had said in his 1947 inaugural address. He had
advocated the adoption of the proposals of a Committee on
State Aid to Public Schools, to simplify the system of state
aids and equalize educational opportunities throughout the
state. He had also urged the passage of a minimum teachers'
salary law and the establishment of scholarships by which
young people would be encouraged to enter the teaching profession. Like most governors before and after him, he had
pressed for increased appropriations for the university and
state colleges.

The pattern of increased expenditures had been apparent
in his proposals either to eliminate or raise the maximum allot-
ment on old age assistance grants and aids for dependent children, and to grant pay increases to state employees. However,

he had urged caution in considering a bonus for veterans, lest it take precedence over more urgent needs.

The 1947 Legislature had responded favorably to a large portion of Youngdahl's program. A new school aid system, simplifying aid grants and increasing them by over nineteen million dollars, had been established. The University had received its highest appropriation in its history, $16,462,496. Other aspects of Youngdahl's program which had been adopted were: the creation of a Department of Business Research and Development; preparation of a state rent control system to operate if and when federal controls were lifted; provision for low income housing and slum rehabilitation; increase in grants for old-age assistance and dependent children, in each case from $40 to $50 a month, and higher salaries for state employees.

The 1949 Legislature could also point to several accomplishments that strengthened the human welfare program. The maximum on aid to dependent children was finally abolished, and the maximum on aid to the aged was raised to $55. Financial aid for Minnesota's Indians, as well as funds to implement the re-settlement of displaced persons, were provided. Increased aids for the blind and tuberculosis victims were granted. In the midst of strong pressure from lobbyists representing both labor and management, the legislators passed workmen's compensation legislation. One bill raised disability benefits from a minimum of $13.50 to $15.00 a week and maximum payments from $27 to $30 a week; and another statute increased maximum weekly benefits to $25 a week for a worker earning $2,750 and more a year. A commission to study the state's marriage and divorce laws was authorized and asked to report to the next legislative session.

Tax Policy

Youngdahl was an expensive Governor. Legislators with an eye for economy had little peace while he was in office. Appropriations for 1947 had totalled $176,064,248, the highest in Minnesota's history; but the 1949 Legislature more than doubled that figure by making appropriations totalling $362,977,903. How to raise the money for Youngdahl's humanitarian program was one of the most difficult challenges confronting the state government.

Two basic issues in tax policy are concerned with the problems of how taxes are to be spent and who pays them. On the first question, Youngdahl was obviously in favor of increased government spending for human welfare. On the second question, his position is more ambiguous. He urged passage of cigarette, beer, and liquor taxes, which are forms of a sales tax and indiscriminate in the matter of the ability of the consumer to pay. He called for increased taxes on iron ore, private utilities and the railroads, thus removing himself from the category of those who try to keep taxes on business and industry as low as possible. He opposed the general sales tax and objected to any increases in the real property tax.

The 1947 Legislature did not have as acute a problem as the 1949 Legislature had to face. Part of the program, such as expanded school aids, was financed out of surpluses. No general revision of the tax structure had been necessary, although there were substantial increases in existing taxes. A new cigarette tax had been enacted and liquor taxes were more than doubled. Other enactments that the legislators had adopted were: slight reduction in the rate on real property; exemption of up to 85% of corporation dividends to another corporation, which meant a reduction of about $350,000 in income; increase of the royalty tax on iron ore from 10.5% to 11%, and a proportionate raise of the occupational tax rate and changes in respect to labor credits on the iron ore occupational tax, all of which were expected to yield additional revenue of about $960,000 a year. The Legislature had failed to change the tax levied against railroads and public utilities. In the case of the railroads this is not unusual. The railroads in Minnesota pay no income taxes, no personal property taxes and no real estate taxes. They pay only a gross earnings tax. Since both the method of taxation **and the rate** have been fixed by constitutional amendments, the legislators have no power to determine the taxes on railroads. The railroad lobby has been successful. The tax rate on railroads' gross earnings has not been changed for 37 years. It is not a mystery why the railroad lobby has fought vigorously against constitutional revision.

In 1949, the legislators had to find ways of increasing taxes by $55,248,000. As surpluses dwindle, and expenditures increase, the tax problem in Minnesota becomes more acute. The 1949 Legislature was the first to feel the growing pressure of this problem. The story of how it was handled illustrates the great power of legislative committees, particularly those dealing with finances, and the need for a reform of legislative procedure in Minnesota.

One of the big problems of the session was whether or not to divert funds from the Income Tax School Fund to pay for other programs. Some legislators favored diverting funds to pay for the soldiers' bonus, which had been approved by a referendum in 1948; some suggested that the University and teachers' colleges could be financed from the school fund; others believed that, if diversion was not authorized, income taxes should be reduced to keep the surplus from mounting. On the opposing side were the educators and Governor Youngdahl, who were determined that no diversions should be authorized.

The decision to divert part of the funds was delayed until the closing hours of the session. The House tax committee procrastinated action on other tax measures until the dedicated fund issue was settled. As a result, there was a five-day deadlock and "legislative jam" that startled the entire state. Pressed for time, the legislators were unable to subject the tax measures proposed by the tax committee to adequate debate. This greatly increased the actual power of this committee, because the other legislators were forced to depend on their proposals. At least one group in the state was disturbed by the record of the committee. CIO observers wrote:

"It is disquieting to know that the 1949 House Tax Committee in the Legislature was one of the most reactionary committees in the entire legislature. Even some conservatives agreed with this indictment.

"The committee functioned as a Big Businessman's chore boy. It produced no new major tax laws. For the first time in the history of the Legislature, it failed to report out any iron ore tax bills. It spent most of its time considering ways and means of cutting loopholes in existing tax laws which would give businessmen tax relief. It refused to suggest any means of paying the soldiers' bonus. As a result, reactionaries were able to jam through a completely unjust tax plan to pay the bonus. . . .

"The full story on behind-the-scenes string-pulling by a small group of three or four men who rigged the financing of the bonus plan is a scandal of no small proportions. The shenanigans of legislators who doubled in brass as employees of big companies who were interested in only one or two bills to help their single company, and the devil take the hindmost — these richly deserve an airing." (Minnesota State CIO Council, **Did You Vote for This Last November, A Report on the Minnesota Legislature and Legislators,** 1949 Session, Mpls., Minn., 1949.)

A "tax package" plan was prepared by Governor Youngdahl and a special caucus of conservative leaders in both houses. It was introduced in the House by Roy Dunn's motion to suspend the rules until the proposed taxes could be voted upon. (The motion was necessary because the rules required three readings of the bills, which had been introduced on the last legal day of the session, thus leaving no time for a third reading.) Since the regulations prohibited the presentation of any alternative proposals while the special rules were in force, house liberals spent three hours fighting the motion to suspend the rules but were unsuccessful.

As finally passed, the plan for increasing income so that the bonus and other items could be financed consisted of:

1. A $5 head tax upon every person who files an income tax return — $4,100,000;

2. A 5% surtax on income, corporate and bank excise taxes — $2,726,000;

3. A "blank check" authorization to levy more property taxes to cover deficits — an increase of 2.34 mills the first year

Displaced Persons Commission meets with Gov. Youngdahl

Gov. Youngdahl confers with the disputants in the Minneapolis school strike

and 2.17 mills the second year was decided upon later — $3,275,000;

    4. An additional five-dollar payment by all banks — $3,000;

    5. A one-cent increase (to 4c) on the gasoline tax — $6,000,000;

    6. A one-cent increase on the cigarette tax — $3,000,000;

    7. A 1% increase (to 12%) on royalty and occupation iron ore taxes — $1,300,000;

    8. A 10% increase on taxes for liquors, wine and beer — $1,600,000;

    9. Revision of labor credits on iron ore occupation tax — $720,000;

    10. Higher fishing and hunting licenses — $900,000.

(The Minnesota Institute of Governmental Research, "The Financial Record of the 1949 Legislature," No. 26, July, 1949, p. 5. Hereafter cited as Minn. Inst., No. 26.)

Youngdahl believed that the program he had outlined should be financed by higher taxes on beer and other items he regarded as luxuries. He reasoned that alcoholic beverages were not only luxuries, but that their consumption was often a contributory cause for the high cost of necessary spending on welfare, law enforcement and public health. Not everyone agreed with him. One day he challenged one of the lobbyists on the subject of his inconsistency.

"You come to ask me to approve the highest appropriation for the University in the history of the state. I would be very happy if you would tell me where to raise the funds, because I want the University to be a fine institution, too. Any ideas?"

The lobbyist, a member of the Board of Regents of the University, was stumped and admitted it. His freedom to make suggestions was limited in part by the fact that he also represented the interests of the brewers.

"Why don't you stop fighting the increase of the beer tax? It seems hardly consistent for you to urge me to grant the University increased funds and then oppose a tax plan I have for paying the bill."

"Are you insinuating that I should resign from the Board of Regents?"

"No, but I think you should go and talk to the brewers and try to persuade them to stop opposing the beer tax plan."

There was no evidence that the man ever abandoned his dual role as spender for the University and saver for the brewers. The incident points up the problem of taxation involved in a program of human welfare. Every citizen wants a humanitarian program — until he feels the pinch in his own pocketbook.

Few were pleased with the tax plan as passed by the Legislature and signed by the Governor. Two groups showed an awareness of the ethical issues involved in taxation — the Minnesota Institute of Governmental Research and the C.I.O. Council. The churches showed no interest in this problem.

One of the thorniest problems in Minnesota politics is the taxation of the state's richest natural resource, iron ore. Necessary to an intelligent understanding of the problems of tax policy in Minnesota is a knowledge of the factors that determine the iron ore tax. Since 70% of all the iron ore mined in the United States comes from Minnesota mines, taxation of mining companies has always been a controversial issue. Taxation committees of the Legislature have long been the object of heavy pressure from the steel companies who own the mines, and more recently from lobbyists representing labor.

The iron ore royalty tax is a form of income tax, except that its rates do not rise as the amount of income increases. The small increases voted by the Legislature in 1947 and 1949 did not basically alter this tax. Critics have questioned whether it is fair to the people that such a valuable resource, which depletes as time passes, should be taxed at such a low rate. The tax proposals of the Minnesota C.I.O. Council called for an increase of the tax from 11% to 23%, which would bring in additional revenue of about $21,000,000. Dissenters argue that too high taxes may drive the steel companies to seek their resources elsewhere, especially since the richer deposits which can be mined efficiently are depleted.

The second iron ore tax is the occupational tax, which is

a substitute for an income tax. Most Minnesota corporations are subject to a corporate income tax based upon profits. However, this tax cannot apply to the iron ore companies. Most of them are subsidiaries of the steel companies, and their profits are consolidated in the financial statements of the parent corporations. The occupation tax is based on the presumed capitalized value of each ton of iron ore produced, rather than the profit derived from producing it. This value is determined by the steel companies, which provide the state department of taxation with what is known as the "Lake Erie price" as the base for the tax rate. This price is established by the first chance sale of ore of prescribed content in the spring at lower lake ports. This tax and the method of compiling it have been controversial, although the use of the Lake Erie price as a basis for computing the value of iron ore was sustained in 1936 by the Minnesota Supreme Court. Some critics say that the Lake Erie price is not a competitive price but one arbitrarily set by the steel companies, controlling close to 90% of the iron deposits and shipments. Others representing mining companies complain that the price has always been higher than the actual annual average price for ore. Critics also question whether the value of a ton of ore properly constitutes a fair tax base related to the ability to pay. (Minnesota State C.I.O. Council, Minnesota's Unfair Taxation of Iron Ore In Comparison With Other Minnesota Taxpayers, a mimeographed report available in the Council offices.)

The third tax paid by the mining companies is the property, or ad valorem tax, based upon the presumed volume and grade of iron ore in the ground. Tax officials have to rely on unverified statements by the companies as to the amount and chemical type of unmined ore which they own.

A national C.I.O. study commission produced figures to show that iron ore tax collections have failed to keep pace with the value of the ore produced and have provided a decreasing percentage of the total tax collections of the state. (Sixteen per cent of the total from 1925-29 came from iron ore taxes and 9.7% of the total during the five-year period from 1947-51). They point out, too, that the proportion of the total taxes paid to Minnesota, commensurate with the total profits after taxes of 20 major steel companies, has been declining. They warn that, if the services provided by the state to the people of Minnesota are to be adequately financed, there must be an increase of taxes on iron ore. A general sales tax would be the only alternative. (Report of the National C.I.O. Commission in the Matter of Minnesota Iron Ore Taxes. Mimeographed copies available at the offices of the Minn. C.I.O. Council, Minneapolis, Minn.)

One of the criticisms of Youngdahl concerned his failure to present a well-developed solution for financing the increased expenditures required for his program, delegating the responsibility to the Legislatures. That Youngdahl gave less attention to taxation problems, such as those connected with the iron ore tax, than he did to his humanitarian program cannot be disputed; but it was not due to his ignorance of the problem of taxation. The criticism should be balanced by the observation that Youngdahl gained detailed knowledge of the problem of iron ore taxation during his judicial career on the Minnesota Supreme Court bench.

CHAPTER NINE

The People's Governor

The governor of a state plays a complex and powerful role. His position as chief executive increases in power even as the functions of the state, especially its welfare projects, continue to multiply. In addition to enforcing the laws and administering the state's program, he is also the interpreter of popular opinion. Public attention is concentrated on him to a greater degree than on any other state officer or party leader. He is looked upon as the champion of the people. Popular interest in him gives him authority within his party. If he is not the actual head of the party, he is at least the figurehead. Charles Beard wrote, "So great is the popular interest in the office that even the most powerful party managers, in making nominations, must be on their guard; they may choose a nonentity or even a man of doubtful reputation for auditor or treasurer, but seldom for governor. They may even be forced by public opinion to choose someone whom they dislike or distrust." (Charles A. Beard, **American Government and Politics,** Eighth Edition, New York, MacMillan, 1939, p. 576). Without a candidate for governor who is known and trusted by the people, the party jeopardizes its chances to win the election.

A man must be "wise beyond wisdom" to wend his way adroitly through the network and snarls of his offices of executive, party leader and spokesman of the people. Without political acumen, a governor would be "clanging brass and tinkling cymbal," even if he had a four-square program and an unblemished reputation.

How did Luther Youngdahl play his complex role? Behind the scenes, was he the G.O.P. figurehead, a party hack? How did he deal with the Legislature? How did he handle the special interest lobbies? Was he primarily the administrator of a legislature's program and the enforcer of its laws, or did he aggressively push into the forefront as the spokesman of the people with a program in the people's interests? Did he make arbitrary use of the power his popularity gave him? In a manner consonant with his high ideals of honesty and humanity?

The answers to these questions gradually became apparent during his first term. In his first inaugural address, he explained precisely how he intended to operate while in office. (See chapter six, p. 140) His crusades against the gamblers and for the benefit of the mentally ill were dramatic displays of courageous and determined action by an aggressive leader who was not afraid of a fight even though it meant venturing beyond the limits set by party policy, and who successfully captured popular interest and support because of his dedication to the humanitarian cause. However, the very fact that those crusades were so dramatic makes them insufficient as evidence. It is also necessary to observe how Youngdahl functioned in the less dramatic but highly vital matters of day-by-day administration of the government, how he dealt with the Legislature on important matters that did not have the color to attract popular interest, and how he operated in party councils.

The Arkansas Bond Deal

A test of Youngdahl's administrative integrity occurred in the summer of 1949, when he uncovered evidence of improper activities by State Investment Board Secretary, Charles Foster, who had been appointed by Youngdahl in 1947. The investment board had held a secret meeting to approve the purchase of bonds from the state of Arkansas. Youngdahl had been opposed to this $5,208,000 purchase on the grounds that Federal bonds are a better investment for Minnesota's permanent trust funds than state bonds. Mr. Foster had altered the minutes of the board to conceal its surreptitious activities.

A. Herbert Nelson obtained the information from a friend and wrote a memo to Youngdahl about it. Youngdahl investigated the matter and, discovering the rumor to be true, demanded the resignation of Foster. Despite the opposition of the other members of the Executive Council, all of whom favored the bond purchase and put pressure on the Governor to keep silent about the whole matter, Youngdahl released the story to the press. He insisted that the issue of "whether we should condone a secret meeting of the investment board with alteration of the minutes plus a secret agreement to purchase the bonds or not" was of sufficient seriousness to require drastic action. (**Minneapolis Tribune,** Aug. 6, 1949.) When the matter of Foster's dismissal was put to a vote in the Executive Council, the other members opposed Youngdahl; Foster remained in his position.

Youngdahl's stand deepened the rift between the conservatives in his party and himself. The Executive Council members were all Old Guard men. The predominantly conservative Hennepin County Republican Club rebuked the Governor and backed the other state officers. However, the Republican State Central Committee unanimously endorsed his action and commended him for his "courage and public spirit in bringing into the open the alteration of records and the secret arrangements connected with the case." (**Minneapolis Star,** Aug. 6, 1949.)

His actions also won the commendation of the Lutheran Brotherhood of the Minnesota Conference of the Augustana Lutheran Church, which passed the following resolution at its convention on September 18, 1949: "Be it further resolved by this convention that Governor Youngdahl be highly commended for his forthright and courageous action in bringing to the attention of the citizens of Minnesota the conditions existing in the investment of some of our State Trust funds and that he be complimented on his insistence that such conditions be rectified for the good of the people of the State and the integrity of our elected officials." (The Lutheran Minnesota Conference of the Augustana Lutheran Church, Minutes of the Ninety-Second Annual Convention, 1950, p. 128.)

Youngdahl and Patronage

Youngdahl's policy regarding the politician's traditional privilege of dispensing patronage was stated in one of his letters: "The merit system prevailed in my administration. What few appointments I made were made not for the political effect but from the standpoint of ability to get the job done." (Luther W. Youngdahl, letter to the author, June 25, 1952.)

The appointment of Myron W. Clark as Agricultural Commissioner ignited political tempers. Youngdahl's failure to promote Bernhard C. Swenson, the Deputy Commissioner, caused Mr. Swenson to resign in anger and brought the charge from a D.F.L. leader that "the appointment of Clark is the pay-off of a political debt assumed for Clark's efforts in Youngdahl's behalf while serving with the Minnesota School Board Association." (**Minneapolis Tribune**, July 21, 1950.) Swenson had the support of leading agricultural leaders in the state, as well as that of farm groups and the D.F.L. party. Youngdahl defended his appointment of Clark before the Southern Minnesota Vegetable Growers' Association convention by saying that he had been determined to get the best man available and relating Clark's record in rural affairs. (**Minneapolis Tribune**, July 27, 1950.)

Another appointment made news, not at the time it was announced but after the appointee took office and began to carry out his assignment. Youngdahl was dissatisfied with Minnesota's supervision of insurance practices. In recent years, a few large companies have dominated the state Insurance Department; and the commissioners have received their information and advice from the persons they should have been supervising. Members of the department were entertained regularly at dinners and cocktail parties. Youngdahl knew that his friend, Herbert Nelson, an insurance man, was aware of the situation and concerned about it. He called him to his office one day.

"How would you like to be Insurance Commissioner? Make the position a guardian of the people's interests and the job is yours."

"Naturally I appreciate your confidence in me, Governor, and I promise you I would do my best to fulfill my oath of office."

"You probably will — in fact, I know you will — take plenty of heat!"

"I'll take the job anyway. I would like to see what could be done in that department if someone got in there and started working with the assumption that he is supposed to be a watchdog for all the people, not just the companies."

Nelson became Insurance commissioner and State Fire Marshall on May 15, 1951. He was not reappointed by Governor C. Elmer Anderson two years later when his term expired. The story of his brief career in government service throws some light on the influencial role that special and powerful interests play in Minnesota's government.

Nelson undertook a study of fire insurance rates and discovered that in Minnesota no adjustment had been made since 1945, whereas in surrounding states substantial rate reductions had been allowed. He learned that Minnesota's fire insurance rates were 25% higher than Wisconsin's. The available evidence indicated that reductions also were possible in Minnesota.

His investigations led to his discovery that seventeen northern counties had rates higher than the rest of the state, because of the forest fire hazard. Figures showed that fire claims were no more frequent in the northern counties than anywhere else and that the higher rates were not justified.

He soon discovered that the department had no trained actuary who could make independent investigations of rate-making practices. The Department hired a New York actuary whose primary income was obtained from insurance companies who used his services. This signified that the Commissioner was dependent upon the talent of insurance companies — and their advice.

The law regarding the examination of domestic insurance companies, to determine the fairness of their rates, was being ignored. Nelson's predecessors had not allowed the rate technicians to participate in the examination of domestic companies.

A few lending agencies and automobile dealers were using coercion on buyers. Under their regulations, it was impossible for the borrower to continue his present policy or purchase insurance from a company of his choice. Nelson uncovered that abuse, too.

One day during his study of fire insurance rates, Nelson received a call inviting him to lunch at a Minneapolis social club with the director of a life insurance company who had been a former insurance commissioner. The conversational approach was polite, but its meaning was unmistakable.

"Herb, I think I'm in a position to give you some good advice. The insurance companies feel that you are going about this business in the wrong way. They think you shouldn't adjust rates without listening to what they have to say about it. It's never been done this way before."

"The facts are clear enough," Nelson retorted. "Take the city of Brainerd. Dwellers there pay $6 a thousand on their dwellings and $7.50 on contents. In a comparable Wisconsin city owners are paying $3.25 on both dwellings and contents. Or what about the people in Duluth? They pay $2.50 more on their homes and $4.00 more on their household goods than people in Superior, Wisconsin, across the bay from them. You insurance people have not justified this discrepancy."

"Well, let me put it this way. 'The boys' don't care for this activity of yours at all. Now understand, I'm telling you this in your own interests. Your re-appointment will be opposed. I'm just giving you this tip."

Nelson refused to submit to political pressure. He requested the insurance companies to adjust their fire insurance rates. He initiated action to reduce the rates in northern counties; and, because of delaying action by the Attorney-General's office, this mitigation was not affected until after he left his post. He appointed his own actuary and insisted that the provision for examination of domestic companies be carried out. He ruled out insurance coercion, enabling borrowers to buy insurance on purchases from any company. Although his ruling was approved by all but a few finance companies and banks, it was abolished by his successor.

Insurance executives wrote letters to advise him on his proposed reforms. One day he told Governor Youngdahl about these letters.

"I know all about them. They send me carbon copies," Youngdahl replied. Yet he had not interfered with Nelson's attempts to reform the department. "Herb, enforce the laws fairly and objectively. Work for the interests of the people. That's all I demand. When people start sniping, you can count on me to back you up. Some of them have tried to impress me with unfounded rumors—obviously trying to undermine you. I'm afraid I was not very tactful with them."

Nelson only had time to begin inaugurating his reforms. He was not re-appointed, perhaps because he was not considered to be desirable by the insurance companies.

Youngdahl was granted the opportunity of filling an important office when Harry H. Peterson resigned from the Minnesota Supreme Court to become the D.L.F. candidate for Governor in 1950. No political repercussions followed his appointment of Theodore Christianson, Jr., son of the late Republican governor. Christianson's qualifications were well-known, and the appointment pleased everyone.

Activities of Church Members in 1950 Campaign

Youngdahl announced his intention to file his candidacy for a third term on May 28, 1950. His statement at the time contained a phrase that became the slogan of his third campaign — "honesty and humanity." His platform revealed that his interest in human welfare and good government had not diminished. In addition to planks on law enforcement, education, the mental health program, youth conservation, F.E.P.C. and others on good government, the platform stressed the reform of marriage and divorce laws, the establishment of family conciliation courts, the passage of a lobbyist registration bill and opposition to a sales tax.

He continued his practice of canvassing the entire state to make his "reports to the people." Commenting on his 1950 campaign one day he revealed, "I think that a man, even in a political campaign, should be guided by honesty and humanity. . . . A public official who fails to make a full, frank report of his administration does an injury to his people. A candidate who distorts the facts is in the same category." (**The Minneapolis Tribune,** Nov. 2, 1950.)

A unique aspect of Youngdahl's 1950 campaign was the activity of church people on behalf of his re-election. Not only was he endorsed by individual church leaders, but there were instances of organized campaigning by church people on his behalf.

A few clergymen approved his candidacy publicly. One Mission Covenant pastor in St. Paul endorsed him from the pulpit; however, his unprecedented action was criticized rather severely by members of his congregation. Alton Motter, Executive Secretary of the St. Paul Council of Churches, sent a letter to thirty-two clergymen inviting their contributions of one dollar toward an advertisement that would appear in the newspaper with the names of leaders from various vocations listed as endorsees of the Governor. Twenty-seven clergymen responded by sending each a dollar.

It was not the first time Youngdahl had been endorsed by a clergyman. His pastor, Dr. Leonard Kendall, pastor of the Messiah Lutheran Church, had sent letters of endorsement in 1946 and 1948 to the Protestant clergy of Minnesota. In explaining his action Dr. Kendall emphasized that he rarely endorsed candidates for any office but that he knew Youngdahl so well that he did not hesitate to endorse him.

There were at least three instances of organized backing among church people. On October 30, a letter of endorsement was sent to all alumni of Gustavus Adolphus College by the "Gustavians for Youngdahl Volunteer Committee." Obviously the appeal was primarily made on the basis of his being a fellow Gustavus graduate; but the letter noted his religious and moral qualifications, and the Committee was largely composed of active Lutherans.

Youngdahl was endorsed also by Protestants United, which called itself "a committee of representative Protestant clergymen and laymen which seeks to uphold and promote the fundamental convictions of Protestant Christians in American civic and religious life." This group sent the following letter shortly before the election:

Dear Co-Worker:

We are writing you on behalf of Protestants United, a group of St. Paul Protestant clergymen and laymen, who are vitally interested in civic matters.

We are writing you because our last meeting brought out the necessity of urging our Protestant people to vote on election day, November 7, to prevent losing the gains recently made for the moral good of our state. At that time we were asked to write all the pastors of Protestant churches as well as Rabbis of Jewish synagogues, urging them that they hold before their people the necessity of voting at the forthcoming election.

It has been repeated time and again that the great issues are often lost, less by the number of voters opposing them than by the many voters who do not cast their ballots. The right of free exercise of the ballot is one of the many boasts of democracy. Real believers in our American Way must vote if we are to retain that right and maintain good government. Will you, therefore, kindly impress on your people that they vote?

It is not the function of Protestants United to interfere in purely political contests. However, we are convinced that the contest for the governorship is not purely a political one. We hope for the re-election of our present Governor in the interest of HUMAN WELFARE. His battles for MENTAL HEALTH — YOUTH CONSERVATION — LIQUOR CONTROL — EDUCATION — GENERAL LAW ENFORCEMENT — to mention but a few of them, are worthy of whole-hearted support by church people. We do not hesitate to urge you to call these issues to the attention of your people and to recommend Governor Youngdahl to them as a Christian churchman who brings his Christian convictions to his high office.

We hope you will pray with us for God's guidance in continuing to give to the people of Minnesota a government built on high spiritual and moral principles.

(Signed)

Irving A. West, Chairman
Alton M. Motter, Secretary

The most extensive of organized efforts of church people on Youngdahl's behalf was carried out under the direction of Alfred France, Jr. It was a project designed to enlist the support of church members in every county. The idea took shape one day when a group of churchmen met with the Governor to discuss how the churches could work effectively in the political arena. Bradshaw Mintener, a Methodist layman and a vice-president of General Mills, was the leader of the group. The Rev. H. L. Stright, Executive Secretary of the Minnesota Council of Churches, also was present.

It was first suggested that Mr. Stright be granted a leave of absence to travel the state for the purpose of organized support for Youngdahl. The group rejected this plan, because Stright's close connection with the Council might give the impression that the Council was identifying itself with a political party; its effectiveness would thus be impaired. Later the name of Alfred France, Jr., a recent graduate of the University of Minnesota, who had majored in political science and had played and active and leading role in campus politics, was suggested to Mr. Stright. Impressed by France's qualifications, Mr. Stright recommended him to Bradshaw Mintener. At the next meeting of the group with the Governor, Mr. France was interviewed and then offered the job.

After first acquiring the names of key church leaders in every county, he sent letters announcing that he would be visiting them soon. Later, when he called on them personally,

he asked them to become county chairmen whose task would
be organizing local support for Youngdahl by personally con-
tacting people and encouraging them to vote and to write
endorsing letters to friends. If the persons first contacted were
unable or unwilling to participate, he asked them for the names
of other possible prospects in the county.

France succeeded in getting the organized support of church
people in 73 out of the 87 counties in the state. France believed
that the most impressive progress was recorded in St. Paul and
Roseau County. In 1948, Roseau County voted Democratic;
in 1950 the "churchmen-for-Youngdahl" effort there was well-
executed, and the county's vote went to the Governor. France
attributed the reduction of the D.F.L. candidate's majority of
19,000 in 1948 to 2,000 in 1950 in St. Paul to the vigorous work
of Protestants in that city. (Interview, St. Paul, Aug. 16, 1951.)

He obtained the most noteworthy cooperation from pastors
and laymen of the following churches: Augustana Lutheran,
Evangelical Lutheran, American Lutheran, United Lutheran,
Northern Baptist, Presbyterian, and Methodist. A number of
Episcopalian churchmen were very helpful. Missouri Luther-
ans, Southern Baptists and Roman Catholics did not participate.
(This does not imply that members of these denominations
did not support him and vote for him as individuals, since
France was describing organized group action only.)

There was one unique instance of support by a church
organization. At its convention in 1950, the Southern Minnesota District of the Evangelical Lutheran Church's Women's
Missionary Society passed a resolution favoring the organization of women for the support of Youngdahl's candidacy.

Church leaders, labor leaders, politicians and educators
were among those who believed that Youngdahl's chief political strength was derived from the endorsement of church
people. Dr. Leonard Kendall said, "he had tremendous support from the church people. This support was largely spontaneous and came from the grass roots of church membership.
They were aroused by his forthright convictions to a new interest in political life. This support resulted in volunteer groups
among church people, whose purpose was to enlist support in

the Governor's campaign." (Interview, Galesburg, Ill., June 13, 1951.)

H. L. Stright said, "I feel that the churches responded to the opportunity of supporting a Christian in politics and that political activities among several ministers was begun as a result of Gov. Youngdahl's program." (Interview, Minneapolis, Minn., Aug. 29, 1951.) Dr. Melvin A. Hammarberg, pastor of the Arlington Hills Lutheran Church, St. Paul, said he had observed an increased political interest among church people, which he attributed to the Governor's influence. He believed Youngdahl won the people's support as a result of his law enforcement crusade in 1947, because he showed he was ready to risk political suicide to uphold his convictions. (Interview, St. Paul, June 26, 1953.)

Dr. Arthur Naftalin, associate professor of political science at the University of Minnesota, was convinced that Youngdahl's religion and his moralistic approach had much to do with his ability to win the vote. (Interview, Minneapolis, June 10, 1953.) Emil Krieg, Editor of **Minnesota Labor** (official organ of the C.I.O. in Minnesota), said, "Youngdahl's chief strength came from church people. He had the reputation for being a God-fearing, deeply religious man. He made it a point to talk to church people, and brought religion into his talks on all occasions." (Interview, Minneapolis, June 11, 1953.) Orlin Folwick, public relations director for the Minnesota A. F. of L., also declared that Youngdahl's religious affiliations made him popular with church people. (Interview, June 17, 1953.) Otto Christianson, executive secretary of the Minnesota Employers Association, who battled Youngdahl on several legislative issues, had a different way of recognizing the Governor's appeal to church people when he said, "The Governor knew it was just smart politics in Minnesota to stress that he was a deeply religious man." (Interview, St. Paul, June 18, 1953.)

Youngdahl himself made efforts to enlist the support of church people, not directly for himself but on behalf of good government and participation in politics. He gave many addresses before church groups on subjects dealing with the relationship of Christianity to politics. He was fond of saying, "We get government just as good or bad as we are willing to pay the price for. Men and women of Christian faith and character must be willing to fight in the open for good government." He never ceased to battle against the indifference among church people toward political activities. In a speech entitled "Do Christianity and Politics Mix?" he said, "We have come to misconstrue this philosophy of the separation of church and state as an unwillingness on the part of people to participate in politics at all. . . . We need Christian politicians in and out of office." In an address given frequently to gatherings of church youth, "Politics — a Challenge for Christian Youth," he said:

"To meet the obligation of Christian stewardship, George and Mary Jane have made some definite plans. They will attend church faithfully, teach Sunday school with real enthusiasm, serve willingly in church offices and perform gladly the many other duties of an active layman. . . . Unfortunately, though, I am afraid they will completely overlook one of the most important areas of opportunity for worthwhile Christian service. I am speaking of politics. As their parents have done, they will stand apart from politics, feeling that political participation is not within the realm of Christian responsibility. . . . I hope fervently that George and Mary Jane will, therefore, come to see that Christian stewardship includes active participation in politics."

He was invited to speak at such occasions as commencement at Gustavus Adolphus College, meetings of the Minnesota Council of Church Women, the Y.M.C.A. convention, a regional convention of the National Federation of Catholic College Students, a convention of the National Conference of Catholic Charities, Reformation Day rallies all over the country, Sunday services in some of the churches, baccalaureate exercises, and many church gatherings.

Some of the people in the state remained skeptical. One critic believed that "Youngdahl was playing to a full house, and he knew it." Other disparagers felt he used religion to his own political advantage. One of the more vicious of the attacks on him was the surreptitious distribution of derogatory printed matter at a Crusade for Freedom rally in St. Paul, at which Youngdahl had invited Billy Graham, noted revivalist, to speak. The spirit of the rally was considerably dampened when the audience found at their seats copies of a sheet containing a denunciation of the Governor by Charles L. Schultze, chairman of "the St. Paul Good Government Group." He was indignant over the way the Governor had turned the Crusade for Freedom into a "revivalist fiasco" and made a political football of religion. He was quoted as saying:

"Citizens of St. Paul should rise in protest against this latest attempt to display himself not only as the governor of the state, but also as the state's top clergyman.

"Throughout his public career, Governor Youngdahl has made every attempt to place himself on a religious pedestal. He preaches from the pulpit when it is generally considered that that sacred place should be reserved only for those who have spent years of theological study and who have been called to the religious profession.

"At least at the last minute when the City Council had exposed Youngdahl's plot, the Reverend Governor, in shining armor, condescended to invite a Catholic priest and a Jewish rabbi. . . .

"The people of Minnesota can go to the polls on November 7th and retire Youngdahl so that he can devote all of his time to revival meetings and preaching and not be burdened with the governor's duties which he so sadly neglects." (Typewritten copy of the full statement in possession of the author.)

Others, not doubting the Governor's sincerity, raised questions about the **kind** of political activity he encouraged. Being an independent-minded man and having no long experience in party government, by his example Youngdahl encouraged Minnesotans to incline toward independent, non-partisan political activity rather than party-group organization. He succeeded admirably, his critics concede, in mobilizing citizens' advisory committees on behalf of specific legislation. His influence among independents was so great that in 1950 they organized a statewide Independents for Youngdahl Committee to work for his re-election. He was less successful, his detractors point out, in drawing new blood into the parties; because his strategy of forming independent citizens' committees tended to discourage, rather than inspire, participation in party politics.

An observer of Youngdahl's political career was Bernhard LaVander, state chairman of the G.O.P. State Central Committee from 1946 to 1950. LeVander, an active member of the Augustana Lutheran Church also, has some convictions of his own about the importance of the Christians being active in politics. However, he is committed to working within the political party rather than as an independent. It is from this point of view that he made the following analysis of Youngdahl's politics:

"Youngdahl appealed directly to the people. Often he went over the heads of party leaders and ignored party organization — he acted unilaterally. He failed to understand the dynamics of party organization and the vital role of the party in American politics.

"He did not consult the party or try to lead the party to accept his program. He launched his program and expected the party to go along with him. Stassen and Youngdahl were a study in contrasts at this point. Stassen always conferred with party heads; and the decisions made were party decisions, even though they were often decisions approving Stassen's views. Youngdahl felt the effects of his unilateral actions from the beginning on the law enforcement program. The party was more incensed at the way he launched it, without consulting anyone, than at his program.

"The effect of appealing directly to the people rather than enlisting the support of the party was not an unmixed blessing. Youngdahl's methods succeeded wonderfully in dramatizing state politics and arousing public interest and support of his program. But the effect was to alienate more and more of the party organization, and he did not draw new blood into the G.O.P. He inspired political activity of many fine and influential people who had not been active before, but they did not become interested in the party. They supported him personally, or features of his program. Hence, when he left office, these persons melted back into the ranks of the voters and their interest in politics died down." (Interview, Mpls., May, 1953.)

Youngdahl has admitted that he was not a dedicated party man, and that he believes very much in political independence. Recently he said, "Of course, I believe strongly in the two-party system of government and recognize the need for a strong party organization, but along with party government goes much pettiness that I dislike very much. Mrs. Youngdahl and I attended party conventions and caucuses faithfully, but we often grew weary of the petty bickering, the request for favors and jobs in return for work done for the party and the narrowly partisan point of view when it came to deciding the stand that should be taken on issues. The party was more important than the people to some of the boys. We would often be glad to be back in the car and on the way home away from that atmosphere." He added that he believed the independent modern voter held the balance of power and that this was a wholesome development in American politics. Gone are the days when the party machine could marshall the votes in solid blocs. People are thinking, listening to political speeches, watching T.V. programs on politics, and reading. They make up their own minds. They can often make their pressure felt most effectively in independent citizens' committees. (Interview, Minneapolis, Oct. 23, 1954.)

Supporters would be quick to defend Youngdahl's approach to state politics. They would point out that the liberal wing of the G.O.P. was firmly under Stassen's control and that Youngdahl and the Old Guard did not see eye to eye. As long as that situation existed, Youngdahl's only choice was to regiment support for his program outside the existing party organization. He was too independent to follow Stassen's orders. They would also defend Youngdahl by pointing out that the weak party system and the non-partisan legislature made it necessary for him to appeal directly to the people. He defended his strategy by referring to this latter situation: "As far as party government in Minnesota is concerned, I was very much discouraged with our non-partisan election of legislators, because it did not give us party responsibility to carry out programs. Therefore, if the Governor wanted certain laws passed he had to go over the legislature to the people, which I did." (Letter, Washington, D. C., June 2, 1953.)

After a comfortable victory in the primaries, Youngdahl went on to win the November election by a plurality of 235,163, which was the largest of his career. He polled 635,800 votes; his opponent, Harry H. Peterson, received 400,637. Youngdahl carried all but Itasca, Dakota and Ramsey counties. Such a sweeping majority had not been recorded since 1928, when Governor Christianson had carried 84 counties.

The Inaugural Address of 1951

Youngdahl's third inaugural address, delivered to the Legislature on January 3, developed his campaign theme of "honesty and humanity in government." He defined those terms as follows:

"When we speak of 'humanity' in government, we think of it in its broadest sense as including every program by which we meet human needs and, by meeting them, undergird our human resources.

"Similarly, 'honesty' in government encompasses not only integrity in financial matters, but also a fair and equitable approach to every practical problem relating to our economic resources."

The first section of the speech dealt with the family, with clarifying his determination to give high priority to proposals for the strengthening of this institution. His recognition of the importance of the home is reflected in his statement:

"It is impossible to exaggerate the calamities that befall a society in which the home disintegrates. The cost in terms of heartbreak and human wretchedness cannot be described. The economic loss defies calculation. Repercussions are felt in added relief loads, increased aids to dependent children and additional costs of law enforcement, including the maintenance of penal institutions. Complications are felt in recreational programs, housing facilities, mental health work, in every area of social welfare. Every other social institution, including our churches and schools, is endangered."

He directed attention to the work of the Interim Committee on Family Life and urged careful consideration of its recommendations. Specifically he requested legislation requiring a period of conciliation before a divorce action may be commenced and the creation of "family courts" establishing procedures which would provide specialized treatment for families endangered by marital strife.

His recommendations concerning other established features of his program followed much the same pattern as in previous addresses. Proposals receiving the most publicity were: the school for mentally-deficient children, commission on alcoholism, minimum teachers' salaries, forestry camp for youth conservation program, F.E.P.C., a commission on the aging, raising of property lien limit from $6,000 to $7,000 and county convalescent homes.

In the section of the address dealing with "honesty in government," proposals most emphatically stressed were cautious consideration of the recommendations of the Efficiency in Government Commission, the bill providing for the calling of a constitutional convention, registration of lobbyists bill, party designation, re-apportionment, increase of income tax exemptions to aid especially those with fixed salaries and wages, and salary increases for state employees.

The budget proposals submitted by the Governor to the Legislature, while more conservative than in previous years, involved appropriations exceeding available revenue. To meet the costs of his program, Youngdahl proposed — in addition to using the surplus in the General Revenue Fund — to raise the taxes on beer and iron ore. He opposed the use of the $53,000,000 surplus in the dedicated Income Tax School Fund for any other than local school aid programs.

Youngdahl's Relations with the 1951 Legislature

From the beginning it was obvious that the Legislature intended to display its independence of the Governor's dominance. In the past he had formed his own legislative bloc of conservatives and liberals who supported his program and had been opposed by the right wing conservatives who controlled most of the legislative machinery. In 1951 it was more difficult than ever to push his program through the legislative mill. Liberals were not enthusiastic about his suggestion to raise the tax on beer (because it was a sales tax that hit the low income bracket of people). Conservatives were more economy-minded than ever. A cool reception met the Governor's proposals to create family courts, and there was little eagerness to pass a power-of-arrest bill, F.E.P.C. legislation, or a statute providing for a convention on constitutional revision. Youngdahl's tax proposals were all but completely ignored.

Midway in the session, he reversed his earlier non-interference policy and began a fighting drive for the passage of his program, employing tactics developed in previous sessions. After a strenuous week spent in trying to woo the support of legislators in private conferences, he took to the radio on February 24 to rally public support. He urged the people to put pressure on their legislators to pass the power-of-arrest and F.E.P.C. bills. In March he called upon them to lobby for the passage of the family court bill and towards the end of the session made a moving appeal for support of the bill providing for a hospital for the mentally deficient children.

Despite his efforts and the fact of his great popularity (considering the big majority he received in November) the Legislature was not moved to pass many of his pet proposals. Defeated were the power-of-arrest bill, F.E.P.C., the family court bill, constitutional revision, adoption of party designation and registration of lobbyists and re-apportionment legislation. Appropriations for the mental health program were smaller than he had requested. The executive budget was ignored by the House. No major tax-raising bills came out of the House Tax Committee. Disagreement between the House and the Senate on the proposed salary increase for state employees delayed all appropriation bills until the final hours, resulting in a much smaller increase than Youngdahl had recommended. The controversy over the budget again brought into sharp focus the crucial role played by legislative committees, especially the House Appropriations Committee, in which fiscal measures originate. Because appropriations bills were retarded until the last hours of the session, the remainder of the lawmakers were compelled to act within minutes on measures deserving careful debate and study.

There were victories, too, for Youngdahl, such as the expanded program of the Youth Conservation Commission, including the approval of a forestry camp and appropriations for it; increased aid for schools, assistance for dependent children and the aged; authorization of county convalescent homes; liberalization of workmen's compensation laws; a salary increase for state employees, although less than he had requested; an expanded conservation program; creation of a Civil Defense department; establishment of interim commissions on alcoholism, the aging, tuberculosis, mental health and youth conservation; and the passage of measures designed to strengthen the divorce laws.

While these accomplishments of the Legislature indicate that Youngdahl's program had not been entirely ignored, the conviction that Youngdahl had been hampered by a recalcitrant Legislature was quite general. There was talk of a rift between Youngdahl and the conservative Republicans. Senator Gerald T. Mullin did not agree with newspaper interpretations of the situation. He wrote, "In spite of press comments to the contrary, Governor Youngdahl enjoyed good relations with a majority of both houses of the Legislature. It is true that on various issues raised by the Youngdahl program, so-called, there was a shifting of support and in some instances vigorous attacks were made on certain portions of his program." (Letter to author, Sept. 11, 1953.) During the week that followed the adjourning of the session, a public clash between Youngdahl and House majority leader, Roy E. Dunn, served to increase the impression that such a rift had developed and that it was the cause of Youngdahl having been check-mated. On April 28 the Governor made two speeches, one before the state convention of the Young Republican League and the other over the radio, in which he charged the Legislature with being controlled by special interest groups. He was quoted as saying:

"Special interest pressure groups, in many cases, decided these issues in smoky hotel rooms — not the Legislature. When the history of the session is finally and completely written, the people will conclude that many of those both within and without the Legislature, who helped shape the course of events, placed greater emphasis on dollars than on lives, on material things than on things of the spirit." (**Minneapolis Sunday Tribune,** April 29, 1951.)

On the following Saturday, Roy Dunn attacked these charges as political trickery and defended the Legislature's stand on taxes and the budget. "The biggest and most pernicious lobby in St. Paul during the session was the government itself and its agencies," said Dunn. "Every time a new appeal was made for public support, more state employees and more people who live off the fat of the government showed up around the Legislature. The members of the Legislature weighed with care every bill that came before it. If they thought it was worthy, it became law. If they thought it wasn't worthy, the bill lost."

Defending the fiscal decisions of the Legislature, Dunn said, "The Legislature provided adequately for every state need and every state activity. The remedy for unnecessarily high taxes is to refrain from unnecessarily high spending. We stood steadfastly against every pressure to levy new taxes, preferring not to fool you, the people, that you can spend and spend and spend and not tax and tax and tax. The Legislature is being criticized by some people, not because they spent too much money but because they did not spend enough money. If those critics want to be known throughout the state as the champion spenders of all time, they are welcome to that reputation." (**Minneapolis Sunday Tribune,** May 6, 1951.)

Press commentators saw in this exchange an open confession of a rift between the liberal and conservative factions of the G.O.P. It was not a new development but an old sore spot that had originated with Stassen's victory over the Old Guard in 1938. The 1951 legislative session made this rift more apparent.

In the early weeks of the session, observers were confident that Youngdahl would succeed in mobilizing public opinion in support of his program to offset the resistance of the Legislature. But this popular support never materialized, at least not in the enthusiastic proportions it attained in previous sessions. Youngdahl claimed that the people's lobby deserved credit for pressuring the legislators into providing for a hospital for mentally-deficient children, but no popular excitement developed for any other legislation.

What was the explanation for this "stalemate"? An editorial in The Minneapolis Star, commenting on the deadlock at the capitol, criticized Youngdahl because he did not take the legislative leaders into his confidence and had a tendency to call them in and tell them what he wanted and to announce his course of action without arriving at the decision jointly with them. (Minneapolis Star, Mar. 13, 1951.) One observer believed that Youngdahl did not understand the legislative process, because he weighed political issues with a judicial mind—he was accustomed to operating as a judge who has the supreme authority to make the final decision on a case. He was criticized for tending to be arbitrary and tactless in handling people with whom he worked. His colleagues had to be "all for him," without qualification, or he suspected them of being opponents and treated them accordingly. He was impatient when opposed and lacked the diplomacy necessary to winning his opponents to his side or maneuvering them into a position where they were obliged to support him.

Special Interest Lobbies

Youngdahl had his own explanation. He publicly stated, a few times during the session and later, that the special interest lobbies were actually in control of the session. He went so far as to single out the utilities, steel, liquor, beer and railroad lobbies. (**Minneapolis Tribune**, March 25, 1951.) In a speech at St. Peter in May, 1951, he singled out one of the legislators from Nicollet County, labelling him "an errand boy of the canning companies," and deploring the fact that some legislators had their "minds made up" before they arrived at the capitol for the session. He urged passage of a bill requiring the registration of lobbyists, because he believed it would bring their activities out into the open so that people could see what is being done to shape the course of legislation. (**Minneapolis Tribune,** May 10, 1951.)

Youngdahl was confronted by a difficult political situation in Minnesota. Many Minnesota legislators are also the employees of corporations and other economic organizations. They are elected to represent the people. They are also hired, usually as lawyers, to represent their clients, and this often means keeping an eye out for their clients' interests during law making sessions. This is possible, because Minnesota laws are much more lenient than Federal laws governing the conduct of legislators. Moreover, it is necessary; because no legislator could live on the salary paid him by the state. This situation makes the legislators more susceptible to pressure than they would be if they did not act in their dual capacity. The consequence is a Legislature which is not as free to arrive at policy benefitting the general welfare as it was designed to be. The comment is often heard that it is a credit to the legislators that there is not more double-dealing than there is, but this observation should blind no one to the fact that the circumstances tend to produce conniving.

There was evidence to justify Youngdahl's attacks on the lobbies. Some of them seemed to care for nothing but unrestricted freedom to make profits. One of them told a member of the League of Women Voters, Mrs. H. Rosser Matson, that he believed every legislator "had his price." Lobbyists like him resorted to the usual methods of bestowing little favors—free liquor, fishing trips, vacations, invitations to dinner—until a legislator was "indebted" to his benefactor and inclined to be prejudiced in his favor. They made effective use of the ample sums of money available to them.

In the opinion of the leaders of the Minnesota C.I.O., the steel trust re-emerged as a powerful lobby and completely controlled the decisions of the Legislature on fiscal matters; other lobbies mentioned in the C.I.O. report on the 1951 legislative session were the railroads, Northwest Airlines, liquor, Minnesota Employers' Association, the Bankers' Association, and the Minnesota Taxpayers' Association, all of whom lobbied against increased appropriations for welfare measures. (Minn. State C.I.O. Council, Report on the 1951 Session of the Minnesota Legislature, special issue of **Minnesota Labor**, Sept. 7, 1951.)

Accounts of committee sessions in diaries, prepared by the legislative representative of the League of Women Voters, give ample evidence of the activities of the lobbyists. (See the League's "1951 Legislative Report," available at the Minneapolis headquarters.)

The Minnesota Employers' Association's capable lobbyist, Otto Christianson, was able to report to members of the group that a great degree of success had been obtained in blocking legislation not favored by the Association's Board of Directors. This group, representing 1,200 companies, seeks to promote legislation "favorable to business and industry and its **right to profits**" (bold face words supplied) according to Christianson. (Interview, St. Paul, June 18, 1953.) A brochure describing this organization states: "Business men know from painful experience that improper legislation can break industry. They know that highly-organized, well-financed minority groups want legislation that will be costly and burdensome to industry. They know that in order to fight these groups, management must provide an effective spokesman to answer the numerous legislative agents hired by anti-business forces. The Association has established itself as that spokesman in the eyes of the Legislature and of Minnesota business and industry." ("You and the M. E. A., What It Is, What It Costs, What It Does," available at the St. Paul office of the Association.) During the 1951 session the Association's lobbyists opposed legislation favorable to labor, that called for increased services to the people, party designation, F.E.P.C., reapportionment and constitutional reform.

Labor unions, too, are rapidly coming of age in the practice of lobbying. Both the C.I.O. and the A. F. of L. have developed lobbying programs in Minnesota.

Orlin Folwick reported that, as a result of the Federation's political action, twelve senators and about 35 representatives opposed by the A. F. of L. had been defeated. Their records were exposed to the unions' members, and concerted efforts to get out the vote were made. The Federation uses the usual lobbying methods, such as testifying to committees; and it also did a limited amount of entertaining at luncheons where labor leaders could present their proposals to several legislators at once. (Interview, St. Paul, June 17, 1953.)

In addition, the C.I.O. lobbied and prepared complete reports on the session, including the voting record of legislators on crucial motions and important bills. The C.I.O. reports disclosed an interest in legislation affecting the general welfare, as well as that affecting the unions specifically. Defending this broad interest, the 1947 report stated: "We . . . believe that we have a responsibility to the schools, the hospitals, the city governments, the state government and all other institutions and groups in which our members have a share of the rights and duties of governing ourselves in a democracy. That responsibility is as much our task as is the job of managing our unions. Therefore, we will participate, cooperatively, with all groups in the solution of the problems before us. The objective will always be the protection and furtherance of individual rights in a constantly improving community." (Minnesota C.I.O. Report on 1949 Legislature, p. 1.)

While this is by no means a thorough report on all the lobbying being promoted, it supports Youngdahl's contention that the Minnesota Legislature is under constant pressure from special interest groups, some of which work for narrowly selfish ends and others for more comprehensive social and political reforms.

It was obvious that the interest groups were able effectively to limit Youngdahl's program in the 1951 Legislature, once more demonstrating the fact that there is no effective way to hold non-partisan legislators responsible to their constituents. They are free to choose whom they shall represent. The Minneapolis Star, commenting on the 1951 session, concluded that it is possible for legislators to work both sides of the political street and to run the show their own way, since they have no responsibility towards a party or its platform. "We witness a situation in which the people elected Governor Youngdahl to office on a progressive, humanitarian program, and at the same time they elect a conservative Legislature which thwarted his program." The editorial advised a return to partisan elections so the Governor would have the support of a majority in the Legislature, thus enabling the people to fasten responsibility on the party in power if it failed to carry out the program as promised in the campaign. (Minneapolis Star, March 13, 1951.)

Youngdahl and Structural Reforms

Youngdahl was aware that structural reforms were needed in Minnesota government to promote more efficiency and truly representative democratic processes; his platforms and public speeches contained recommendations along that line. During his first term he had appointed a Constitutional Commission, as approved by the 1947 Legislature. Minnesota's original constitution was written in 1857 and has been amended 75 times. Some of its provisions are obsolete, some are at variance with the Federal Constitution, and still others are more properly the subject of legislative action. The Commission had reported to the Governor late in 1948, recommending such changes as: granting the Legislature power to call itself into session and prolong the 90-day limitation on length of sessions; extending the terms of office for Governor and Lieutenant-Governor to four years; a short ballot for state offices; stronger taxation powers for the Legislature; and changes in the rates and methods of taxing railroads. (League of Women Voters, You Are the Government: A Handbook for Minnesota Citizens, St. Paul, Minn., 1949, 86-89.) The Legislature had failed, in 1947, to pass even a bill which would have enabled the citizens to vote on whether or not a constitutional convention should be held. The bill had been placed on General Orders of the Senate, but the pressure of the railroad lobby had kept it from being acted upon.

The 1947 Legislature had done no better with re-apportionment legislation. One bill, H. F. 827, had passed the House and expired on General Orders in the Senate after 28 senators voted against it. It would have added 10 additional state representatives from urban counties but no extra senators. The Constitution of Minnesota requires the Legislature to re-apportion the entire state every ten years, but the provision has been ignored since 1913. The purpose of re-apportionment is to insure an equal representation for every 1,000 citizens in the state. At every session, the conflict between the city people seeking fair representation and the rural people seeking to preserve the status quo has been won by the predominantly rural Legislature. Failure to re-apport the Legislature has resulted in a situation now in which 50% of the legislators are elected by 35% of the population. Minneapolis has only 68% of its rightful representation in the House. St. Paul has 77% of its rightful representation in the House. (The Minneapolis Star, Dec. 30, 1953. The information was taken from an editorial on a report of the League of Women Voters, "Re-apportionment in Minnesota: Democracy Denied.")

The 1947 Legislature had created the Efficiency in Government Commission of nineteen citizens, which was assigned to study the organizational problems in state government and report to the next session of the Legislature. The report of "the Little Hoover Commission" was submitted to the Governor and legislators late in 1950. Youngdahl was criticized for not conducting a more vigorous campaign on behalf of its recommendations. His inaugural address contained a section on efficiency and economy in government but no recommendation for action on the report. The Governor had appointed only one member, the chairman, Bradshaw Mintener, to the Commission and had had little to do with its creation. One organization believed that his indifference proved fatal to the recommendations, because most of them affected the executive branch; and the history of outstanding state reorganizations in this country shows that they succeeded only when the proposals were militantly sponsored by the Governor. (The Minnesota Institute of Governmental Research, "Reorganizing the State Government of Minnesota," Bulletin No. 29, July, 1952, p. 5.)

The report found that, despite two previous reorganizations, Minnesota still retained a sprawling organization consisting of 35 major departments and 70 boards, commissions and offices. It called for organizational changes that would place all major departments under heads appointed by the Governor, thus increasing the Governor's accountability for the manner in which the state is governed; it called attention to over 200 changes in organizational procedure and methods that would result in saving over $4,000,000 as well as increasing efficiency; it recommended the short ballot, a department of legislative services, a four-year term for the Governor and all department heads, discontinuance of dedicated funds and a single appropriations bill to be prepared by the Governor and sent to the Legislature along with his budget, and many other changes. (Minnesota Efficiency in Government Commission, **How to Achieve Greater Efficiency and Economy in Minnesota's Government,** St. Paul, Minn., 1950.)

The People's Lobby

It is apparent that Youngdahl did not stress structural reforms as the means to remove the political and legislative roadblocks that stood in the way of rational and representative government. For this he was criticized by political scientists and the Minnesota Institute of Governmental Research.

Youngdahl resorted to direct appeals to the people, thus depending upon his personal popularity to arouse the rank and file citizen to a new level of political activity. He frequently advocated "a people's lobby," consisting of interested citizens coming and going constantly and expressing their opinions on impending proposals directly to the legislators, as a force offsetting the pressure of special interest groups. The role of his citizens' committees has already been mentioned; so apparently he recognized that organized activities were necessary and that individual, unco-ordinated actions were insufficient. Youngdahl's farewell address contained some important comments which revealed that his method of bringing the citizens into an active part in government was based on a conscious political philosophy and an awareness of political realities. Since his words are a vitally comprehensive expression of his views on government, the sections in which he explains his position are quoted as follows:

"I have always felt that the governorship was a partnership with the people — a partnership that obligated me to go down the line for our Minnesota programs without sacrifice of principle, or compromise with special interests. I know that many of our fine programs would have been scuttled by certain self-interest groups were it not for your help. . . .

"There is something in the Minnesota character that rises above all party lines to back programs that involve human values. No law compels people to give of their time and energy in the interest of human conservation and honesty in government the way you have. Your wonderful support has come because of a sincere desire to meet the 'unenforceable obligations' of citizenship, those things that are done not because of the compulsion of law, but because of an inner wish to do more than is asked in the service of fellow men. This is one more example of the spirit that makes democracy strong and vibrant and living. It is the source of power that dictators with their slave states can never understand or know. It is the spirit that will sustain democracy through every dark hour and crisis and insure the ultimate triumph of the cause of human freedom. . . .

"Government has grown more complex with the years. Neither the administration of the affairs of the people nor the writing of laws is the easy task it once was. It has been necessary to delegate authority. The result is that government has drifted farther and farther away from the people to a point that would bewilder our forefathers.

"As government becomes more complex there are more areas of cooperation carried on without public understanding and awareness at every level of government. And as we get tied up in more and more details of government based on a state constitution long in need of revision, it is difficult for administrators and legislators to keep close either to the public pulse or the activities of the very departments for which they are responsible.

"To get government closer to the people, each time a major new program arose, I appointed advisory and action committees composed of both plain citizens and professional experts in the field. I believe that the utilization of such citizen committees is essential in the operation of modern democratic government. They provide the necessary vehicle for public expression and education relating to the problems with which government must deal.

"Unfortunately for the general welfare, the growing complexity of legislative and administrative activity makes governmental policies more susceptible to manipulation by special interests. These operate quietly behind the scenes. Their motivation is advancement of themselves at the expense of the public. Here is what gives this such frightful significance: government today has the responsibility for activities such as the education of our children, rehabilitation of the handicapped, care of the mentally ill, assistance to the aged, the poor and the helpless, the dependent and neglected child and the youth of our state. It is legitimate, it is proper, it is necessary, that groups in our society organize themselves to state their case, to protect themselves, to make sure they are treated fairly by government. But it is not fair or proper if they strive to win benefits from government at the expense of decent care for the handicapped, the sick, the poor, the blind, and the education and rehabilitation of youth. . . .

"People who wouldn't steal a dime out of a blind man's cup, who wouldn't take food from a child, who wouldn't hurt a sick person, often do so in effect when their interests clash with those of the people. They often strive to undercut these worthy programs of help to the unfortunate. . . . Under the guise of advocacy of efficiency and economy they press their case for the special interests. . . . Without a feeling for the human responsibility of government, efficiency and economy frequently become only catchwords used by representatives of special interests to block programs needed for the welfare of the people.

"That is why the people must be alert and vigilant to make sure that governmental policies are maintained for the best interests of all the people. In sharp contrast to the selfish lobbies . . . there is another lobby — one in which I have put my trust every time. It is the people's lobby. It doesn't operate behind closed doors. There are no membership dues, no formal organization. It is open to every citizen who realizes that the price of our liberty is eternal vigilance on his part. When enough people are ready to join the people's lobby, progress comes for good humanitarian government." (**Minneapolis Star,** Sept. 26, 1951.)

Social Action Program of the Minnesota Council of Churches

The most highly organized instance of political effort by church groups during Youngdahl's administration was the social action program of the Minnesota Council of Churches. Its operations are not the only instances of organized church activity, but the Council's program is representative and characteristic of the Protestant churches within its membership.

The Council serves as the Protestant agency for state-wide cooperative functions of various kinds and is supported by seven major denominations, a number of local councils and congregations, and individuals. In order of the size of their contributions, the church bodies financing its support are: Methodist, Congregationalist, Episcopalian, Presbyterian, Evangelical and Reformed, Evangelical United Brethren, and the Disciples of Christ. No Lutheran bodies have membership in the Council, although five out of every eight Protestants in Minnesota are Lutherans. (Note: In 1951, statistics showed that Lutherans numbered 542,821; all other Protestants combined totalled 341,864. See "Minnesota Points the Way," **The Christian Century,** LXIX, No. 21, May 21, 1952, 612 ff. The article explains the Lutheran non-participation in terms of its traditional isolation from other Protestants, based on doctrinal grounds. There is another possible explanation. Since the Lutherans are the dominant Protestant group in the state, they feel no urgent necessity for strengthening their position by affiliation. They are more in a position to give than to gain. This explanation is borne out by the fact that Lutheran groups in New England, where they are in a minority, are members of state councils and that several of the national Lutheran bodies belong to the National Council of Churches.)

Among its several activities, the Council has in recent years developed a social action program involving legislative activities. The Council's political action program began in 1947. The anti-slot machine campaign had aroused Protestants to an unprecedented level of political concern. The spontaneous nature of the churches' activities in that situation assumed definite shape when the Council created a social action committee to organize support for the bill.

In 1950 the Council's migrant worker committee arranged a study of conditions among Minnesota's seasonal migrant workers, who enter the state seeking employment in the fields —growing and harvesting sugar beets and potatoes in the Red River Valley, and peas, beans, onions, corn and carrots in the Minnesota River Valley. The results of the study, which was made by Dr. and Mrs. David E. Henley, were shown to legislative leaders and the Governor, and a code for migrant labor camps was proposed. When growers and canners exerted pressure on lawmakers, expressing opposition to the legislation, the Council's social action and migrant workers' committees went into action. Conversations were held with key legislative leaders and state department heads, and regular progress reports on the bill were mailed to pastors and ministerial associations. When the bill was passed, the Council's efforts were generally given a large share of the credit for the victory.

Political action on behalf of the migrant labor camp code set the precedent for the establishment of a legislative information service during that session. A Macalester College student, William Gerberding, was employed on a part-time basis to follow the trail of and report on legislation "of interest to the Christian conscience." Gerberding read bills, interviewed members of the Legislature and attended committee hearings; but he did not act as a spokesman to the legislators or anyone else, inasmuch as the views of the Council were concerned. His assignment was not to persuade legislators, but rather to keep churchmen informed on developments. He sent out regular reports on the progress of legislation, and arguments for and against current bills, to approximately 4,000 leaders throughout the state. When a crucial point was about to be reached in the progress of a bill of special interest to the churchmen, he immediately issued a bulletin to key persons, and sometimes even dispatched telegrams urging prompt action. A study of the six reports he sent out is indicative of the issues that he and Council leaders believed to be legislation of interest to the "Christian conscience." Law enforcement, liquor control, F.E.P.C., youth conservation commission forestry camp, family court, mental health and the migrant workers' code, received the most attention. The reports also contained a few references to constitutional revision and other structural reform matters, and welfare legislation; but there were no notes on labor legislation or tax bills.

John M. Wilson of the Council made it clear that the legislative secretary was no lobbyist in the popular sense of the word. His function was to keep the churches informed, but not to pressure the legislators, Mr. Wilson explained. The Council meticulously avoids any type of demonstration that might make it suspect of indulging in pressure politics. It fears that church people would be unduly alarmed at the prospect of an excursion into politics and would be apprehensive about supporting such a program by the Council. (He and Mr. H. L. Stright explained this in interviews on August 29, 1951.)

Resignation and Acceptance of Federal Judgeship

The end of Youngdahl's gubernatorial career came with surprising suddenness in July, 1951, when the papers announced his appointment to the position of United States District Judge in Washington, D. C., by President Truman. Youngdahl indicated his intention of resigning as soon as the United States Senate confirmed his appointment. The announcement came after President Truman had a half-hour conference with Youngdahl and Senator Hubert H. Humphrey.

In a formal statement explaining his decision Youngdahl said that the emotional and physical strain of being governor was so great that he would find it impossible to run for a fourth term; he also mentioned "the challenging opportunity to perform service in a great federal judicial system" — since the judicial field was his first love he was glad to have an opportunity to get back into it. (**Minneapolis Tribune**, July 6, 1951.)

There were behind-the-scenes political developments that put Youngdahl into a difficult situation, and the appointment gave him a graceful way out. It developed as a matter of common, though little-publicized knowledge, that Stassen had asked Youngdahl only a few days before to head up the Stassen-for-President movement in the state in preparation for the Republican presidential primary election the following March. Youngdahl wanted no part of the Stassen movement, but his refusal to help the man who had given him his opportunity in politics would have looked like political treachery. Another development further complicated the Governor's situation. A Youngdahl-for-President movement was rapidly taking shape among his own supporters, and a split in the liberal ranks of the G.O.P. was thus threatening to develop. (Verne Johnson, Interview, Minneapolis, June 18, 1953.)

Some also believed that the failure of the conservative Republican leadership to support his program was also a factor that helped him decide to resign. ("Youngdahl Move Jolts Minnesota," a news item written by W. Torkelson in **The Christian Century**, LXVIII, No. 34, Aug. 22, 1951.)

His decision jolted the people of Minnesota. Some were deeply disappointed that Youngdahl should pull out in the middle of his unfinished fight for good government. Others accepted the decision in good grace, feeling that the Governor (for reasons given above) had no other practical alternative.

An evaluation of his career appeared in **The Minneapolis Star** shortly after the announcement of his appointment. It is in many ways an adequate picture of the impact he left on Minnesota citizens:

"Governor Youngdahl has reshuffled the political deck and left the game. He may be the first winner the rest of the boys are happy to see pick up and leave.

"It is safe to wager that there isn't a Minnesotan unaware of the fact that the popular Youngdahl won solid support for his anti-gambling campaign shortly after his first election in 1946.

"Since his first election as Minnesota's chief executive, Youngdahl has been a controversial figure in state politics. Damned for his liberalism by some elements of his own Republican Party, he swept criticism aside and with support from all shades of voters won three terms as governor. And there seemed little doubt that a fourth term was his — until his dramatic announcement Thursday.

"His political career has been one of unbounded success, so unbounded that those Republicans who disliked him accepted him because he was unbeatable. And those D.F.L. opponents who tried to beat him on election day often showed up on the side of his program when the votes were tallied in the legislature.

"Whatever he did and wherever he went his popularity grew. He doesn't drink, smoke or approve of strong language. He is as much at home in church as on the political rostrum, and his strong religious convictions have been an unbeatable asset among church-going Minnesotans.

"His earnest convictions sometimes irked his political foes who found — when they tangled with Youngdahl — that the voters looked upon their efforts as reflections not against Youngdahl but against religious convictions. Dur-

ing the 1950 campaign one of the newspaper editors opposed to Youngdahl suggested that he had heard too much
of Youngdahl's slogan, Honesty in Government. 'He
should take up Cedric Adams' slogan of honest-to-goodness
goodness,' the editor chided. But nobody could accuse the
Governor of insincerity. He pounded home his record and
his program, and the voters expressed their approval.

"With Youngdahl out of the picture, one observer has
suggested, Republicans can go back to being Republicans
and Democrats to voting for Democrats." (Minneapolis Star,
July 6, 1951.)

The regard with which the people of Minnesota held their
governor was reflected in the results of a Minnesota Poll.
Youngdahl was rated as the best governor in the past twenty
years, getting 45% of the first place votes. (Minneapolis Sunday
Tribune, Sept. 9, 1951.)

CHAPTER TEN

Federal Judge and
The Lattimore Case

"Luther Youngdahl, practicing constitutionalist and Christian, fierce defender of the rights of heretics, sat firm upon the bench and fought off a berserk attack upon the integrity of our judicial system."

A well-known Washington commentator, writing these words in the **New Republic** (July 11, 1955, p. 6), was referring to Judge Luther Youngdahl's recent decisions in the case of the United States against Owen Lattimore. This case drew Youngdahl into the thick of one of the bitterest controversies in American history — a post-war extremity commonly called "McCarthyism." As a consequence, his new position in the federal judiciary was far from being a quiet post removed from the stresses and strains of American politics.

Owen Lattimore, the Johns Hopkins University professor and expert on the Far East, had been labelled by Senator Joseph R. McCarthy of Wisconsin as "the top Soviet espionage agent in the United States." Although this charge was never substantiated, Lattimore was accused by the Government of perjury, allegedly committed before the McCarran Senate subcommittee in 1952 during his attempts to defend himself against the charge that he was "pro-Communist." This case found its way to the docket of Youngdahl's district court early in 1953. The judge's decisions on the case attracted national attention. In order to understand their real significance, they must be seen within the context of Lattimore's "ordeal" and the atmosphere of post-war politics.

The Post-War Political Mood

Many Americans want their politics simple. They want one, clear-cut, monstrous evil to be exposed as the cause of their ills — an evil clearly defined and sharply contrasted with the good they believe in. They want to be able to choose between two camps, divided on the basis of simple and dramatic issues. They want their victories to be clean-cut and decisive. At times in American political history this simplification has been used to advantage, but its results are usually temporary and superficial. Simplification has usually operated effectively in war-time politics. In 1917 German imperialism was the one, colossal evil, and the Kaiser was the devil to blame; on the other side was Uncle Sam, who would save Democracy for the world. In 1941-45 Hitler, Tojo and Mussolini were the unholy triumvirate, and fascism and totalitarianism were the evils to be exorcized. During the decade following the end of the second world war, Communism was the evil to blame; and the fear of it almost, but not quite, swept away rational deliberation involving readjustment, and the consideration of programs necessary to cope with the complexities of post-war politics.

The course of post-war events was frustrating and even frightening for Americans who wanted their politics simple. The defeat of the Axis powers did not result in a clean-cut, decisive victory that would allow Americans to feel free to go about their own business. Acting quickly to extend their influence, the Communists dropped the Iron Curtain over the Eastern European countries and began to exert heavy pressure along the border countries between the East and the West. By the time the United States had taken a firm stand in Europe, China had slipped into the Red orbit as the Chinese Communists drove the Nationalist Government from the mainland.

Thrust into a position of dominant power by its involvement in the war, the United States was forced to challenge the Communists' ambitions to extend their influence. There were hard choices to face and limitative decisions to be resolved by the government, making it difficult for Americans to picture Uncle Sam in his usual role of spotless champion of democracy. The Government found itself in compromising positions where it chose to support fascist-like reactionaries, rather than permit a small, vulnerable country to fall to the Communist revolutionaries. Democratic reformers were deserted in situations where there existed a "vacuum of power," which had to be filled by the strongest men available, men like Bao Dai and Sigmund Rhee. Foreign policy was based upon the assumption that Communism was the great evil that must be checked. If, in doing so, an injustice is done here — poverty left untouched there — and the forces of reaction supported somewhere else, it must be understood that this was a portion of the price that must be paid to arrest the advance of Communism and to make possible later and more stable reforms. Americans found their nation involved deeply in the bargaining, compromising and even plotting, that prevailed in world politics. They were confronted by problems so complicated and immense that they began to feel singularly insecure. Involvement in the world situation was going to be costly, even dangerous — as the Korean war was to prove. Somehow the American people had to be inspired to believe that it was necessary.

Whether or not it was deliberately fostered by the people in positions of power, fear of Communism became the motive force that spurred the United States into decisive action. Consideration of a means to halt Communism became the overshadowing issue in post-war politics. Americans again had one, bad enemy and a single issue by which to assize men and events. There were accusations against the Democratic administration for bungling Far Eastern policy. Truman and Acheson, his secretary of state, were roundly criticized for allowing China to become Communistic. There was loud, frightening talk of Communist infiltration into vital areas of American life. When the Alger Hiss case broke, the fear that Communism was an internal danger became stronger than ever. Hiss was a high-ranking official in the state department, trusted and respected by the Democratic administration. An ex-Communist, Whittaker Chambers, exposed his connections with the Communist underground. Hiss denied Chambers' allegations and, in the course of doing so, made statements that resulted in his conviction on perjury charges. When Truman dubbed the investigation of the Hiss case a "Red herring" and Acheson affirmed his personal loyalty to Hiss after his conviction, the stage was set for a full-scale hunt for Reds in the state department.

At this point the junior Senator from Wisconsin, Joseph R. McCarthy, stepped into the picture. More decisively than any other individual, he related and developed the conversion of Communism as a threat on the international scene to a threat also within the United States by focussing national attention on "the Reds-in-government" issue. He knew how to exploit the advantages of simplification; and he played movingly on the heart-strings of the American people, which were a-tingle with confusion and uncertainty and fear. McCarthy's approach was simple. He posed the question, is Communism a danger within the United States? Those who disagreed with him found themselves running desperately to find the facts to dispute the charges that he circulated to keep his issue alive. Those who agreed with him found it difficult to dispute the next step in his logic — ruthless methods must be used against so ominous an enemy. A tough ex-Marine, skilled in rough methods, was the man to fight the battle — not mild, reasonable, scholarly men.

McCarthy's method involved making charges that were sensational enough to merit headlines. While a great majority of the accused eventually were able to deflate the charges with facts, a lingering suspicion about their loyalty was left behind. In the meantime, the Senator was off in another direction making new charges. The unsubstantial nature of McCarthy's attacks made it very difficult to fight them off. His charges were like big, red bubbles filled with an odorous gas. Eventually they burst when they were touched by hard, real facts, but they left a lingering odor behind. No sooner were the bubbles deflated than the bubble blower was inflating new ones and releasing them in another direction.

McCarthy opened his attack on the State Department with a bright red bubble. On February 9, 1950, in a speech at Wheeling, W. Va., he said:

"While I cannot take the time to name all of the men in the State Department who have been named as members of the Communist party and of a spy ring, I have here in my hand a list of 205 that were known to the Secretary of State as being members of the Communist party and who nevertheless are still working and shaping the policy of the State Department."

(Alfred Friendly, "The Noble Crusade of Senator McCarthy," **Harpers**, August, 1950, p. 34. These were McCarthy's exact words, as quoted in the Wheeling Intelligencer, released to the largest radio station in that city, and substantiated by affidavits of two of the station's officials who monitored his delivery of the speech.)

The State Department immediately asked for the list so that an investigation could begin; but McCarthy, his aim of getting attention achieved, immediately modified his original figure. There were fifty-seven "card-bearing Communists," he said; later he again changed the figure to eighty-one. His charges shifted so fast that, by the time his sources were traced and evidence marshalled to refute them, a great deal of suspicion and confusion was created. People began to think, "Where there is smoke, there is fire." When he named specific persons, he was prudent about his charges, making them under the protection of Senatorial immunity or in such a manner as to create the suspicion without incriminating himself for libel. McCarthy succeeded in creating enough furor to bring about the formation of a Senate sub-committee, under Sen. Millard Tydings of Maryland, to investigate his charges.

The "Ordeal" of Owen Lattimore

McCarthy's attack on the State Department began to focus on Owen Lattimore. He first named him as one of the Communists in the State Department in an off-the-record remark to the press, after a speech in Denver in February. Later, at a meeting of the Tydings committee, he referred to him as a "pro-Communist" whom he regarded to be a very poor security risk, inasmuch as Lattimore had been working for the State Department and had access to its files. In a secret executive session of the committee early in March, he claimed to have the name of "the top Soviet espionage agent in the United States," stating that he was willing to stake his whole case on this man's guilt. (Newsweek, April 3, 1950: He said, "Look, let's go off the record for a moment. I'm willing to stake my whole case on this man. If I'm wrong about him, then I am discredited as a witness. All I ask is that you dig into the files. You'll be convinced.") The committee asked J. Edgar Hoover to prepare a summary of its files on Lattimore. These files had no evidence to support McCarthy's charge, but this did not deter him. On March 21, in another off-the-record remark at a press conference he named Lattimore as the Soviet agent. The news seeped out, and the professor was embroiled in a bitter battle to save his reputation.

Who was Owen Lattimore? At the time of McCarthy's attack on him, he was in Afghanistan on a mission for the United Nations. His permanent position was that of Director of Walter Hines Page School of International Relations at Johns Hopkins University in Baltimore. For years he had been a student of the Far East and respected as one of the few authorities on Mongolia and other remote Asian areas. He had written eleven books and hundreds of newspaper and magazine articles in his attempt to arouse interest in this area and to spread knowledge of it in the United States. From 1934 to 1941 he was the editor of a magazine, **Pacific Affairs,** a publication of the Institute of Pacific Relations. The Institute was organized with units in several countries, including Russia, and constituted an international forum for the exchange of ideas on problems confronting the regions bordering the Pacific. The American unit had a good reputation as a research institution and was a recognized source of independent studies of the problems of the Far East. Its chairman in 1950 was

Gerard Swope, Honorary President of International General Electric. Among its trustees were General George Marshall, W. R. Herod of International General Electric, and C. K. Gamble, a director of Standard Vacuum Oil Company. **Pacific Affairs,** as a matter of policy, printed articles from various countries and by authors of a variety of viewpoints — some leftist and some conservative, but most of them by moderate or scholarly men who had prepared factual studies for publication. Lattimore's former connection with this organization caused him a great deal of vexation, because it was suspected of being a Communist front organization.

Two of Lattimore's books were used by McCarthy as evidence of his pro-Communist sympathies. In 1945, he published a book called **Solution in Asia,** in which he made known his views as to what would constitute a sound Far Eastern policy for the United States, after the war. In it he maintained that Communism must be regarded as a more or less permanent factor to consider in Asian politics. Its influence in Asia must be regarded as competitive rather than subversive. American policy must not be limited to forbidding Asians to be attracted to Communism. It must be extended to offer a powerful counter-attraction. A policy of drift might easily result in giving national support to aggressive special interest groups that found profitable a prolongation of Asia's economic dependency upon and subordination to the Western powers. He urged a policy that would be favorable to the development of independent and local capital and industry, and which would give businessmen in the Orient an opportunity to build up their own private enterprises. He insisted that the United States government must face the fact that the Kuomintang was changing rapidly from a coalition party to a landlord party, and that consequently the Communists in China were attracting a wider, more diverse following. He predicted that some sort of compromise between the Communists and the Kuomintang might have to be devised because of these facts. The closest thing to pro-Communist views that McCarthy could find in the book were statements to the effect that Russia and her Communist system had gained status in Asia and that many Asians regarded Russia as "democratic." Lattimore also urged that all major world policy be discussed with the Russians and warned against giving the impression that the United States intended to help restore colonialism in Asia. The second book, **Situation in Asia,** published in 1949, was an elaboration of this thesis: the United States and other Western powers can no longer control the Asian situation. An independent bloc of nations had developed there. Our chief aim should be to keep those nations from falling completely under the dominance of Russia. Therefore, our policy should be to increase our power of attraction for the Asian nations.

Lattimore, a former political adviser to Chiang Kai-shek, had urged vigorous support of the Nationalist Government until late in 1946, when he finally became convinced that the Kuomintang could never regain control of China. In 1950 he frankly stated his views on China policy to the Tydings committee. He said he believed it would be catastrophic if China were completely absorbed by the Soviet Union, that it was futile to hope for a Nationalist Government's reconquest of China, and that American policy must, for the time being, encourage an independent nationalism in China (even if it is a Communist type) capable of standing up to the Soviet Union. In the long run the United States must do everything possible to stimulate conditions which would make possible the survival of a third force, a democratic group within China. In his mind, apparently, absorption of China by the Soviet Republics would be more disastrous from a political point of view than the fact that China is governed by Communists. His subordination of ideological to political considerations, in his recommendations, helped to create the suspicion that he was pro-Communist.

McCarthy claimed that Lattimore was an employee of the State Department and, more than that, its chief architect of Far Eastern policy. Lattimore's governmental appointments were the following: He was appointed by President Roosevelt as a member of the Pauley Reparations Mission to Japan, after the war, and served for about four months on the payroll of the State Department. He participated in a two-day panel discussion of problems relative to China, in October, 1949, along with General Marshall, Harold Stassen and John D. Rockefeller, Jr., and others. When requested by the Department, he submitted a memorandum on China policy after the conference. On June 5, 1946, he lectured on Japanese problems at the State Department. In July, 1941, he was appointed as political adviser to Chiang Kai-shek, at the suggestion of President Roosevelt. He served in this capacity for a year beyond his original appointment of six months at the request of the Generalissimo. From 1942 to 1945, he was Deputy Director of Pacific Operations and then Consultant for the Office of War Information. While in this position, his official duties included accompanying Henry Wallace on the mission to Siberia and China that resulted in a controversial report, with which Lattimore claimed not to have been involved.

In answer to McCarthy's contention that he was the chief architect of American policy on the Far East, Lattimore indicated in his testimony that the policy of the State Department and his recommendations had very little in common. He referred to the last chapter of his book, **Solution in Asia,** as a catalog of recommendations ignored by the Government and told the Tydings Committee, "What I cannot be accused of is advice that has influenced the policy of the United States in the Far East. I wish that I had in fact had more influence. If I had, I think that the Communists would not now control China." (**Ordeal by Slander,** Boston, 1950, p. 88.) Also challenging McCarthy's contention were statements from four Secretaries of State, placed on file by Senator Tydings. Cordell Hull, James F. Byrnes, Gen. George Marshall and Dean Acheson all denied knowing Lattimore or being aware of any influence he was purported to have had on their policies.

Lattimore's political views, at least as stated in the two above-mentioned books and in **Ordeal by Slander,** give the impression that he is a thoughtful man who drew his conclusions from years of direct contact with the peoples of the Orient and from a large fund of factual information about their situation. He was careful to leave a tentative note in his views, in the event that further information should turn up or the situation should change. The shift in his views between 1945 and 1950 reveals that he was ready to change his mind when a new situation developed. He was willing to face the fact that political situations are seldom simple and that the choices confronting the American people are not between two sharply contrasted alternatives but rather are options between a relative good and a relative evil. He was trying, in his own best judgment, to face the facts about Chinese Communism and formulate conclusions on those facts, even though his conclusions did not fit the prevailing mood of fear of Communism. His views were those of an intelligent scholar — and of him McCarthy remarked, "I might say that if we study him, we cannot help but see that here is a brilliant individual. **That is what makes him so dangerous." (Congressional Record,** Senate, March 30, 1950, p. 4385.)

McCarthy made that statement during a four-hour speech before the Senate on March 30, in which he dealt with his case against Lattimore in detail. He announced his intention of documenting two charges: that Lattimore is a Soviet agent and is or has been a member of the Communist party, and that he is the architect of American policy on the Far East. To support the first of his charges, McCarthy displayed affidavits from men who alleged that Lattimore had close connections with Communists and other subversives, was regarded by them as one of their allies, and, as one affidavit claimed, was actually a Communist. To support the second charge, McCarthy alluded to Lattimore's connections with government officials and quoted from Lattimore's writings and from an article about his views printed in a magazine called **Plain Talk.** In his testimony before the Tydings Committee in April, Lattimore painstakingly marshalled evidence to contest each allegation in McCarthy's case against him. His defense of himself, as he summarized it in **Ordeal by Slander,** is in marked contrast with McCarthy's speech printed in the Congressional Record. It made the latter look like a flimsy fabrication. Lattimore and his legal counsel actually counted ninety-six lies, not wrong opinions but misstatements of facts, in the speech. Apparently McCarthy found Lattimore's testimony unpalatable. He did not stay to hear it through to the end.

At the end of the questioning of Lattimore, Senator Tydings announced that the committee had been shown a file on him prepared by J. Edgar Hoover, and that it was the opinion of the committee members that there was nothing in that file to show that he was or ever had been a Communist or connected with espionage activities.

Lattimore's case took a turn for the worse when Louis Budenz, ex-Communist converted to Catholicism and a professor at Fordham University, appeared to testify. He was the man McCarthy had promised would give evidence that Lattimore was a member of the Communist party and subject to its discipline. The nub of his testimony was that Earl Browder and Frederick V. Field had said in his presence that Lattimore was under Communist discipline. When asked for an example of an order Lattimore had received, Budenz claimed that Lattimore was assigned to organize writers to produce enthusiastic stories portraying the Chinese Communists as well-meaning "agrarian reformers." Budenz bolstered this slim evidence with long excursions into the nature of the Communist underground in the U. S. These digressions had nothing to do with Lattimore directly, but they helped to create an atmosphere of suspicion. Budenz also resorted to an amazing attempt to undermine Lattimore's rebuttal by warning the committee that Communist agents are sometimes given special dispensation permitting them to attack the party line. He further warned that people who are still Communists will lie when testifying and therefore cannot be trusted as witnesses. Despite this latter statement, his value to McCarthy's case was temporarily deflated by the testimony of Bella V. Dodds, an ex-Communist; Earl Browder and Frederick V. Field, well-known Communist and suspected Communist. None of them knew of Lattimore as a Communist and had never heard his name mentioned by party leaders as a friend of the party. Field denied that he told Budenz that Lattimore was under Communist discipline. Lattimore later answered Budenz in detail.

The Tydings sub-committee's investigation ended in July, when it issued a report calling McCarthy's charges "a fraud and a hoax" upon the Senate and the American people. Hickenlooper and Lodge, the Republican members of the committee, did not sign the report. The Department of Justice reviewed Lattimore's testimony and concluded that it would not merit a prosecution for perjury.

Why did McCarthy direct his fire at Lattimore? Where did his charges originate? Lattimore, in his testimony before the Tydings committee, stated his belief that McCarthy was resurrecting the same charges that Alfred C. Kohlberg had been making since 1944. Kohlberg was an importer of laces and linens and had amassed a large part of his fortune out of China. He was a key figure in the China Lobby, a pressure group that advocated all-out support of Chiang Kai-shek. In 1945 he had tried to gain a dominant voice in the Institute of Pacific Relations, but he was defeated in a proxy fight which yielded him only sixty-six votes from the two thousand members of the Institute. The Institute was defended at that time by such persons as Sumner Welles, Arthur H. Dean, Robert Gordon Sproul and Ray Lyman Wilbur. Kohlberg began to build up a picture of the Institute as the "evil genius" of American policy, and of Lattimore as its chief exponent. The dispute aroused the interest of the FBI and resulted in an investigation of charges involving Lattimore. To substantiate his statement, Lattimore gave the Tydings committee an eleven-page analysis showing in parallel columns the Kohlberg charges and those of McCarthy. They were so much alike that in places the wording was identical. Kohlberg founded his own magazine, **Plain Talk,** to promote his propaganda campaign against the Institute and other opponents of the policy of all-out aid to China. McCarthy's Senate speech on March 30 leaned heavily on material from this magazine. He inserted into the Congressional Record two entire articles from **Plain Talk.** The pattern of simplification was obvious in Kohlberg's logic: Anyone who was opposed to all-out support of the Nationalists must be sympathetic to the Chinese Communists and maybe even a Communist himself. Since Lattimore opposed his policies, Kohlberg undertook to discredit him.

McCarthy seemed to have "lost his gamble and fallen flat on his face," as Lattimore had predicted he would when the facts were told. Not only did the committee decide adversely on his charges, the press generally treated him in an unfavorable light. Commentators deplored his methods. Public figures in government, education, labor and other areas expressed themselves publicly against him. Despite this censure, McCarthy emerged with a large public following. A Gallup poll at the end of May revealed that 84% had heard of McCarthy's charges against Lattimore; 46.4% approved of his methods, and 34.5% disapproved. His popularity increased, rather than diminished, after the Tydings committee had exonerated Lattimore. McCarthy labelled the committee report a "whitewash" and moved right into Maryland during the Fall election campaign to help defeat Tydings by charging that he had been lenient on the Communist issue. The Maryland voters responded and elected Tydings' Republican opponent. Apparently the Senator from Wisconsin had struck a responsive chord in the hearts of the people. The "Reds-in-government" was a live issue. The Senate created a subcommittee on internal security in December. Senator Pat McCarran was named chairman.

The McCarran committee set out to investigate the administration, operation and enforcement of the Internal Security Act of 1950, and other laws relating to espionage and sabotage and the "effects of subversive activities within the United States." In July, 1951, it began its hearings, and it was soon obvious that the committee was deeply interested in the Institute of Pacific Relations — eager to ascertain whether or not it was infiltrated by Communists and their fellow travelers and how much influence it had on U. S. public opinion and Far Eastern policy. Interest in its investigation was heightened by the clamor of alarm over the Korean war. Aroused at the costliness of the distant conflict, the nation was aroused to a mood for searching out the persons responsible for the course of events that led to the Communist aggression.

The McCarran committee had more evidence than the Tydings group. It had learned that old minutes, correspondence and memoranda of the Institute were stored away in a barn in Massachusetts. It seized the material without obtaining legal permission from an IPR official. For seven months the committee studied these documents and called witnesses to testify about the Institute and Owen Lattimore. The picture that took shape depicted the IPR as an organization entwined in a powerful Communist web of influence and that its magazine, **Pacific Affairs,** as a vehicle for Soviet propaganda, written in such a manner as to avoid Marxist cliches. The IPR appeared to have had a subtle effect on the State Department's strategy in the Far East. Since this strategy had failed, the IPR was held responsible for the China disaster. Since Lattimore had a position of great influence as editor of its magazine, he was charged with a major part in the tragic turn of events.

The testimony of witnesses and the material in the IPR documents raised serious suspicions about Lattimore's relationship to the Communists. Only one witness, Louis Budenz, went so far as to label Lattimore a Communist. (Is it not significant that Budenz, up to 1950, had not reported Lattimore to the FBI? Nor had he listed him among others whom he charged with wrecking our foreign policy, in a 1949 **Collier's** article. After McCarthy attacked Lattimore in 1950, he inserted a brief reference to Lattimore in his manuscript of a book on the China situation). Lattimore categorically denied Budenz's charges and demanded that both his and Budenz's testimony be referred to the Justice Department and examined for possible perjury, since one of them was lying. Budenz's testimony was not so referred, while Lattimore's was. (Brian Gilbert, "New Light on the Lattimore Case," **New Republic,** Dec. 27, 1954, p. 8) Another witness, former Red Army Intelligence Officer Alexander Barmine, testified that the chief of Russian military intelligence told him that Owen Lattimore and Joseph Barnes were among "some of our men working in China under cover." (**Chicago Tribune,** July 31, 1951) Harold Stassen, former Minnesota governor and President Eisenhower's adviser on disarmament, revealed that at a two-day meeting at the State Department in October, 1949, Lattimore had proposed a policy that Stassen considered as an aid to the Communists. Despite his pleas, Ambassador Philip C. Jessup, who presided at the meeting, had stated that he believed the "greater logic" lay with the Lattimore arguments. Stassen claimed that almost every detail of the Lattimore program had been carried out in succeeding months. Lattimore had advocated the recognition of Red China, and the discontinuation of economic aid to Chiang Kai-shek had been proposed by Acheson and Jessup. Stassen's testimony supported previous evidence given by Prof. Kenneth Colegrove of Northwestern University at Evanston who also attended the meeting. Colegrove said that a preliminary briefing by state department officials indicated that the experts had been assembled to be indoctrinated in favor of Red China and against the Nationalists. He said that many of those present were high ranking officials of the IPR and named Lattimore as one of seven who quickly became a dominating influence. He said Lattimore advocated immediate American recognition of the Chinese Reds and economic aid to all communist and non-communist countries of Asia. (**Chicago Tribune,** Sept. 26, 1951) Colegrove said he resigned from the IPR in 1943, when the Communist line became apparent. Others also testified that the IPR was influenced by the Communists and charged Lattimore with Communist sympathies.

The documents found in the Massachusetts barn revealed evidence damaging to Lattimore. There was a letter from Lattimore to Edward C. Carter, General Secretary of the IPR, dated July 10, 1938. In it were statements that looked incriminating when interlinked with the testimony of the witnesses. Lattimore wrote: "For China, my hunch is that it will pay to keep behind the official Chinese Communist position—far enough not to be covered by the same label—but enough ahead of the active Chinese liberals to be noticeable. . . . For the USSR—back their international policy in general, but without giving them or anybody else an impression of subservience . . ." Other documents revealed that Lattimore had agreed with the Director of the Soviet Council of the IPR that **Pacific Affairs** "ought to find more suitable subjects for publication than anti-Soviet articles," and had taken pains to edit Soviet-sponsored articles to make them less obviously Soviet propaganda. (New Republic, Feb. 14, 1955, p. 21)

Lattimore was called to testify on February 26, 1952. He came to the witness stand an angry man. He had prepared a fifty-page statement to refute the testimony that would ruin his reputation if it were true. He had issued the report to the press the day before, and it was obvious that he planned to hit back and hit hard. From the beginning, the hearing was a difficult one. Before Lattimore testified, Chairman McCarran, who had read the news release, made a statement in which he implied that Lattimore was using Communist tactics of invective and disparagement against the committee. This made Lattimore more bitter than ever.

In his statement he said, ". . . I am not and have never been a Communist, a Soviet agent, sympathizer or any other kind of promoter of Communism or Communist interests . . ." This categorical statement later became the basis for his indictment on the charge of perjury. As he had defended his position before the Tydings Committee, he again minimized his influence on U. S. policy-making. He claimed to sanction the containment of the Communists, a strong Point Four program, and peace. The aspects of his testimony that received the most press space, however, were the provocative expressions he used to describe those who had testified against him. For instance, Time interpreted the Lattimore statement as an angry denunciation of the inquiry and as "derisive invective." It reported that Lattimore described McCarthy as "the Wisconsin whimperer . . . a graduate witchburner;" Stassen was "irresponsible . . ." and "a perpetual presidential candidate;" Knowland was "the Senator from Formosa." Budenz was perjured and immoral. Compared with its review of Lattimore's 1950 testimony, this Time article was far less sympathetic in lay-out and tone. (Was the magazine's management by now convinced of the truth of the charges, or did the story's tone reflect the fact that the magazine had become very critical of the Truman administration's Far Eastern policy and was building up support for the Republican party in the coming presidential campaign?)

Angered by Lattimore's attitude, committee members interrupted him with indignant questions so persistently that it took him three days to finish his statement. There was a marked difference, obvious to those on the sidelines, between the committee's handling of the witnesses who contributed to the picture of the pro-Communistic ilk of the IPR, as contrasted with Lattimore and the way Lattimore was handled. Ten more days of questions followed. Using the old IPR documents, the committee was able to focus questions on events which had occurred ten or more years earlier. Lattimore did not have the advantage this data gave the committee, but this did not prevent the committee from probing his memory of the events. At least one observer believed that McCarran was determined to prove his belief that Lattimore was guilty and to catch him in false testimony. Lattimore's use of "intemperate and provocative" expressions such as calling the Nationalist Chinese "driftwood on the beaches of Formosa," and his uncooperative attitude, made him appear to be an arrogant man; but his supporters described him as a man who had been badgered into a state of indignation over the harsh treatment he had been accorded since McCarthy opened his attack on him.

Lattimore had claimed, in his testimony, to be ignorant of Communist activities and propaganda within the IPR. In the cross-examination, committee counsel Robert Morris was able to create a different picture. He produced a list of twenty contributors to Pacific Affairs, identified by previous witnesses as Communists; Lattimore denied knowing that they were party members. Morris asked him when he learned that Frederick V. Field was a Communist. Lattimore said he did not know it unil 1940 or 1941. Morris produced a letter which made clear that he had known Field's ideology as early as 1939. When Morris produced a report of a meeting in Moscow in 1936, at which Lattimore stated he would like to meet the Russian demand for a more definite line in articles, Senator Ferguson questioned him as follows:

Ferguson: That line was the Communist Party line, wasn't it?

Lattimore: In my opinion, no.

Lattimore: What line was it . . . if it wasn't the Communist party line?

Lattimore: The line of the Soviet Council of the IPR . . . nothing Communistic about it.

McCarran (Banging gavel): Answer yes or no.

Lattimore: I believe the Russians have at various times followed lines . . . that had nothing Communistic about them . . ."

(In **Ordeal by Slander** Lattimore described the 1936 meeting as a fruitless attempt to persuade the Russians to participate in the research and discussion of the Institute with more of a "give and take" attitude. He said that he had published an article containing an uncomplimentary personal reference to Stalin which had angered the Russians. They were also incensed at him for publishing a "Trotskyist version" of events in China. This may explain the Russian pressure on Lattimore, at the Moscow meeting, in different terms altogether).

Lattimore said he had never knowingly published the writings of Communists, except one article he had labelled as such, and those prepared by members of the Soviet Council of the Institute. Morris produced a memorandum to show that in 1939 the Soviet representative on the IPR executive council had urged him to publish the writings of a man known as "Asiaticus," who was actually a German Communist named Hans Mueller. Lattimore insisted he had never thought of "Asiaticus" as a Communist, whereupon Morris produced another document in which Lattimore was quoted as saying, "In the next issue of P. A. there is to be an article by a Communist writer . . ." In that issue, an article by Asiaticus appeared.

It was also possible for Morris to produce evidence that McCarthy's statement claiming that Lattimore had had a desk in the state department was a true one, and that Lattimore's statement that he had never taken care of the mail of Lauchlin Currie, former assistant to President Roosevelt, was false. Lattimore had occupied this position, and his desk had been in Currie's office in the state department. Lattimore then confessed to a faulty memory. In the third week of his cross-examination, Lattimore was confronted with a list of a hundred persons, fifty of whom had been identified as Communists or followers of the party line. He insisted that he had not been aware that any of the fifty were Communists when he had dealt with them. Since the questions covered a period of from ten to twenty years before the hearing, his lapses of memory are understandable.

The McCarran subcommittee proceeded to publish its report in July, 1952, after seventeen months of deliberative and prolonged hearings involving sixty-six witnesses and thousands of documents. It concluded that the Institute of Pacific Relations had been pro-Communist and pro-Soviet and that its program had frequently furthered Russian aims and subverted United States interests. The committee also resolved on two cases of alleged false testimony. One of the persons accused was Owen Lattimore.

The report called Lattimore "a conscious and articulate instrument of the Soviet conspiracy," and stated that he had not told the truth on six separate matters. It recommended that the Department of Justice prosecute him for perjury. In fact, it was rumored that McCarran demanded that the Department prosecute. Since he was chairman of the Senate Judiciary Committee, his demands carried authority. McCarran's questioning of James P. McGranery, whom the President had appointed as the new Attorney-General, during hearings of the Judiciary Committee, made it obvious that he would not approve of McGranery or anyone else as Attorney-General if the candidate were unwilling to prosecute Lattimore. He asked: "If it should be related . . . that you were opposed to presenting the matter of Owen Lattimore to a Grand Jury, would there be any truth in it?" McGranery replied, "There would not be, sir."

In the meantime, Roy Cohn, later a key figure in the "Army-McCarthy" hearings, came to work in the Justice Department, at the recommendation of McCarran. He prepared the first, and key, indictment against Lattimore. The Justice

Department placed the case of Lattimore before a federal grand jury, and it indicted him on seven counts of perjury on December 19, 1952. The trial was set for May 11, 1953, in the District Court for the District of Columbia.

Apparently the McCarran committee had been able to discover no evidence that Lattimore was a Communist, Soviet spy, or even a fellow traveler.

The Justice Department's key indictment accused Lattimore of perjurying himself in denying that he had ever been "a sympathizer or any other kind of promoter of Communism or Communist interests." The other six counts referred to minor statements of fact about which he allegedly had lied:

Count two: he lied in saying that he had known prior to 1950 that a man named "Chi" was a Communist;

Count three: he lied when he said he had not known in the late thirties that "Asiaticus" was a Communist;

Count four: he falsified when he denied he had knowingly published articles by Communists (excepting Soviet writers);

Count five: he answered erroneously when he said that his luncheon date with Russian ambassador Oumansky was not held before Hitler invaded Russia;

Count six: he had maintained that he had not taken care of Currie's mail at the White House while Currie was away;

Count seven: he said that neither he nor anyone in his group had made any pre-arrangements with the Communist party in order to get into Yenan.

Luther Youngdahl's Role in the Case

The case came before Judge Youngdahl on March 30, 1953, when arguments on several motions (including one to dismiss the charges) were filed by the defense. Realizing the importance of the case, Judge Youngdahl allowed the litigants all the time they felt they required to present their oral arguments, which amounted to two full days. The law firm of Arnold, Fortas and Porter was re-inforced at the trial stage by former Senator Joseph C. O'Mahoney and William D. Rogers. The chief prosecutor for the Government was Leo A. Rover, who was aided by John W. Jackson, George J. Donegan and Edward F. Hummer.

Judge Youngdahl has admitted that he worked more assiduously on this case than on all but a few of the problems that have ever faced him. On May 2, he delivered his opinion; and the next day, the country was astounded as the news of his decision swept from coast to coast.

The most important statements in the opinion were advanced in connection with the first count, which legal experts regarded to be the key charge and the most controversial. Youngdahl affirmed his conviction that the first count was "fatally defective," because it violated the First and Sixth Amendments of the Constitution.

The Sixth Amendment protects the accused in upholding his privilege to be informed of the nature and cause of the accusation against him, permitting him to prepare a defense and protecting him from "double jeopardy." (being tried twice for the same crime). A subsidiary rule of the Federal Rules of Criminal Procedure requires that the indictment "shall be a plain, concise and definite written statement of the essential facts constituting the offense charged." Youngdahl reasoned that charging a man with lying about his sympathies violated this constitutional protection:

"Defendant in the first count is charged with lying in denying that he was a sympathizer or promoter of Communist interests. It seems to the Court that this charge is so nebulous and indefinite that a jury would have to indulge in speculation to arrive at a verdict. Sympathies and beliefs and what they mean to different individuals involve concepts that are highly nebulous and speculative at best. I presume a person could sympathize with a belief and still not believe. To probe the mind in a situation like this would give rise to nothing more than sheer speculation on the part of the prober. It is fundamental that a jury should not be asked to determine an issue which can be decided only on conjecture." (Note: United States vs. Owen Lattimore, Criminal No. 1879-52, Cited as D.C., 125 F. Supp. 295) The entire opinion is found in the appendix.

Further legal argument would have been unnecessary, as later developments in the case proved, but Youngdahl's opinion continued with the observation that Count One is in conflict with the First Amendment and "restricts the freedom of belief and expression which the Supreme Court in the Rumely case clearly points out as a limitation upon Congressional inquiry." The First Amendment to the Constitution provides that: "Congress shall make no law respecting an establishment of religion, or prohibiting the free exercise thereof; or abridging the freedom of speech, or of the press; or the right of people peaceably to assemble, and to petition the Government for a redress of grievances." Youngdahl was aware of the broader political issues at stake in the Lattimore case, and he did not let the atmosphere of fear of Communism deter him from taking the opportunity to strike a reverberating blow in defense of freedom of belief. Public excitement was at a high pitch on the Reds-in-government issue, and McCarthy was riding the crest of his popularity; Youngdahl was taking a risky step when he came to the defense of the rights of political heretics. By dealing with the case in terms of the First Amendment he provided another instance to show that the judicial system is not as removed from a political role as the doctrine of the separation of powers suggests. The courts often assume an aggressive role as shapers of the political climate and the social philosophy of the nation. Youngdahl was in a familiar crusader's role when he delivered the following words:

"The First Amendment protects an individual in the expression of ideas though they are repugnant to the orthodox. Communism's fallacy and viciousness can be demonstrated without striking down the protection of the First Amendment of discourse, discussion and debate. When public excitement runs high as to alien ideologies is the time when we must be particularly alert not to impair the ancient landmarks set up in the Bill of Rights. 'The greater the importance of safe-guarding the community from incitements to the overthrow of our institutions by force and violence, the more imperative is the need to preserve inviolate the constitutional rights of free speech, free press and free assembly in order to maintain the opportunity for free political discussion, to the end that government may be responsive to the will of the people and that changes, if desired, may be obtained by peaceful means. Therein lies the security of the Republic, the very foundation of constitutional government.' (De Jong vs. Oregon, 299 U. S. 353, 365)

"If we weaken the safeguards afforded under the Bill of Rights we impair our position with the democratic forces in the world fighting against the tyranny of Communism. 'Safety of society depends on the tolerance of government for hostile as well as friendly criticism, that in a community where men's minds are free, there must be room for the unorthodox as well as the orthodox views.' (U. S. vs. Rumely, 345 U. S. 41)

"In our proper concern for the internal and external threat of Communism and in pursuing our efforts to strike down this threat, we should endeavor to be consistent and not attempt to require a conformity in thought and beliefs that has no relevancy to a present danger to our security. During the past few years the experts have had many conflicting and divergent views on foreign policy. Many thoughtful people and patriotic American citizens in 1938 and 1939 were not enthusiastic about our getting into the war. Violent changes in the thinking of our people occurred in a short period of time before and after Germany broke with Russia. 'Attempts of the courts to fathom modern political meditations of an accused would be as futile and mischievous as the efforts in the infamous heresy trials of old to fathom religious beliefs . . . It is true that in England of olden times men were tried for treason for mental indescretions such as imagining the death of the king. But our Constitution was intended to end such prosecutions. Only in the darkest periods of human history has any Western Government concerned itself with mere belief, however eccentric or mischievous, when it has not matured into overt action; and if that practice survives anywhere, it is in the Communist countries whose philosophies we loathe.' " (Communications Ass'n vs. Douds, 339 U. S. 382, Jackson dissenting)

Youngdahl also threw out Counts Three, Four and Seven as being subject to the same defect of vagueness and expressed "serious doubt whether the remaining counts two, five and six can ultimately pass the test of materiality so as to present a jury issue." He granted the defendant's motion asking for a bill of particulars on the remaining counts and set the date for trial at October 6, 1953.

With the key charge dismissed, the Government knew it had no case against Lattimore, so the Department of Justice appealed, with the intention of trying to get the most important part of the case restored. Senator Arthur Watkins intimated which approach the Government's counter-attack would take when he said, immediately after the charges were dismissed by Youngdahl: "When he talks about the Constitution and free speech he is entirely missing the point. The question simply was whether Lattimore lied to a Senate sub-committee and, if so, whether he had lied about material matter." (New York Times, May 3, 1953, p. 1) Lattimore was being tried for lying about his beliefs, not for holding certain beliefs. Late in the summer the Department of Justice filed its request with the Federal Court of Appeals for the District of Columbia, for a re-instatement of the four counts dismissed by Youngdahl. In a sixty-one-page brief, the Government's lawyers attacked Youngdahl's reasoning. This summary contended that the first count of the indictment restrains no speech and condemns no views, but merely attempts to hold Lattimore accountable on his oath to testify truthfully; it reasoned that the First Amendment grants no license to commit perjury. The vagueness or indefiniteness of the first count is not at issue, the brief said, because the sole concern in a perjury case is whether the defendant knew that his testimony was false. A jury should be responsible for determining what "sympathizer" or "promoter" of Communism and Communist interests actually meant to Lattimore and whether his statement, according to his own meaning, was false.

The nine judges on the Federal Court of Appeals for the

Youngdahl receives a plaque in special recognition for his work for racial equality

Gov. Youngdahl at a Law Enforcement Conference

Luther Youngdahl is sworn in as judge of the U. S. District Court for the District of Columbia

Gov. Youngdahl sets fire to various restraints at Anoka State Mental Hospital

District of Columbia recognized the importance of the case. The Court usually sits in panels of three to hear most cases, but in this instance they sat **en banc** with a full compliment of nine, a procedure reserved for only important occasions. In its opinion, delivered in July, 1954, the Court re-instated two of the counts, but it upheld Youngdahl's dismissal of the crucial First Count by a vote of eight to one. Still the Department of Justice persisted. The prosecuting lawyers were convinced that Lattimore meant to lie in denying his Communist sympathies; they believed that he consciously had worked closely with the Communists and that, when he denied it, he lied. Consultation between Leo Rover and the newly-appointed Assistant Attorney General William F. Tompkins resulted in the decision to re-phrase the charges and ask for a new indictment. The problem as they saw it was to make its charge that Lattimore lied more specific so that the jury would have a more objective basis for its decision. The prosecution attempted to do this in two ways: by dropping the charge of "sympathy" with Communism and adding the charge "follower of the Communist line" and by defining what the terms "follower of the Communist line" and "promoter of Communist interests" meant.

This time the charge contained two counts. The first count alleged that Lattimore lied when he denied that he was "a follower of the Communist line." It averred that in his views on political, diplomatic, military, economic and social matters, there can be found expressed in his statements and writings from 1935 to 1950, several hundred instances in which he followed the Communist line. This meant, wrote the Government, that he "followed in time, conformed to, complied with and paralleled the positions taken, the policies expressed and the propaganda issued on the same matters by the Government of the Soviet Union, the Comintern and its successors, the various Communist governments, parties and persons adhering to Communism and accepting the leadership of the Soviet Communist Party." (Count I, paragraph 5) The second count charged him with lying when he denied having been a "promoter of Communist interests." The Government defined such a person as one who "knowingly and intentionally contributed to the growth, enlargement and prosperity of Communism by acting to further, encourage and advance those objectives of political, diplomatic, military, economic and social interest of the Government of the Soviet Union, the Communist party of the Soviet Union, the Comintern and its successors, the various Communist governments, parties and persons adhering to Communism and accepting the leadership of the Soviet Communist party." (Count II, paragraph 5) On October 7, 1954, the Federal Grand Jury indicted Lattimore on these counts.

If the McCarran sub-committee had furnished the Department of Justice with any evidence proving that Lattimore had actually carried out orders from the Cominform, the case would have been easier to prosecute; but no such evidence was produced.

The next development in the case was a dramatic attack upon Judge Youngdahl by U. S. Attorney Leo Rover. In an extraordinary legal move on October 23, 1954, Rover accused the judge of bias and prejudice against the Government and requested Youngdahl to withdraw from the case. For two hours Youngdahl listened to Rover's accusations, expounded before a court-room packed with lawyers and others interested in the issue. Observers were amazed at his composure. Impassive, except for a hardly visible tightening of the jaw muscles and clenching of the fingers when Rover occasionally pounded the podium and shouted his charges, Youngdahl listened mutely as Prosecutor Rover accused him of "astounding language" in his 1953 opinion. "The Government is not trying to put Lattimore's mind in a straitjacket!" Rover roared, according to Time. "We are trying to convict him of lying under oath." Youngdahl's opinion was "a gratuitous insult to the Government. You picked out what was favorable to the defendant and left out what was unfavorable. I want a judge with an open mind and not a judge who has already expressed himself as you have done." (Time, Nov. 1, 1954, p. 18) Pounding the podium, he protested, "The judge seems to be interested only in the defendant and pays no attention to the right of the public—my client." (New Republic, Nov. 1, 1954, p. 8)

Lawyers often accuse judges of prejudice **against the de-**

fense, but it was very unusual for a federal prosecutor to accuse a federal judge. Youngdahl could have avoided a great deal of exertion and annoyance at this point, and without losing face. When faced with Rover's accusation, he could have stepped aside, as judges usually do when their objectivity is challenged. Instead he chose to hear the argument about his bias and decide the question himself. Federal practice forced this most difficult choice upon Judge Youngdahl. It was not possible to withdraw from the case for the limited purpose of having the question of bias put before another judge. He, himself, had to render a decision on the legal sufficiency of the affidavit concerning his own prejudice, or to an attack upon his integrity. (Note: Monrad Paulsen, member of the faculty of the Law School of the University of Minnesota, supplied this information for the author). Commenting on the judge's decision Dr. Monrad Paulsen wrote, "It took great courage to face up to the government's challenge. No lawyer would feel comfortable in deciding a question involving his own interests. It is particularly difficult to face such a question in a time of great public excitement. One would be well aware of the professional criticism forthcoming. Let me say that for most lawyers of integrity sharp substantial criticism from your colleagues can be much more painful than the wolf howls of the irrational." (Note: Letter of Sept. 28, 1955) The judge worked through most of the night and all of the next day to prepare his answer. Late in the afternoon he stepped into the court-room and delivered his memorandum opinion.

In his answer, Youngdahl noted that the affidavit relied on certain language in the 1953 opinion. He did not deny that he had used certain words quoted in Rover's affidavit, but he did deny the inference drawn from the quotations—namely, that those words gave "fair support" to an inference of bias. He reviewed a decision of the Supreme Court to substantiate the point that an inference of bias against a judge "must be based upon something other than rulings in the case." (Berger vs. United States, 255 U. S. 22, 31) Youngdahl also observed that the Federal Court of Appeals had not found anything that would support a charge of bias, and yet the

Government had not asked the Supreme Court to review its action. "Hence," he concluded, "the Government must have believed that there was no valid basis within the judicial process for pursuing further review of my rulings in the case." Youngdahl then delivered his hard-hitting opinion on what lay at the bottom of the Government's move:

> ". . . The affidavit is based upon the virulent notion that a United States judge who honors and adheres to the sacred Constitutional presumption that a man is innocent until his guilt is established by due process of law has 'a bent of mind' that disables him from conducting the fair and impartial trial to which both the accused and the Government are entitled. The affidavit is therefore so patently and grossly insufficient that I cannot escape from the conclusion that **the purpose of the affidavit is to discredit, in the public mind, the final action of our courts, or else to intimidate the courts themselves.** (Emphasis supplied) It follows that those who made or authorized the certificate that the affidavit was made in good faith acted irresponsibly and recklessly as lawyers and officers of the Government.
>
> "Under my oath to preserve sacred Constitutional principles, I can properly do no less than to strike the affidavit as scandalous.
>
> "It is so ordered."

This attack upon Youngdahl's competence to judge the Lattimore case was widely publicized as an attack on the freedom and integrity of the courts. Some believed it was a thinly-veiled attempt to subordinate the judiciary to the executive branch of the government. Others viewed it as a typical episode in the Administration's frenzied attempt to prove McCarthy's sweeping charges, which had a tendency to shrink when challenged. Marquis Childs, Washington correspondent, probed the Washington grapevine and came up with a story that told of political machinations within the Republican Party. In a syndicated column dated November 12, 1954, he wrote: "Behind the (Rover) accusation is a drama of politics involving high ambitions and fierce partisanship. It reached a climax early this year when on two separate occasions Judge Youngdahl was approached by a spokesman close to the Eisenhower administration with the suggestion that Youngdahl resign from the bench and return to his native Minnesota to run for the senate against the Democratic incumbent, Senator Hubert Humphrey. While Youngdahl will discuss no phase of the case, this information comes from unimpeachable sources, and there can be no doubt of its authenticity. Youngdahl's friends believe the charge of prejudice is a reprisal for refusing to run for the senate." A Minneapolis newspaperman predicted privately that the next move by the Government would be an attempt to impeach Youngdahl. Fortunately for all concerned this prediction did not prove true. It may be that the bias charge was prompted by nothing more sinister than an overdose of zeal to fight Communism and a desperation born of the Government lawyers' frustration in striving to convict a man they believed to be guilty.

In October, the defendant's lawyers again filed motions to dismiss the new counts framed by the grand jury; and on January 18, 1955, Judge Youngdahl again dismissed the charges. This time he limited his opinion to a dismissal on the grounds of vagueness, which he said made unnecessary a determination of their constitutionality under the First Amendment. The substance of the crime charged the defendant, he said, "is defendant's lack of belief in the truth of his testimony as of the moment he made it. For a jury to conclude that perjury has been committed, in fact, it must determine what the words meant to the defendant at the time he offered them as his testimony, and then conclude that the defendant did not at that time believe in the truth of such testimony according to the meaning he ascribed to the words and phrases he used." Since the Government supplied the definition of "follower of the Communist line" and "promoter of Communist interests" after Lattimore's testimony before the McCarran committee, and since Lattimore refused to accept the Government's definition and offered one of his own, and since the phrases are subject to varying interpretation, Youngdahl concluded that only "by groundless surmise could the jury determine which definition defendant had in mind. . . . This count, even with its apparent definition, is an open invitation to the jury to substitute, by conjecture, their understanding of the phrase for that of the defendant. . . . With so sweeping an indictment with its many vague charges, and with the existing atmosphere of assumed and expected loathing for Communism, it would be neither surprising nor unreasonable were the jury subconsciously impelled to substitute its own understanding for that of defendant. . . . To require the defendant to go to trial for perjury under charges so formless and obscure as those before the Court would be unprecedented and would make a sham of the Sixth Amendment and the Federal Rule requiring specificity of charges. The indictment will therefore be dismissed." (Note: U. S. vs. Lattimore, cited as 127 F. Supp. 405)

The Federal Court of Appeals again upheld his action, this time by a split vote of four to four. There was one vacancy on the bench which the Administration had not yet filled. It is possible that the outcome might have been different if a man who was sympathetic with the Government's probe had been appointed in time. A five to four vote could have reversed Youngdahl's decision.

Finally, on June 28, 1955, Attorney General Brownell announced that the case against Lattimore would be dropped. By interesting coincidence, the **Minneapolis Tribune** printed — directly under its editorial on the case — an article by Doris Fleeson entitled, "Loyalty Issue Has Lost Its Old Political Wallop." The issue, like McCarthy, had run its course.

The Significance of the Lattimore Case

But like a ravaging flood, it had left tragic scars behind it. The length to which McCarthy, McCarran and his committee, and the Government were able to extend their powers in pressing charges against Lattimore is a measure of the intensity of the fear of Soviet Russia and Communism in the United States during the decade following the war. Highly questionable procedures were practiced and evils tolerated that should have been immediately checked. A review of them is in order.

The use of "the big lie," under the protection of senatorial immunity, to impugn the reputation and career of men who were to the "left" of the accuser, should never have been tolerated. This scandalous practice usually sullied the reputations of men in far darker colors than their acts or opinions warranted. Even when the facts that refuted the original charges were broadcast, the truth never quite managed to overtake the falsehood in the battle for the headlines. In Lattimore's case, McCarthy's charge that he was the top Soviet agent was never pressed, and no attempt to prove it was made.

It is true that Lattimore held and advocated vigorously opinions about the Far Eastern situation that many believed to be dangerous to American interests. It may be true that he had exerted some influence on State Department policy — although the evidence on that theory is far from conclusive, it being a composite of unfounded allegations, quotations out of context and conflicting testimony. Perhaps his views resembled the so-called Communist line enough to warrant suspecting him of promoting Communist interests; but this conclusion is difficult to sustain unless one were previously convinced that Lattimore was pro-Communist; the evidence is too much of a patchwork of allegations and isolated quotations and parallelisms between his views and those of people known to be Communists or more sympathetic to Communism than McCarthy thought they should be. At one point, Lattimore's writings were described as Communistic but so carefully worded that the usual Red clichés were deleted! Budenz even strained credulity by suggesting that Lattimore's anti-Communist views should be taken as evidence that he was actually a Communist under special dispensation to criticize Communism. Most comprehensive of all is the belief that Lattimore was less alert to the dangers of Communism and its conspiratorial methods than he should have been in the light of recent history, and that he protested too loudly his innocence of Communist aims and intrigue. He was detected making several mis-statements of facts. Here again, it must be remembered that he was being asked to extract from his memory, spur-of-the moment recollections involving his thoughts, beliefs and achievements during a period of time some ten to twenty years before he was questioned. McCarthy and others today have the advantage of judging his views with the hindsight given them by the passage of time. It is easier to be a Monday morning quarterback than to be on the field calling the plays.

Oppressive and costly as the experience was for Lattimore, the question is not merely a matter of one man's fate, of whether or not he was guilty enough to be pressed with charges for five years, of his becoming reduced to financial insolvency, and of having his reputation permanently smeared. The larger concern should emphasize that this probe came dangerously close to an attempt to stifle the expression of opinions on controversial questions. China policy in the forties was, as Lattimore himself realized, a controversial issue growing out of an ambiguous and complicated situation. Mistakes were made, but to be mistaken is not to be a traitor to one's country. To advocate a position that attempted to cope with the complexities of a situation, rather than one that was the product of an emotional fear of Communism, is not necessarily to sympathize with Communism. To be to the left of someone who is to one's right is not a crime, and it does not make one a Communist. Lattimore was as much the victim of the American passion for simplification as he was allegedly the dupe of Communists.

Another abuse that was highlighted during the Lattimore case was the subtle transformation of the process of informative legislative investigation into a method of public prosecution of suspected persons, by procedures less than fair. The formal intention of congressional investigations is the obtaining and publicizing of information helpful in achieving good government; during the Red probes, the hearings were used to further the political aims and philosophies of the investigators. The legislative investigation can never be an appropriate substitute for a court trial if it is to accomplish its legitimate role. In order to obtain the necessary information for legislative purposes committees could not allow cross-examination of witnesses or the introduction of other witnesses at the request of those who come before. To do so would result in a hopelessly bogged down procedure that would get few results for the cost and time involved. On the other hand, a proper trial of fact must be conducted in such a way as to provide protection for individuals allegedly guilty of misdeeds, and this means cross-examination of witnesses and witnesses for the accused and other protections. The use of congressional investigations for establishing the guilt of American citizens is one of the most dangerous threats to civil liberties and to justice that has developed in recent years. Even if Lattimore had been allowed unrestricted freedom to introduce witnesses on his own behalf and his counsel to cross-examine witnesses, the hearings would still have been a travesty of due process of law; and it is doubtful that they did much to improve the internal security of the nation.

The law against perjury was mis-used. Perjury is defined as lying under oath. The laws against it are designed to make it costly for witnesses to lie and to insure getting accurate information as a basis for sound legislation, but it has always been possible to use the law to repress dissenters. The Government can direct its questioning in such a manner as to trip up a witness on small points of fact and thus make him liable for an indictment on a perjury charge. The McCarran committee asked witnesses questions framed to pry out all possible details concerning Lattimore's activities. Old files of the Institute of Pacific Relations were combed for incriminating evidence on him. Using this information, the committee subjected Lattimore to the longest cross-examination at any congressional hearing. Despite the fact that their witness did not have a chance to consult the IPR files to refresh his memory, the committee managed to find only six statements in which Lattimore might have lied. Some were so vague they were later thrown out of court. The rest were so minor that Judge Youngdahl later was skeptical as to their materiality. Senator McCarthy, in testimony before the Tydings Committee, made it obvious that the objective of the hearings on Reds in government was to "get" Lattimore and others on charges of perjury. He said:

"It is hard to get them for their criminal activities in connection with espionage, but a way has been found. We are getting them for perjury and putting some of the worst of them away. For that reason I hope every witness who comes here is put under oath and his testimony is gone over with a fine tooth comb, and if we cannot convict some of them for their disloyal activities, perhaps we can convict some of them for perjury." (Quoted in **New Republic**, Dec. 27, 1954.)

The attempt to obtain a conviction on a charge stated in vague, ideological terms was an extreme measure prompted by the fear of Communism. The vagueness of the charge reflects the fact that the term Communism has become an emotional representation of all that is menacing in the minds of many Americans, rather than a specific, rational symbol. Had Lattimore been tried and convicted on the charge of lying about his sympathies and interests, the precedent for charging people with a multitude of vague mental crimes would have been established.

Another unfortunate development in the case was the attack on the independence of the judiciary which was implied in the Government's charge that Youngdahl was biased and prejudiced in favor of the defendant. The challenge to Youngdahl's presumption that Lattimore was innocent indicates how completely the congressional investigations had departed from the constitutional premise and were operating on the assumption that a man is guilty until he proves himself innocent. Had the attack succeeded in intimidating Youngdahl, the courts might have been left weaker in their ability to protect the individual harrassed by repercussions originating in the expression of his views during the heat of debate on national policy.

A sixth evil is eloquently described by Archibald MacLeish: "What has been happening in the United States over the period of the past five years or more makes it tragically evident that the danger (to individual freedom) is now both real and present. There has been a massive, almost glacial, shift away from the passion for individual freedom and toward a desire for security of association, of belonging, of conformity." ("Loyalty and Freedom," **American Scholar**, Autumn, 1953, p. 394.)

This is the most insidious evil the American people have tolerated. They have allowed themselves to fear making forthright statements of opinion; they have allowed themselves to become suspicious of independent-minded men who are not afraid to voice convictions based upon free inquiry into the facts; they have allowed themselves to smirk at scholarly men as McCarthy did, implying that because they were erudite, they were dangerous. (A revealing comment was made by Mr. B. M. Miller, a McCarthy supporter, at the National Rally for McCarthy in Constitution Hall in November, 1954: "Of course I don't have a long string of degrees; if I did I wouldn't be here tonight." Laughter followed. The anti-intellectualism of McCarthy's crusade was never more manifest). The dark tide of unreasoning and almost hysterical apprehension that flowed over the nation in recent years has left behind it a grim testimony to the ease with which the American people allowed fear to govern them when the course of events prove trying. This atmosphere of trepidation shows how uncertain is their faith in the democratic process of discussion, the freedom to disagree, and due process of law. Even educational leaders succumbed. Fear of McCarthy was almost as strong as fear of Communism. Those who saw in Lattimore and Hiss the shades of commissar agents were matched by those who saw McCarthy as a reincarnation of Hitler in American guise.

The question of what the long range effects of McCarthyism are will be debated for years to come. Already some are of the opinion that the status of civil liberties slipped lower and that McCarthyism abetted tendencies toward less freedom that are present in a highly organized and complicated society. Others argue that McCarthy and his friends prompted a reaction that will have the long range effect of strengthening the American democratic tradition. (Note: Professor Charles Alan Wright argues this viewpoint in a book review of three books on McCarthyism in **The Progressive**, April, 1955 p. 37-38).

It is true that there is a massive strength in American democracy that moves slowly to throw off those who would destroy it but eventually manages to put its demagogues in their places. Certainly, too, the McCarthy episode was dramatic enough to arouse interest and activity; and perhaps such dramas are necessary to offset the deadening effect of the frustration citizens feel when they realize that politics nowadays have passed almost beyond the control of the people into the hands of power blocs that do their work quietly but with alarming effectiveness.

What must not be forgotten is that all along the course that the McCarthy flash flood followed were sturdy dikes to stem the tide — not many of them, but there never have been many even in the United States. All over the country people still had the freedom to sternly criticize McCarthy in the open to as many as desired to listen, and there were those who used their right. There was the press. Its record was not unblemished since, in the course of reporting the hearings, it contributed to the sensationalizing and spreading of the charges that damaged the reputations of the witnesses; but most of the time, while it was reporting the news McCarthy's charges made, it was speaking bluntly and warningly about McCarthy's methods. There was Johns Hopkins University, which was victimized financially by the Lattimore proceedings but nevertheless did not pre-judge his case or fire him. There were Lattimore's colleagues, headed by Dr. George Boas, who organized a defense committee and raised $36,000, much of which they contributed themselves. There were 1,800 Americans who contributed gifts averaging $20 to the defense fund and many others who expressed themselves in public statements advocating a fair hearing to the defendant. There was the law firm of Arnold, Fortas and Porter that defended Lattimore at a cost of exhausting months of labor and, since it charged no legal fees to Lattimore, contributed an estimated $250,000 in legal service, for which they could rightfully have collected; thus they demonstrated that the American bar is still represented by those who value justice above material considerations. There were Professor Lattimore and his wife, who could have played mouse but instead chose to stand up and fight valiantly for not only their reputation but for the right of teachers and authors to speak and write about the events that are shaping our times.

Last, but not least, there was a judge who refused to be stampeded by the popular excitement aroused by McCarthy's charges and the potent danger of Communism and who would not be cowed by an ill-considered attack on the integrity and independence of the courts — Luther W. Youngdahl, "practicing constitutionalist and Christian and fierce defender of the rights of heretics."

CHAPTER ELEVEN

Christianity In
Minnesota Politics:

An Evaluation

PART I

Youngdahl as a Christian in Politics

"Christianity and politics can mix" — this is a recurring theme in Luther Youngdahl's thinking.

Some cynics may believe they hear in this slogan the echoes of a popular and false version of the Christian faith, the pleasantly incredulous mood of which is caught in the ditty:

"Early to pray
(What a surprise)
Makes a man healthy,
Wealthy and wise."

They fear that Youngdahl's theme is a slogan appropriated in the banal belief that Christianity will make a person successful in everything he does.

Warily these skeptics watch for indications that he has fallen into the error of thinking that the Christian faith endows the believer with superior wisdom to enable him to avoid political blunders and miscalculations. Suspiciously they dig around for evidence of the type of faith which mistakenly assumes that Christianity provides a complete set of rules to automatically create perfect justice. Their uneasy skepticism is understandable, because well-intentioned and decent Christians often have made both of the errors they fear. It may gratify them to discover that Youngdahl found resources in his faith, quite apart from these erroneous conceptions, that proved relevant to his political career.

However, the very fact that Youngdahl was successful and also recognizably Christian makes an interpretation of his career difficult. One could easily conclude that it was his Christianity that made him successful or that all Christians would be as successful as he, if they were as zealous and courageous as he was. This over-simplified and illogical conclusion can be dispelled forthwith by imagining what sort of political

273

prospects a state like Massachusetts or a city like New York might have offered to a man with a Scandinavian name and a philosophy similar to Youngdahl's. There are many factors in a man's success. Youngdahl succeeded in Minnesota during the years 1947-51, and this is noteworthy and a credit to him. It does not necessarily prove that there is a perfect correlation between practicing Christianity and achieving success.

The following evaluation of Youngdahl will not be concerned with his success. It will be concerned with the question: which insights and resources of the Christian faith did he discover to be significant and helpful as he applied his faith to his political life?

One is tempted, for another reason, to avoid the delicate task of evaluating his career. Each person is unique, and every situation calls for an approach adjusted to itself. Christian love, while absolute in its demand for obedience to God at all times, is relative in that it must manifest itself in terms of the people's requirements and the limited resources available for those needs at the time. It would be easier to say, "Here is one man who, in his own way, tried to be a Christian in a particular situation," and let it go at that. Yet, there is much to learn by standing apart to evaluate, if it is accomplished without presumption and with the desire to be helpful.

If we take a profile of a Christian politician based upon the analysis in the Introduction and use it to evaluate Youngdahl's politics, we will discover the factors he found in Christianity that proved relevant in politics. This profile can be briefly sketched as follows:

1. The Christian politician's strategy is based upon his respect for government as the instrument whereby God enforces his law of mutual assistance in human society and his realistic acceptance of the presence of sin and the resultant necessity for governmental supervision. He therefore participates willingly, if not always light-heartedly, in the political process of conflict and compromise. He regards this process as a necessary restraint upon the self-will of interest groups in a society, and even upon himself and his own party. He

recognizes the relativity and imperfections of every party, proposal and law.

2. The Christian politician regards his work as a calling from God in which he is duty-bound to serve his neighbor. He therefore aggressively seeks to accomplish more good than the pressures of self-interest groups can achieve; he is not content with the measure of welfare and justice attained by conflict and compromise. He speaks for unrepresented groups and strives for the under-dog, without questioning whether they can help him politically. He appeals to the consciences of men, not just to their self-interest. He subordinates his personal ambition to his public duty.

3. The Christian politician's program evolves out of his concern for people and his respect for government as an instrument of law. He therefore presses for policies beneficial to people, and for proposals designed to strengthen the ability of the state to be lawful and orderly.

4. The Christian politician is active in the Church, submitting himself and his program to the judgment of God's Word and the discussion of the human situation in the fellowship of Christians.

Youngdahl's Sense of Vocation

It is apparent, from the evidence collected, that Youngdahl performed the duties of his office with a strong consciousness of Christian vocation. He believed that politics was a calling in which he was obligated to serve God faithfully and wisely and was explicit about relating his belief in the Protestant idea of the calling to his job. He brought a crusading zeal into his office. He preached his political ideals and program wherever he went, taking advantage of every opportunity to persuade Christian people to become active in politics, not merely because it was their patriotic duty but because it was their **Christian** responsibility. He had a high regard for the political office, despite his distaste for competitive politics. He credited his Lutheran training with being the source of his inspiration.

Those who questioned his motivation, interpreting his

career in terms of a very strong ambition to be a success, are not to be ignored. Only a person with a shallow view of human nature would discount the drive of a man's ego. Yet, it must be said in defense of Youngdahl that he was willing to risk his success in politics on behalf of his law enforcement program, at the very inception of his career, when he had no guarantee of what the outcome might be.

Youngdahl's Concern for People

Youngdahl's political program was cogently summarized in the phrase, "Honesty and Humanity." His campaign speeches, messages to the Legislature and reports to the people, over the radio and on the platform, bear ample evidence that his program was strongly humanitarian. His tax policy, his insistence that laws be enforced, his advocacy of social welfare measures, his fight for civil rights for minority groups, his endorsement of a program of increased funds for education, and his youth conservation program, were all means of implementing his concern for preserving the human resources of the state. Minnesota's wealth was regarded as a means to that end. The management of the state's government should be efficient, honest and sound, thus enabling the state to serve its people more effectively. His most vigorous efforts were expended in the crusade for those aspects of his program that were directly concerned with people and their needs.

In advocating his program, Youngdahl was motivated by a concern for people that grew out of his Christian faith. He believed it was a proper demonstration of faith to be concerned with the welfare of others and to practice love for one's neighbor.

Youngdahl's critics could be cynical and point out that it was just clever politics to sponsor policies favoring the youth, the aged, and the handicapped. It is the easy road to popularity. Yet it must be noted that Youngdahl's consideration for people prompted him to advocate human interest programs in advance of public pressure for them. Some of his proposals, such as youth conservation, mental health, and family courts, were of a pioneering nature in state politics. His genuine concern is also verified in his readiness to espouse the cause of minorities which lacked political power to return him a favor, such as the Indians, the small Negro population, and the displaced persons. He confronted the people of Minnesota with their needs and challenged them to do something about the situation. He was more than the spokesman of the dominant factions. He was a community conscience, bringing the law of love for neighbor to bear upon state problems and appealing to the people, on ethical grounds, to act according to this law.

Government as an Instrument of the Law of Love

Youngdahl's advocacy, and the people's support of a human welfare program for the state of Minnesota, implied a readiness to utilize political power in advancing the cause of human welfare. Youngdahl was never very explicit about this point, yet it is obvious that he believed the people had the right to use the political power vested in them to obtain human benefactions. In effect, this means that the law of love is not an elective matter for Christians, but binding upon all men, including those who would be selfish. It is reasonable that men should use collective means to aid one another in periods of distress. Furthermore, to depend on voluntary methods of meeting human needs is not an entirely justifiable social policy, because people are concerned mostly for their own welfare and must often be coerced into helping their neighbors and treating them fairly. When Youngdahl saw a human need being neglected, he apparently assumed that people either would not or could not handle it on a voluntary basis and that the state would have to set up a program to assume the human obligation. The state therefore becomes, by Youngdahl's interpretation of its responsibilities, a check on human selfishness; and it prods people out of their self-concern. It also becomes, in that area, an instrument of order for accomplishing social tasks in a systematic and smoothly-organized fashion. Behind Youngdahl's program was the coercive power of the state. Let us consider various aspects of Youngdahl's program to illustrate this fact.

Youngdahl regarded laxity in enforcing the laws against gambling, and also those controlling liquor sales, to be socially harmful. In advocating law enforcement, he was requesting that the people of Minnesota approve the employment of government power in promoting the welfare of the people. If they still believed that gambling should be prohibited, they should approve of having enforceable laws.

Similarly, he proposed measures that would strengthen the regulation of liquor sales and consumption. In his opinion liquor was a harmful and dangerous commodity, the use of which should be carefully regulated by law. Therefore, he proposed such measures as the uniform closing hours bill and the "power of arrest for liquor inspectors" bill. If the people believed as he did, they should not hesitate to make use of the coercive power of the state to promote their concern for human welfare.

By advocating a youth conservation program, Youngdahl was requesting that the resources of the state be made available to alleviate community conditions that lead to delinquency, and to provide help in rehabilitating young people who were in need of readjustment. The forces of law and the power to tax were to be applied in "coercing" the people to provide a better program for youth.

His mental health program called for a revision of policy based on the enlightened concept that mental illness was curable; and for a hospital and clinical program that would effectively implement this policy. This program recognizes that the mentally ill continuously confront their fellow citizens with God's call to service, and that their requirements are so excessive that resources beyond the income of the immediate family are needed to meet it. It is expedient that the state, by its power to tax, call upon the entire citizenry to assist their neighbors in distress.

Youngdahl was a strong advocate of conciliation as a

means of restoring disrupted human relations. Therefore, he staunchly defended Minnesota's labor relations law. He even urged the formation of family courts as a legal measure, to require conciliation procedures in families threatened by marital strife. Since agencies, such as the churches and social welfare societies, apparently were not able to persuade people to seek this method voluntarily, it was proper that the state use its power to enforce such a procedure for saving homes.

He advocated an F.E.P.C. law, because he believed it was a matter of **right** that men of all races and creeds be treated fairly. Even though he recognized that inward respect for people is unenforceable, he was prepared to use the power of the state to insure outward observance of fair treatment and equality in matters of employment, housing, political and social rights. These instances are sufficient to indicate both the depth of Youngdahl's concern for human welfare and the height of his political belief that the state should promote human goals.

In connection with this matter, the problem of tax policy should be discussed. It is far more than a technical problem dealing with the raising of funds for the government. Basic problems of justice are involved. As we have seen, on the question of the spending of tax money, Youngdahl stood with those who believe that the government should finance human welfare; on the question of who shall pay the taxes, he took a more ambiguous stand. His political philosophy obviously made him more concerned about spending for human goals than about the equally important and equally ethical problem of fair distribution of the tax burden required to finance the program. Although he has been criticized for not being enough concerned about the question of who shall pay the taxes, it is not too far-fetched to say that his middle-of-the-road policy at least showed that he was aware of the problem and tried to suggest taxes that would spread the burden.

Youngdahl was realistic enough to see that it was not advisable to have a law that the community would not support; yet he believed it was good political administration to bring the will of the community to bear upon individuals who did not voluntarily practice what the community expected of its citizens. While he legislated for measures that would expand the program of the state into new areas of service, he worked on the assumption that the state should do no more than the people were willing to entrust to it. "If the people do not like the law, let them repeal it," he said on more than one occasion. This reflects his implicit recognition that the justice achieved by the state is always relative.

"Honesty in Government"

"I believe the key to success in politics is to follow one's conscience in doing what one thinks is best for all the people. . . . People soon learn whether their leaders are sincere. When I say that Christianity works in politics I mean applying the Christian conscience to every decision one makes and every act one performs. . . . The teaching of my church which helped me the most in politics was that there is a right and wrong and a sharp line between the two; that sin cannot be compromised with. . . . Of course, there should not be a stubbornness and refusal to listen to other views, but there should not be any need to compromise on principles." (Letter of June 25, 1952.)

That the above statements were taken seriously by Youngdahl is not hard to establish. He believes that "politics is the machinery by which society makes its moral decisions." At the outset of his career, he announced that he intended to follow his convictions even if it meant his defeat in elections.

He bulwarked his words with action. He launched a law enforcement program that was in accord with his convictions, even though it was bitterly opposed. His campaigns for election were conducted as "honest reports to the people." He told them where he stood on current issues and reported on the accomplishments of his previous administration. He backed up his campaign promises with vigorous attempts to get his program approved by the Legislature. He disavowed any participation in the familiar practices of "political trading" in order to further his aims.

As an administrator, he insisted on a high level of integrity from all the officials responsible to him, as exemplified by his support of A. Herbert Nelson and his stand on the Arkansas bond deal. He appointed men on merit rather than as a reciprocal reward for political support. (While Nelson was his friend and a zealous campaigner for Youngdahl, his record as an administrator supports Youngdahl's claim to appointing men of integrity.) He continued the practices of previous administrations with regard to civil service, open and competitive bidding, and the stressing of efficient stewardship of state business and monies.

His insistence on law enforcement was also an expression of his political honesty; if laws are going to be on the books they should be enforced, or it is obvious that the integrity of government will be undermined by insincerity. Youngdahl believed in judging legislation on its contribution to the welfare of the state, not on its political effects.

Youngdahl's insistence upon political honesty and his courage in following his convictions are characteristics worthy of high praise, and the political world could well use more people whose ethical principles originate from a basic belief in the theory that the politician is a servant of God and obligated to live by high moral principles in his political life.

This must not overshadow the fact that Youngdahl oversimplified the moral problem in politics.

He believed that the difference between right and wrong in politics is clear-cut and that there can be no compromise with sin. The problem, in other words, was not discerning what was right, as much as finding the courage to do it.

It may be true that most people summon enough courage to obey their sense of right, but that is not the only problem. To know what is right is more of a problem. The social situation is very complex, and the solutions found for problems are relative and imperfect. In politics, there are always several groups affected by a policy — some adversely, at least from their own viewpoint. Human needs of many types clamor for attention, resulting in the conflict between several values. Human selfishness leaves its corrupting mark on all things. The consequent developments tend to obscure the difference between right and wrong.

Jerry Voorhis, a member of the United States House of Representatives for several terms, wrote out of his own experience when he described this difficulty:

"Before I was elected to Congress . . . I imagined that . . . there would be a clean-cut choice between a right way and a wrong way to vote upon issues. I imagined that some bills would be right and others would be wrong. I expected to vote for the ones that were right and against the ones that were wrong. There were times when I did feel that way about my votes. But far more often it just did not turn out that way. Democratic government, even at its very best, is a process of compromise and reconciliation of the various opinions of many different people. And therefore the difficult and usually unsatisfying task of the individual representative is to work unceasingly and wisely for the absolute right in which he believes but to make his choices and decisions from day to day not between white and black but between light and dark shades of gray. . . . Strenuous and frequently discouraging as the campaign for election is, hard as are the long, long hours of work, distressing as are the interferences with one's family life, nevertheless all of these could be borne with a comparatively calm mind were it not for the **searing experiences** (bold face supplied), repeated day after day, of trying to determine just what is the most nearly right thing to do on questions that require a simple 'aye' or 'no' when the roll is called." (**The Christian in Politics**, New York. 1951, p. 96.)

Youngdahl, too, may have been aware of this difficulty of choosing between alternatives, neither of which was completely creditable. There were times in his career when he was faced with complex problems. It was not an easy task to decide how to handle the meat-packers' strike. He spent long hours around conference tables trying to reconcile employer and union viewpoints. He had to make decisions on legislation involving a conflict of principles, such as the bill repealing the prohibition of liquor sales to Indians (see page 186) and the no-strike bill (see page 167). The point must be made that he did not stress the problem overtly when explaining to church people the relation between Christianity and politics. He does not speak in terms like "the agony of decision" or "the searing experience" of choosing what is most nearly right. One of the heavy prices paid by a Christian who becomes involved in politics is this loss of innocence, this awareness of one's own implication in — and assent to — actions and policies that are often a compromise. Youngdahl does not speak of it. He displayed the courage to stand for what is right. It must also be noted that courage is a necessary requisite to becoming involved in the difficult and even heartbreaking political struggle, and to continuing bravely to uphold policies that seem most commendable — although tomorrow those policies might prove to be faulty and require alteration, leaving their advocates subject to harsh criticism. It is this type of courage that church people need. They would have it in the measure that they believe that God's grace atones for their sins and that their salvation does not depend upon their own perfection but upon God's love for them.

Youngdahl's over-simplification is revealed in another way. He tended to construct a view of the political struggle as one between "good people" and "selfish interests." Political victory would be achieved by rallying the "good people" to the cause; this would result in the rout of "selfish pressure groups." The moral struggle (as he conceived it) was between two camps — the legislators and lobbyists who opposed humanitarian and honest policies, versus the voters, citizens' groups and legislators who supported those policies. (Note: See especially his farewell address, p. 225f.)

Youngdahl's efforts to arouse lethargic people to political action is laudable. One of the afflictions in American politics has been — as Father James Kellar of the Christopher movement has put it — that "most good people are taking care only of themselves while most evil people are trying to take care of everyone else." The so-called "good" people have not been as good as supposed. While living "pure" lives within the law themselves, they have been too selfish to care about others or be concerned about promoting ethical politics. Youngdahl succeeded in arousing in them a greater interest in politics.

There is a common tendency in America to blame some individuals and groups for all the evils, and to praise others for all the good. Midwest farmers, in the late nineteenth century, blamed "Wall Street" for their ills. Americans blamed Hoover for the depression in the thirties and censured the Democrats for "twenty years of treason" in the fifties. Youngdahl blamed the pressure groups in Minnesota for frustrating his program.

But it is not that simple. The moral struggle in politics is not between one group and another — Democrat vs. Republicans, special interest lobbyists vs. the people's lobby, church members vs. non-church members. All are guilty of self-seeking in one form or another. Sin corrupts everyone. Self-love persistently distorts every viewpoint. This is one of the insights into politics that results from Christian realism.

In an off-the-record informal gathering not so long ago, a well-known United States senator framed a remark that reflected his awareness of the moral problem in politics. "A politician's strongest temptation in Washington is not to succumb to bribery in his desire for financial gain. More insidious and powerful is the temptation of power. Getting the limelight and knowing that one's actions affect many lives — these stimulate the lust for power."

Youngdahl may also have understood this allusion to sin in its political form. Again, however, his utterances to church people about Christianity and politics do not contain warnings to them that they are involved in the sinful predicament of mankind and that they must always be on the alert for symptoms of corruption motivated by self-love. He did not explain to them that the political process of conflict and compromise was inevitable, because of sin — and that it might even be regarded as "God's instrument of order" to hold selfishness in check. He did not tell them that all proposals and programs are only relatively superior answers to the problem.

More than his words, however, the story of his career — and the political situation in which it developed — is indicative of a vitally important truth. Even the best of Christians fall short and leave undone the things that should be done. Christians, too, become involved in situations that are not unambiguously good. All human beings are limited and imperfect. It is ingenuous to expect well-intentioned and courageous men to be entirely free of self-love, illusions, and the desire for power. Realism is needed — and the humility to accept human limitations. Lacking the charitable viewpoint, we become pretentious about our own abilities and "starry-eyed" about human possibilities. This can only lead either to terrible abuses (in the name of our own private brand of righteousness) or ennervating cynicism. The story of Youngdahl is a good antidote for the kind of naivete that regards virtue and justice as "simple possibilities." (Note: There is a pertinent discussion of Christian realism in Reinhold Niebuhr's **Christian Realism and Political Problems,** New York 1953.)

Youngdahl's Political Wisdom

Politics has often been defined as the "art of the possible." Although the definition ignores the influence of the sense of justice upon politics, it stresses the necessity for political wisdom. A realistic appraisal of human nature and a thorough understanding of the political process are essential to a Christian citizen. His faith supplies him with no ready-made answers. A Christian must learn to evaluate the political situation and be willing to use his knowledge to attain his goals. He may not always like the methods of accomplishment; he may be required to participate in the process of conflict and compromise against his inclinations; and he will always be confronted by the problem of determining when the means, which he has been using in good conscience, have ceased to serve the end he had hoped to achieve. There is no escape from this dilemma and the political process which creates it. There is no easy solution to the problems of conscience which it creates.

We have seen that Youngdahl believed that the key to success in politics is in following one's conscience, without basic compromise. This is the keystone to his political strategy. While it led him toward over-simplification of the moral problem in politics, it did not prevent him from operating effectively within the political structure in Minnesota. As we evaluate the political wisdom of Youngdahl, we must bear in mind the focal points of political power in Minnesota government.

The Governor. As was indicated in the Introduction, the chief executive wields a great deal of power. That description of executive authority is largely substantiated by what we see in Minnesota. The non-partisan nature of the Minnesota legislature puts an even greater emphasis upon the power of the governor.

Scarcely any attention is paid to the candidates running for the legislature, because they advocate no specific platform. The governor and other state officers are the ones who campaign for a party platform. Thus popular interest is centered almost entirely on the governor and his program. He is expected to formulate the people's desires and clarify the issues.

Since the major parties do not control the legislators, the people are more dependent than ever on the governor to offset the pressure of special interest groups. Because th governor is the one who attracts the public's eye, the parties must select a man who will win the people's confidence. In Minnesota, this gives the governor considerable power within the party councils.

The Governor of Minnesota operates within a semi-centralized type of government. Offices, such as the Attorney-General, the Secretary of State, the Treasurer and the Auditor are elective positions not subject to his control. These officers are members of the Executive Council, along with the Governor and the Lieutenant-Governor. The Governor has law-enforcement powers, can make budgetary recommendations, makes key appointments, and presents the legislative program in his inaugural message.

Youngdahl's natural talents enabled him to capitalize on — and effectively use — the power inherent in his office. He was especially adept at formulating policy on issues that were not yet in the public eye but were close to the people's hearts. He worked for law enforcement and mental health reforms, for example, before either of them had become popular public topics. He made issues out of them. His sense of timing was such that he recognized when public opinion was on the upswing and was primed for a program while more cautious politicians would be inclined to drag their feet. He did not merely assize public opinion; he mobilized it while it was still latent.

He used his power as a spokesman for the people effectively. His ability as a speaker enabled him to appeal directly to the people for approval, and to swing their support his way. He recognized his role as creator of a legislative program and pushed vigorously for the passage of his recommendations. He used his prestige, as the chief law enforcement officer, to advocate more rigid enforcement and to administer the program after its adoption. He also employed his official powers and personal prestige to exert pressure on participants in industrial disputes and yet won universal respect for the understanding manner in which he used his powers.

In the light of these observations, Youngdahl's comprehension of the power of the Governor, and his astuteness in using it, redound to his credit as a political strategist.

The Legislature. The Minnesota Legislature was designed to have considerable initiative and power in formulating public policy. (Note: See general description of the legislative branch on p. 117 of the Introduction.) We are not heartened by what we see when we examine the Legislature's operations. It has yielded its initiative, in constructing public policy, to the Governor; and consequently it tends to be obstructive rather than cooperative in its relation to the Governors' programs. The major action is handled by committees dominated by the seniority system and subject to local and special interest pressures. It is natural for the public to lose track of bills in the legislative maze; and lobbyists consequently have more power than they should have, because they contrive to be on hand almost constantly. The Minnesota Legislature no longer is truly representative. Rural legislators have a preponderance of seats, creating a situation that is not only unfair but illegal; because the constitution requires re-apportionment every ten years. The tendency to agree with George Graham is strong, when he says: ". . . No sins which can be charged against city dwellers can compare in sheer wickedness with the brazen abuse of their political powers by the rural politicians of America, who will not allow the men, women and children who live in metropolitan centers to have equal representation in state legislatures." (Morality in American Politics,) New York 1952, p. 149) Unfair representation introduces an element of disorder that has undermined the power of government to hold selfishness in check. It is illusory to think that rural politicians will have enough detachment to adequately represent city dwellers, especially on some issues. The political effects of having a nonpartisan legislature have been described. The disorder in the legislative branch is compounded by that feature, because the people have no organized means of counter-acting the special interests when the party has no control over legislators. A strong political party can resolve compromises that balance the claims of various groups. This is almost impossible when the legislature is non-partisan. Even though the legislators caucus as "conservatives" or "liberals," they are not taking action as a result of commitments to the people during the campaign but as individuals making their own decisions.

Youngdahl was required to deal with a legislature over which his party had no firm control and which could only be rendered responsive to public opinion if special efforts to arouse the people were made. He had no assurance that the legislators would support his program. In this situation, the special interests became his chief antagonists.

Mental hospital meeting of superintendents with Gov. Youngdahl

Gov. Youngdahl signs the order integrating Negroes into the National Guard

He used two approaches—personal persuasion and pressure on the legislators and, when that failed, direct appeal to the people. Due to the conservatives' opposition to his free-spending program, Youngdahl attempted to form his own bloc of legislators to support and sustain his program. His direct appeals to the people were remarkably successful. It usually is difficult to animate public opinion to the extent of inspiring people to put pressure on their legislators, but he succeeded. Yet, as a continuous procedure, this method is unreliable. It is possible to stimulate an occasional surge of public action strong enough to offset the constant pressure of special interests, but this action is rarely sustained for long. Youngdahl's methods worked very well in 1947, during the anti-slot machine fight. They were successful again in the equally appealing crusade for mental health. In 1951, his system was less effective.

Did he have any alternative? Probably none that would be superior, within the existing situation. What occurred during his administration underscores the necessity for reform of the structure of Minnesota government. Faulty structure makes it possible for the elements of power-lust and selfishness to get away with multiple abuses. Reapportionment, party designation for legislators, constitutional revision, and departmental re-organization are some of the reforms that are vitally needed if road blocks to justice and sound public policy are to be removed. The Christian politician in Minnesota and elsewhere must be willing to work for these reforms, even though they are not dramatic issues packed with human interest. Out of a spirit of respect for government as an instrument of order, the Christian must work for these reforms.

Youngdahl was not entirely indifferent to the problem of structural reform, but his welfare legislation took precedence in his interest and on his agenda. He included proposals on the necessary reforms in his messages and occasionally referred to such issues in his speeches; but he made no special appeals, refraining from using his immense prestige to arouse public opinion. He did not link up his proposals in the field of governmental reform with moral convictions, as he did so effectively in presenting his social legislation. Except for constitutional revision, he created no citizens' committees to arouse support for these reforms.

It may have been more dramatic and appealing to a man of deep human feeling to work for mental health and other social legislation, but the victories he won there can only be temporary and partial if the whole structure of government makes it difficult to secure responsible leadership for these programs, and for public morality to find channels to express itself in promoting humanitarian legislation. What might have happened, if Youngdahl had used his great prestige with church people to direct their attention and zeal toward structural reform and to convince them of the moral issues at stake, would make interesting speculation. Perhaps if he had campaigned a fourth time, he would have made that the next item on his program; for he showed increasing impatience with the frustrating process of government as time went on, directing his attention more and more frequently toward the need for structural reform.

Political Parties. The fundamental role of political parties in American democracy, and the weaknesses of those parties, has been described briefly. In Minnesota the parties are more ineffectual than ever, as we have seen. They have no control over aspirants to county offices, or to state legislative posts, nor can they control the platforms on which these candidates choose to run. Since the parties do not campaign for them or contribute to the campaign expenses of legislators, they have even less power to discipline them than is customary. An example of this lack of power is the fate of the recommendation, by both parties, that party designation be restored to state legislators. It may be concluded, from this description, that a governor would have less than the usual amount of help (or hindrance) from a bi-partisan organization in Minnesota.

Yet, it is necessary for a gubernatorial candidate to rely on the indorsement of a party if he is going to conduct a successful campaign for election. He may participate in the primary without factional support, but the party gives its full support to the successful candidate in the general election campaign.

Youngdahl won Republican support, not because he was a faithful party wheel, but because he had built up a good reputation in civic life and on the bench. In a state where political independence is admired, it is not uncommon for a party to choose as its candidates, men who have earned a reputation for integrity, leadership and civic-mindedness in non-political activities. Since Youngdahl had been chosen for this reason, rather than because of his party loyalty, the balance of power between himself and the party was weighted in his favor. Despite Harold Stassen's firm hand on the state G.O.P., Youngdahl could be independent if he chose. He did not hesitate. He made it clear from the beginning that he was "beholden to no man or group," and he struck off on his own path on more than one occasion. These deviations strengthened his prestige with the public, but it lessened his influence in the party. Some may criticize Youngdahl's light regard for party politics, but they cannot deny that he won elections.

He admitted that he was not a thorough-going party politician and intimated that he believed in political independence. He has many, if not most, of the characteristics of the political independent described in the Introduction. His conception of the moral problem in politics, his crusading zeal, his formation of his own bloc of supporters, his impatience with the complicated and compromising processes of party and pressure politics, his deep concern for people, and his ability to inspire a "layman's revival" of interest in politics among the rank and file of the citizens—all of these traits substantiate his designation as an independent.

The limitations to the strategy of the independent have already been described. In Youngdahl's career and the Minnesota situation, it seems to have been an effective strategy—more effective than is usually the case. At this point, however, we are not primarily concerned with evaluating the potential success or failure of Youngdahl's political independence. It is more relevant to ask whether or not his concept of Christianity led him to adopt the role of the independent. Did he interpret the principles of Christianity in such a manner as to imply that political independence was "more Christian" than partisan politics?

Apparently he did not commit himself in specific terms, yet some of his political traits are deeply rooted in his Christian faith and heritage. His crusading zeal, his concept of the moral problem in politics, and his deep concern for people are expressive of the earnest Christianity he has embraced as his faith. It is not too far-fetched to suggest that Youngdahl found the role of the independent more congenial to his Christian perspective than partisan politics would have been.

This supposition must not lead to the conclusion that political independence is more Christian than partisan politics, and nowhere does Youngdahl express such a view. On the contrary, it can be maintained that the effectiveness of the Christian vocation can be expressed as suitably—and often more adequately—by the party member, in comparison to the independent who must often be aware of his solitary position.

A Christian is not frightened by the compromise and conflict within party politics—not if he is more concerned about effectively serving his fellow man than about keeping himself pure and unspotted. He looks for the circumstances in which he can promote the most good. If he is convinced that partisanship has a direct influence on the shaping of policy and the choosing of political leaders, he will become a member of the party and absorb a share of the power inherent in such deliberations. He may not approve of everything he sees or all the activities in which he participates. Not everyone in the party will be motivated by high ideals; and there will be no dearth of internal conflict, in the struggle for control. The neophyte party member may have difficulty deciding when to speak out—and when to remain silent and "go along" with the party. He may become impatient with the sluggish pace with which the party moves toward enlightenment. He will have to watch while his party campaigns for men whom he opposed in party councils. But he accepts these contradictions as the burden of responsible citizenship; because he fears that if he rejects party policies, someone lacking in conscientious motivation will move into his place and take control. It is a rugged life, but he will not withdraw from it.

Minnesota politics—politics all over the nation—definitely requires both the independents, who crusade for worthy programs, and the "party wheels," who carry on the undramatic processes of day by day politics. Often the independent can arouse public interest out of its lethargy, but his work will make no permanent contribution if there are not a sufficient number of conscientious citizens within the parties—where the power is concentrated, and wielded—to sustain the programs launched by the crusaders. Let the party politicians be willing to acknowledge that they need the irritant action of an independent on the war path, but let the independent refrain from disdaining the faithful party worker whose preseverance lubricates the political machinery, day by day, week in and week out. They need one another, and they both need the sustaining grace of God and the perspective that the Christian faith provides.

Special interest pressure groups have considerable political power. Several circumstances added together create a situation in Minnesota which enables special pressure groups to wield a great amount of political power. The weak party system cripples the major parties' potential ability to "play off" one group against another and to formulate a balance by compromise and bargaining. The non-partisan legislature makes it difficult to prevent lobbyists from unduly influencing lawmakers. Because legislators must depend on other means of support than party funds during campaigns, and inadequate legislative salaries during their terms in office, they are susceptible to employment offers from pressure groups. A number of the legislators serve in the dual capacity of lawyers or public relations men for private concerns and elected representatives of the people. The complicated legislative process allows the lobbyists—who are on the scene—an advantage over the public in bringing influence to bear upon committees at strategic times.

The groups with the most money at their disposal can wield

the most influence, not necessarily by outright bribery (which is more infrequent than most people imagine) but by virtue of having enough people employed to contact lawmakers. The groups with the most at stake exert themselves the most vigorously to put pressure on the legislature. In Minnesota, the most effective lobbies were business and industrial groups with much at stake in tax and labor legislation. In recent years, labor union lobbies have increased their activities and their effectiveness. Groups like the League of Women Voters must rely more on the appeal to conscience and reason.

In Youngdahl's mind the special interest lobbyists were "the bad boys" of Minnesota politics. He fought them openly and expressed himself boldly in exposing their activities. Because strong political parties were unavailable as a check on these groups, he sought other means to offset their power. Inspired by his great faith in "the people's lobby," he relied on building up a wave of public opinion so strong that it would express itself in individual action of one sort or another, such as letter-writing and lobbying. (Note: See farewell address excerpts p. 225f.) He valued his citizens' committees as a method of persuading the general public to return to active roles in government.

There is no question that special interest lobbies wield more power than is legitimate and right, and that they are so often so overwhelmingly dominated by selfish interest that they can be characterized as the villains of politics. But here, too, the danger of over-simplification confronts us. Lobbying in itself is a legitimate activity. It provides constituents with a means of informing legislators of their needs, and of defending themselves against unjust legislation. The objective of lobbying is therefore ambiguous when analyzed in ethical terms—it is a mixture of the good and the bad. It is vitally important, as George Graham has observed, for leaders of economic groups to recognize a public responsibility to keep their special interests and loyalties within bounds of the general welfare of the people. If they do not, a more tightly organized government and greater limitations on their freedom will have to be devised. (Note: **Morality in American Politics,** p. 305) The need for inner integrity within the leadership of special economic groups is just as necessary as it is within political parties. Rules, laws, and restrictions can always be bypassed by unscrupulous men. The Christian faith creates the inner will to serve, rather than be served, and thus is a source of potent vitality for American politics.

The voter. Finally, there is the almost forgotten voter who still retains an important share of political power. In Minnesota, Youngdahl had many characteristics that made him popular with the average voter, and with the Scandinavian voter in particular. It was not only the charm of a Swedish name that attracted them, but also his personification of many of the virtues admired in Minnesota—love of the outdoors, robust physique, honesty and humaneness, and a cultural outlook and moral perspective that appealed to the voters. However, this does not make him unique. Other candidates for office have possessed all or most of these qualities.

Youngdahl is unique in that he attracted the support of the church people. Whether or not he recognized the political strength of this bloc of voters or deliberately bid for their vote, he was the sort of politician that church members were pleased to see in office. He was able to interpret their will and formulate a program that would win their support. The numerical extent to which church people supported him remains to be measured statistically. However, Youngdahl's popularity with them suggests that there exists, in the church membership of a community, a reservoir of political power which sincere, outspoken Christians in politics could release.

Youngdahl's own membership in a church and his Christian family heritage helped to shape his outlook, even if only indirectly.

Youngdahl's opportunities to discuss public policy with a group of church members, assembled for that specific purpose, were infrequent. The meeting with the Minnesota Council of Churches committee, to discuss the migrant workers' situation, is one of those rare instances. To what extent he submitted to "the discipline of discussion," or committed himself to supporting an official proposal of the church body on a social issue, is problematic. Nevertheless, his participation in the life of the church contributed indirectly to the shaping of his ideas, for he often acknowledged the influence of prayer, the Bible, and preaching, on his life.

Youngdahl's eagerness to make frequent personal contacts with people, as well as his warm and enthusiastic platform manner, must be considered assets in evaluating his political strategy; for his appeals for the support of the people had the effect of making the voter feel that his own role in politics was important.

PART II

Evaluation: The Churches' Role in Minnesota Politics, 1947-1951

The Minnesota church picture reflects the divisions in American Christendom. There are nine Protestant denominations with memberships of over 10,000 and several smaller ones; the seven Lutheran groups range in size from 195,833 to 20,344; the Roman Catholic membership is about 726,000. The Lutheran churches comprise a dominant element, because so many of the immigrants who established pioneer homes in Minnesota came from the Scandinavian countries and Germany. They would be more dominant if there had not been a strong tendency to isolate themselves from other churches and to be passive in shaping social policy. Some of the Lutheran groups have been deeply influenced by evangelical revivals and Pietism, movements that stress the subjective religious experience and underplay the role of the Christian in society.

The Minnesota Council of Churches has been described previously as the cooperative organ for all major Protestant groups except the Lutherans. Its political action program has emerged within the last ten years, but behind it there is a long tradition of social concern that is characteristic of the Protestant council of churches movement.

Two limitations must be borne in mind when considering the following analysis of the political activities of Minnesota churches. First, no intensive examination of the political action program of each major group has been made. Attention is centered on the Augustana Lutheran Church, because it is the church which numbers Youngdahl among its members; and on the Minnesota Council, because it is the organ of cooperative action for most of the Protestant bodies. The other limitation exists because no instrument for measuring the political effects of church activities has been devised; this circumstance eliminates any attempt to evaluate the **political power** of the churches—the extent to which their activities shaped the course of events cannot be charted.

The main concern is not with the churches' **success** in affecting Minnesota politics; rather it involves a relative appraisal of the kind of legislation the churches supported and the type of activity with which they were associated. From the analysis of the activities of the two groups mentioned above, and from isolated instances of activities of other groups on various issues, it is possible to raise some questions about the role of the churches in politics anywhere in America. These questions may be suggestive enough to make it obvious that the churches need to analyze what they are doing and not doing in politics, and the reasons why.

Types of Legislation of Interest to the Churches

Graph A pictures the extent of church activity on behalf of thirteen legislative issues that were much publicized during Youngdahl's administration, some of which he strongly advocated and others of which he did not.

GRAPH A
EXTENT OF CHURCHES' INTEREST AND ACTION ON LEGISLATION

	NONE AT ALL	ISOLATED INSTANCES	PULPIT USED TO URGE ENDORSEMENT	INFORMATION SPREAD BY MAIL OR PULPIT	RESOLUTIONS, PETITIONS, LETTER-WRITING CAMPAIGNS	TESTIFYING AT COMMITTEES, CONFERENCES	SUPPORT OF LOBBYING GROUPS	PRESSURE TACTICS
ANTI-SLOT			A O	SC A LC O	SC LC A (8)* O	SC LC A		O
LIQUOR CONTROL			A	SC	SC A	O SC	A O	
MENTAL HEALTH			O	SC	A (8)* LC SC	Uni-tarians SC		
YOUTH CONSERVATION		O A (2)*		SC	SC	O		
FAMILY COURT		A (1)* O		SC	SC			
F.E.P.C.	A A	O		SC	SC	O		
AID TO DEPENDENTS	A	O		SC				
MIGRANT WORKERS †	A			SC	SC	SC		
NO-STRIKE BILL	A A				SC‡			
OTHER LABOR BILLS	A SC							
GOVERNMENTAL REFORM	A SC O							
BEER TAX	SC O	A (1)						
OTHER TAXES	A SC O							

† (State Council study initiated action)
‡ State Council Labor Committee only
A —Augustana
SC—State Council
LC—Local Councils
O —Other church groups
* Indicates number of congregations taking action

Instances of Political Action

Support of the anti-slot machine bill. By far the most extensive, dramatic and effective political activity of the churches occurred during the law enforcement campaign of the 1947 session. This campaign resulted in the formation of social action committees by a few local councils of churches, as well as one which was organized by the Minnesota Council. Representatives of denominational bodies and other clergymen, speaking for themselves (but in effect representing the churches), testified at committee hearings and held conferences with legislators. One clergyman went so far as to give warning that a significant number of church people would take action if the bill were not passed out of committee onto the floor. Congregations forwarded resolutions and petitions endorsing the banning of slot machines. Church councils and social action committees organized letter writing campaigns. Church papers and pulpits were utilized to spread information about the bill and to urge the people to support Youngdahl's crusade.

Support of the United Temperance Movement

The U.T.M. conducts a sustained legislative lobby. Its leaders supply lawmakers with information on liquor consumption and its effects, draft bills for presentation by legislators in agreement with their views, testify at committee hearings, confer with law-makers, and supply churches with information on the progress of liquor control legislation. The organization is supported by several Protestant groups. The Lutheran Minnesota Conference of the Augustana Church supports it. In 1951, it appropriated $400.00 in its budget for the U.T.M. It receives a report from the organization, adopts it, and inserts it in its annual minutes. One of its pastors, Reuben Ford, recently was president. Many of its congregations continue to allow its representatives to speak, arranging for free-will offerings for its work to be received at worship services—a procedure which harkens back to the days of the Anti-Saloon League. Other

Protestant churches preserve a similar relationship with the organization. This type of association actually serves as a lobby for the churches.

Unitarian Committee on Mental Health. The work of this committee originated in the sensitive conscience of a woman whose first-hand experience with conditions in the state mental hospital motivated her to urge that her church do something constructive about them. The woman was Engla Shey; and her efforts illustrate the fact that there are occasions when one lone individual, with compassion and a conscience, can energize a whole humanitarian movement. Her entreaties led to the establishment of the Unitarian Committee on Mental Health, which was prudent enough to conduct a careful study of conditions in the hospitals. The report captured Youngdahl's attention and convinced him of the necessity for hospital reform. The committee continued to perform the roles of "watch-dog" and "helpmeet," as the Governor's "crusade for forgotten souls" progressed.

Minnesota Council of Churches Migrant Workers Committee. For a number of years the Minnesota Council of Churches has conducted an annual religious and recreational program for the many migrant workers who are seasonally employed to harvest and process vegetables for canning companies. Its staff soon discovered that living and working conditions among the migrants were sub-standard. The Council appropriated funds for a study. The study resulted in recommendations for a migrant labor code, with the committee testifying at the legislative session. When it appeared that the bill would be defeated, the committee began to hold conferences with key legislators and administrators and to organize state-wide support for the bill. Youngdahl became interested in promoting the measure and it was passed.

Churchmen for Youngdahl. A unique type of activity among churchmen was the well-organized statewide campaign on behalf of Youngdahl's candidacy in 1950. Although this movement was officially endorsed by only one church organization, it was actively supported by pastors and laymen of several denominations. Some clergymen allowed their names to appear in an advertisement endorsing Youngdahl. One even defied precedent by endorsing him from the pulpit. The significant feature of the program was the retaining of an organizer to concentrate full-time on the campaign for several months. He was Alfred France, Jr., an Episcopalian.

Legislative Information Service of the Minnesota Council of Churches. This project was undertaken for the 1951 legislative session, on a part-time basis. The legislative representative, William Gerberding, did not lobby to the extent of trying to persuade lawmakers to adopt proposals the Council favored. His assignment involved keeping an eye on the advancement of legislation of interest to churches and sending out news bulletins on the progress. When crucial points were approaching, he dispatched wires to key leaders. His bulletins urged the support of several types of legislation. His work was not carried on in isolation. The Council also had a social action committee that endorsed several types of legislation—in its own name, rather than under the authority of the supporting churches—and urged legislators to vote favorably on their recommendations.

Individual churchmen on citizens' committees. Youngdahl was able to gain the cooperation of many church people through the citizens' committees he organized to stimulate support for such projects as law enforcement, youth conservation, mental health and social welfare. The role of the organized churches in this type of activity is indirect—principally to inspire and teach its members to be good citizens and to take advantage of every opportunity to work for good government. One Lutheran pastor was on the Commission for the aging. All major religious groups were represented on the Displaced Persons committee. Catholic priests have served on the state human rights commission, as have Protestant ministers and Jewish rabbis. Churchmen were leading participants in the Governor's conferences on youth. There were both clergymen and active laymen on the mental health committees.

Individual churchmen in political parties. There are people who are both active Christian laymen and active participants in major political parties—probably far more of them than is generally imagined. Some of them enter partisan politics with a sense of Christian vocation, as Bernhard LeVander did. They have their eyes wide open and know the rough realities of party politics, and they become involved in all the activities of the party councils; but, at the same time, they are conscious of a sense of responsibility for the public welfare that is inspired by their Christian faith.

Gaps in the political action program. The widest gaps in church political activity occur on the local level and in state denominational headquarters. There are few local social action committees in congregations, and some denominations (notably the Lutherans) do not have state social action commissions. The lack of committees indicates that church action is sporadic, impulsive and delayed. When someone stirs up enthusiasm about an issue (as Youngdahl did) the churches will impulsively pass a resolution. Their proposals often are not carefully phrased, because no committee has thoroughly studied the matter. Occasionally (as in the case of the Minnesota Lutheran Conference on the mental health program) a church body will come forward with a belated resolution commending a program for which someone else has fought. This conveys the impression that the church is too timid or too unconcerned to get into the fight before the issue is decided. Some churches even failed to participate in the anti-gambling crusade, on the assumption that the church should remain aloof from all political controversies.

Evaluation of Churches' Activities in Politics

These political activities of Minnesota church groups should suggest questions that church members everywhere in the nation might ponder.

Are churches willing to help shape public policy by discussing issues within their own fellowship and by declaring

their positions on these issues so that politicians can consider them?

By their activities, Minnesota churches confirm the impression that they are not deeply convinced that political action is a proper project for them to undertake. It is true that they were aroused to intensive activity on behalf of some issues, like gambling and liquor control; but these subjects are well-established, in the Protestant mind at least, as "moral" issues. When the appeal for their support was broadcast, it was not at all difficult to get action—even to the extent of lobbying for the legislation. On most other issues, little or nothing was done. When the Minnesota Council of Churches sent out bulletins on other legislation, it acted with cautious restraint, explaining and emphasizing that it did not lobby. At times the churches acted belatedly, issuing statements favoring legislation **after** it had been passed.

There are other evidences that the churches lack an intelligible conception of their task in relation to the state. Some churchmen failed to make the important distinction between activities involving the use of pressure (lining up votes against a candidate or bill unfavorable to their policies) and the appeal to conscience (pointing out the moral issues in proposals and urging politicians to support the cause of justice.) Thus on some occasions the church leaders avoided lobbying, confusing it with pressure tactics; on other occasions, they ventured beyond lobbying and employed the political threat (to line up votes). Their reaction was dependent upon the issue involved. Some church leaders regarded lobbying by churches as improper, regardless of the fact that face-to-face testimony has been a traditional means for Christians to bear witness in the world. Minnesota churches avoided using methods regularly employed by their own denominational leaders in the nation's capital. These inconsistencies are evidence of the churches' lack of certainty toward their role in politics.

This uncertainty also is revealed in the procedure by which churches arrived at policy statements on political and social issues. A majority of the state's church groups have no study commissions to keep the membership informed and to serve as an agency for preparing policy statements on behalf of the church. Local political action committees are an exception, rather than the rule. The Lutheran churches, especially, are lacking in any systematic method of policy formation. Occasional resolutions on social issues are presented to state conventions of the churches; but they are introduced on the floor late in the session, after many other matters have wearied the delegates. As a consequence, there is little or no genuine discussion of the issue. More frequently than any churchman desires to admit, policy statements are formulated by denominational leaders or small committees—with no clarifying statement to the effect that the policy has not been discussed by the constituency of their church. The procedure is sporadic and impulsive, rather than well-planned and firmly-grounded in an unfaltering conviction regarding the churches' role as the witness to God's law.

The story of what Minnesota churches have accomplished, by supporting some aspects of Youngdahl's program, encourages the belief that the churches could have a significant role in the formation of public policy. If church people might be taught that there are moral issues in all social issues, it would be possible to conduct a consistent political action program. They have been convinced that gambling and drinking contribute to evils they deplore. Their consciences have been made sensitive on those issues; and, as a result, it was not difficult to arouse them to vigorous activity in support of legislation compatible with their convictions. Social welfare and human rights are beginning to concern them sufficiently to arouse some political activity; but few church people see an issue of justice involved in tax policy, or possibilities for more orderly government involved in structural reforms. It was even more of an effort to promote action in most Minnesota churches on behalf of such social legislation as mental health, youth conservation and family courts; and nothing at all was done about taxation, party designation and similar issues.

It is highly expedient that the churches, on the local scene, begin making apparent to their members that they are responsible for ensuring that justice is done and that government is kept orderly and effective. Christians should be concerned about any political condition that undermines the power of the state to curb selfishness. Any social situation which neglects the needs of some people, even if they represent only an unpopular or weak minority, is a problem for the agenda of a church meeting. The Christian law of love is not primarily a matter of prohibiting activities that some people enjoy—it is a positive concern for the welfare of everyone. The churches' forthright discussion of political questions, at the World Council assemblies, needs to be carried on at a local level, too. Youngdahl managed to break down some of the resistance of church members who were reluctant to engage in vigorous political action close to home.

Do the churches help produce conscientious citizens? They accomplish this objective much more effectively than they assist in shaping public policy directly. Yet, Youngdahl was news—partially because so few church members who choose public careers are as explicit and deliberate about carrying their convictions with them into their political jobs. Because he was determined to demonstrate the political implications of his religious heritage, Youngdahl's convictions shaped the destiny of a whole state. His rise to power meant that his church indirectly played an important part in Minnesota politics. But being instrumental in shaping the convictions of a governor, his church was influential in framing public policy in Minnesota.

Why is Youngdahl the exception? Is it merely because he was more outspoken than most Christians in politics? Or is it because church members are not privileged to hear—often enough—the kind of teaching and preaching that urges the acceptance of civic duty as a calling from God? Are the churches too complacent about having members whose citizenship is limited to voting? In defense of their claim to be nonpartisan, have the churches fostered the belief that the most suitable role for a Christian is that of the independent who remains aloof from partisan politics? Have the churches made sufficiently clear that there are many stations of service in politics—not just those of voting and office-holding, but also party activity and lobbying?

The political power of the churches is not exerted most effectively by indirectly creating a moral climate, or by directly applying political pressure on lawmakers, or by pastors preaching about political issues. It is most effectively demonstrated in the actions of individual church members who perform conscientiously in the political station to which they feel called. These people have two effects; they activate the latent power of other Christians, and their opinions and decisions have a salutary effect on public policy. While it is true that the Christian politician would have a rugged time of it in a community where he is a part of a small minority, it is equally true that the Christian community in the churches is activated by its members who have been given special political responsibilities. The church is a body, and each member serves the whole body in his own way. The politician serves as a sentinel, ready to summon the other members to action when the occasion demands it.

American representative government depends largely on the quality of the men who serve in it. It depends on the intelligence and moral alertness of the voter, the devotion of the party worker to the common good, the integrity and astuteness of the legislator and executive, the devotion to justice in the hearts of its judges, and the self-discipline of those who represent special interests in our society. These are expected to answer the decrees of their own consciences, even more than they are expected to be responsive to the appeals and pressures of public opinion and special interests. Especially is this true of elected representatives. The American people entrust them with the task of governing them, for specified periods of time. While it is possible for the public to defeat an unsatisfactory public official when the next election rolls around, that man is free to act according to his conscience (to a greater or lesser extent, according to the office he holds) until that day of reckoning. If he is the kind of a man who ignores the "Thou shalt" of his conscience and instead submits to the enticements of personal power, or cringes before the threats of powerful interests, or is blandly indifferent to or unaware of the temptations and perplexities of his office, government is weaker for his being in office.

Harold Laski has rightly said, "The sole unwavering guarantee of democracy lies in the fact that every decision is made under the sanction of conscience." When men no longer make conscientious decisions, democracy will fail. By nurturing spiritually-sensitive citizens, the Church endows the State with people who are equipped to make suggestions of high moral value during the process of arriving at political decisions. These people, in turn, have immeasurable influence in their positions of leadership and can promote justice by inspiring the Christian people, whom they represent, to support them.

Luther W. Youngdahl of Minnesota marches up the high road, in the history of his state, as a governor who was a living symbol of that kind of Christian citizen.

Appendix

An Enduring Democracy

Reprint in its entirety of a prize-winning oration, AN EN-
DURING DEMOCRACY, delivered in the Triangular Oratorical
Contest at Augustana College, May 2, 1919, by Luther W. Young-
dahl representing Gustavus Adolphus College.

Democracy is the watchword of the age. A century and a
half ago a new nation was born dedicated to the ideals of
freedom and self-government. The French people desiring to
honor this new nation and to recognize the principles for
which it stood placed an heroic figure symbolizing the spirit
of liberty at the entrance to its chief harbor. Little did they
realize how brilliantly the rays from the lamp which that
figure held aloft should penetrate the gloom of old world oppression, illuminating its dark corners and stirring new emo-
tions in the ears of men.

It marked the dawn of a new epoch. Rapidly the ideals of
America spread over the civilized world, alarming the despots,
autocrats and junkers who schemed to combat the new-born
spirit of the West. It soon became clear that two forces, so
antagonistic, must sooner or later struggle for existence. We
have just witnessed the culmination of that struggle.

It is too early for our minds yet to completely grasp the
deep significance of the cataclysm that occurred when the
German hordes poured out over the fields of Belgium to burn,
ravish, and murder. The horror of it swept over France,
across the channel into England and thence over the Atlantic
to America itself; it crept over Poland, the Balkans and Asia
Minor; it turned Russia into a mad-house, and today threatens
a great portion of the rest of the world with a like fate.

Out of it all, however, there stands forth one ideal, expressed in one word that tells us that it has not all been in
vain. That word is today on every lip. It is Democracy. Thrones
are tumbling on every hand; crowns are being cast into the
scrap heaps and emperors and kings are fleeing in the night.
Democracy is indeed the watchword of the age.

Does this mean the beginning of better things for men? Or does it but mark an epoch which in time will pass? Has Democracy come to stay, or will it as its forerunners, pass and again give way to tyranny? What does the future hold in its embrace?

There is a rule which seems to run throughout human history which might be applied to the questions that are in our minds. That rule is, "That which deserves to survive will survive." For 6000 years of authentic history autocrat kings and militant junkers have sought to trample out the fires of liberty that have burned forth here and there.

Leonidas and his three hundred companions perished, but the liberty of Greece lived on. Arnold Winlerud received the spears of the foemen in his heart as he cried "Make way for Liberty," but Switzerland stood free. Nathan Hale was hanged; his compatriots left their blood stained footprints amid the snow at Valley Forge, died with Arnold in the charge at Saratoga, hungered, suffered and bled through seven years of bitter war, but America was born. France saw her streets run red with blood, her liberty snatched from the hands of a people by a despot whom she herself had reared and educated, but the despot died a broken prisoner on a lonely island; and the Republic of France lives.

The Hohenzollern, with his mighty armies, equipped with all the hellish and cunning ingenuity that a conscienceless and scientific mind could produce, bade defiance to the world and determined to make himself the supreme warlord of the universe. His mighty armies poured over the borders of France and like the scourge of God pillaged, destroyed, burned, ravished and murdered. The forces of civilization were thrown back until that fateful date on the shores of the Marne when Marshal Joffre, echoing the spirit of France, gave forth the words that passed from lip to lip over the French armies, "They shall not pass." Whole regiments of Frenchmen perished where they stood that day but the Huns did not pass and the world was saved from the dominance of the Hohenzollern.

Liberty has endured, because in the happiness it has given it has demonstrated that it deserves to live.

Two thousand years ago a cult sprang up amid the hills of Judea; its leader was the Master himself. The rulers said, "We must destroy this man and his teachings for He is detrimental to our interests." They crucified him one day on a lonely hill just outside of Jerusalem. They went home that day feeling satisfied that they had ended Jesus and His teachings, but in three days the word went like wild fire from village to village, "He has risen from the dead." In three months He had 3,000 followers in Jerusalem alone. In three years His teachers were all over southern Europe and His doctrines were knocking at the courts of Rome itself. In three centuries Christianity was the state religion of the Roman Empire and today it stands as the recognized religion of all the civilized world.

When the world war began men said that Christianity had failed and that the war would bring a new form of worship, but somehow as the soldier knelt in the silent watches of the night face to face with death, the comfort of its saving grace touched his heart and made him feel secure. As he lay upon the battlefield torn and bleeding, the cooling touch of the hand of her whom the soldier called the Rose of heaven, that gentle spirit, who inspired by his love for men and wearing his cross upon her head as her emblem, helping friend and foe alike, soothed the frayed nerves and silently but eloquently testified of him. And away back of the battle-line in some distant home and beside some distant fireplace sat a brave little woman, secure in the faith that come what may the everlasting arms would be about her dear one and that everything possible would be done to ease and comfort him.

Christianity has come through the war stronger for the tests to which it has been put. It has been tried in the fire. The dross of human notions that time has mixed with the pure gold has been burned away, but the gold remains cleaner and brighter than ever.

Human freedom and Christianity represent the two ideals of civilized men; they have endured because they have been gold pure and clean; because of the joy and comfort that they have brought to the race, they have deserved to live. Will Democracy, measured by the same rule, survive?

Unfortunately there are many today who seem to believe that in the mere word Democracy there is a magical saving grace. "Democracy in itself, means neither the ruin nor the salvation of the land." It is but a means to an end. The mere mouthing of the word, without a true conception of its meaning cannot cure any ills. A maze of misconception has grown up regarding its meaning. These misconceptions have in some cases been written into our laws and in others have served to form the foundation of agitators and demagogues.

Thousands of our sons lie sleeping in foreign soil and beneath foreign skies in order that the world might be safe for Democracy. The power of militarism is broken; the danger to Democracy from the outside for the present can be utterly disregarded. The dangers from within are real and definite. To shut our eyes in the midst of them is fatal.

Under the free and easy laws of our country, surrounded by unbounded natural resources and with an unparalleled growth of population; with wonderful material advances in the way of inventions and with humanity's increasing need for products a century ago unheard of and unforeseen, the opportunities for money making have been exceptional. Men have become millionaires overnight and enthused with their good fortune they have forgotten their comrades of yesterday and immediately proceeded to live as no king or potentate in ages gone by even dreamed. Others envious, have sought to equal or excel. The building of great fortunes, most of which have been unearned and either the result of accident or good fortune or methods that to say the least are questionable, have resulted in laying the foundation for a money aristocracy perhaps in some cases more cruel and oppressive than the old aristocracy founded on blood.

On the other hand those who have been less fortunate, and who have fallen into the great class of workers, bereft of their tools by science, ruthlessly at times robbed of their rights, have become sullen and discontented. Glib-tongued agitators have found an easy and ready hearing; the wrongs have been magnified, the privileges minimized; class distinction has been harped upon until we have begun to believe that there are two or three distinct classes in the United States, forgetting that Jim Hill the Capitalist of yesterday was the day before that, Jim Hill the section hand and shutting our eyes to the fact that the door of opportunity still stands wide open to all.

Labor and capital are both essential in modern civilization; they are not natural enemies, as we have been led to believe; they are natural friends. It would be better for both if they would realize how necessary each is to the other's comfort and happiness. In an effort to cure the evils of class distinction, class hatred and class oppression that have arisen, many sure cures and legal hobbies have been proposed, none of which have met with any satisfaction.

To find the cure, we must go deeper; we must sheer off from the notions and misconceptions that have grown up about our Democracy among our own people and seek for the true meaning of the word. Is it not this? Democracy is the equality of opportunity and the equality of rights. The first idea is true and worthy. The second, I believe, has been overemphasized and in its place I should like to suggest an old thought in new words.

It would be EQUALITY OF OBLIGATION.

When the storm of pent-up human passion, engendered through years of despotic but efficient training, broke forth four years ago, engulfed Europe and threatened the very liberty of America, we forgot about our rights and remembered our obligations. The youths of the land were called into the first line, in the training camps, on the battleships and in the trenches, the sons of rich men and poor men slept, fought, suffered and died comrades. The silk stockings and the cotton socks alike were exchanged for the army wool. Artificial barriers, class distinction, class jealousy were obliterated, and under the solemn obligation that they owed alike they stood forth one united band, girded and prepared to fight and where need be, die for Democracy.

In the second line, were the men and women at home, who served in the Red Cross work, in the Y.M.C.A., in the shell factories, who gave and then gave more, all inspired not with the thought of rights, but of sacred obligations.

If Democracy is to endure, it must stand the test of fire and steel; more, it must prove its worth. Two thousand years ago, the Master, teacher of Galilee, said, "He that would be greatest among you, let him be servant of you all." Service rendered by one man to another not because of any right that one man might have to expect from the other, but rather because of the sacred obligations that each member of the human Fraternity owes to each other member was the central thought in his teaching. It has endured the vicissitudes of twenty centuries; it is worthy to form one of the pillars of our Democracy.

If the employer of labor thought less of his rights, paid less for efforts to enforce those rights, and remembered more the sacred obligations that he owes to his employee, how different the lot of the employee would be, how happier his home conditions, how more contented every workman, how much more interested in the business of the employer, and how much more efficient a workman. If the employee, could but for a moment lose sight of his right as an individual, and think more of the obligations that he owes to the employer, how much less there would be of strikes, lockouts and disorders.

This conception of Democracy must become our slogan. EQUALITY OF OPPORTUNITY AND EQUALITY OF OBLIGATION. Our educational system is splendid, it must be made better and more universal; there should be more legislation to prevent the passing of vast fortunes from generations to generations and less of direct taxes upon the people. The natural resources should be preserved as far as reasonably possible, in order that the future generations might participate in their enjoyment. The door of opportunity must be opened to all alike but with it must go the obligation. He who is given the opportunity equally must also share the obligation equally. This portion of our conception of Democracy must equally be built up into our public schools; it must be taught to our young through universal training; it must be made to form the foundation of our laws. We shall have thus combined into our democratic system of government the two ideals for which men have gladly gone to death, the ideals which have given men the only assurance of real happiness, the one political, and the other religious. We shall have laid a firm foundation for an enduring Democracy.

The test of fire and steel is over. The rattle of musketry, the thunder of cannon, the death cry and victory-shout alike are hushed. Soon the gentle pasque flower will bloom upon the fields so recently drenched with blood. Democracy's sons have fought well; the test of fire and steel has been heroically met. Let us, still comrades in arms, as earnestly and heroically labor, to make our Democracy meet the second and greater test. In the bettered social conditions, in the larger measure of prosperity, peace and contentment, in the nearer approach to the hope and dream of all ages that a time shall come when poverty, oppression, social and political inequality shall have passed, when the measure of a man shall be, neither what he has nor who he is, but what he does, may we prove Democracy's worth and justify our faith that it will endure.

—Luther W. Youngdahl

Inaugural Address

EXCERPTS FROM THE INAUGURAL ADDRESS OF
GOVERNOR LUTHER W. YOUNGDAHL
DELIVERED AT A JOINT SESSION OF THE
MINNESOTA LEGISLATURE,
WEDNESDAY, JANUARY 8, 1947.

The fighting has officially stopped!

The President of the United States has just declared the cessation of hostilities in the most destructive war of all history. Victory in this war has come to us since the Legislature last assembled. Our young men and women no longer face the horrors of modern war. Thanks be to God, most of them are home again. We who have survived the terrific struggle have a profound obligation to the thousands who did not come back. It is our sacred duty to carry on now with the same steadfastness and devotion which they so unselfishly gave in war. Because of their sacrifice, we are able to meet here today—an assembly of free people. We prove ourselves worthy of their sacrifice only as we consecrate ourselves in the highest degree to the great tasks of building the peace.

The men, the women, and the children of Minnesota worked long and hard at home, in field, in factory, and in mines to support our fighting men. Because of the efforts of all those who worked and fought and died, the world today has a hope for peace through the United Nations. We pray God that it may succeed!

Aesop, in one of his fables, tells of a lion and a goat quarreling at a water hole as to which should drink first, although there was plenty of room for them to drink together. As they were preparing to fight it out, they looked up and saw some vultures wheeling low above them, waiting for the battle and its aftermath. So, says the fable, they decided to drink together. The vultures fly low over the world today. They have picked the bones of previous civilizations that have fought it out. That shall be our fate, too, unless we learn to live together.

We meet here in this fifty-fifth session of the Legislature during one of the most crucial and difficult periods of American history. In the wake of war are many problems. This first postwar Legislative session presents to us, as the chosen leaders of the people, a heavy burden of responsibility. But it also presents an opportunity for real service by establishing a record of constructive achievement that will be far-reaching in its effect upon future generations in Minnesota. The task will not be easy. In our all-out participation in the war so recently ended, we have had to neglect many services and activities which are vital to the well-being of our state. Now that the fighting has stopped, we must marshal our energies and resources to meet these needs.

Never before in the history of this state has the Legislature faced so many serious needs for our schools, for the mentally ill, and for welfare and other services. These demands confront us at a time when our state income is falling from temporary high war levels. Sky-rocketing costs have aggravated the situation. We know what has happened to our family budgets as a result of the deflated value of the dollar. What affects us in balancing our family budgets, affects as well the operation of the state's business. For example, costs of clothing for those in our mental institutions have risen as much as two and three hundred percent.

Despite these increased costs, we must meet the impelling needs. Money that is carefully appropriated for our schools, for certain essential activities in home building, for public health, for care for the mentally sick, for dependent children, for the blind and for the recreation and guidance of our youth, is not an expenditure in the real sense of the word. It is an investment in the character, stability and happiness of our people. I feel confident that the great majority of the people of Minnesota are determined that we shall meet these needs, and that they are willing to pay for them through as fair a method of taxation as can be devised.

The war caused many strains and disruptions of our economy. Now Government and Industry are busy reconverting an economy of war into one of peace. In business and finance, we

Luther Youngdahl and his children prepare for a fishing trip

Hunting in Northern Minnesota

Fishing at Youngdahl Point

quickly see the need for this economic reconversion. But we are not always so ready to see the importance of bolstering our moral and spiritual resources, which, in the disillusioning aftermath of war, suffer a slump. We must have the vision to encourage those activities which build up the decencies of human life—the spiritual qualities that redeem man from brutality and give him moral dignity and worth.

General Douglas MacArthur, as he accepted the surrender of the Japanese militarists on the Battleship "Missouri," pointed to the basic need of the world. He said that we required a moral regeneration—that it must be of the spirit if we are to save the flesh. Yes, men are redeemed spiritually through the still, small voice of conscience, properly disciplined by the teachings of home, church, and school.

Therefore, let us resolve to strengthen these institutions. We have advanced far in penetrating the frontiers of science. The frontier of the next few decades which we must explore is that of the field of human relations. There is no alternative if the world is to survive. And we must begin right here in our state —Minnesota—and in our home communities and families.

We have long talked about World Brotherhood. It was a beautiful ideal. Today, it is no longer an ideal, but an absolute necessity. The fate of civilization hangs in balance. We must have World Brotherhood, or else! The war has brought home to us the grim picture of what that "or else" means. The thousands upon thousands of starving Greeks; the hollow-cheeked Frenchmen eating thistles; the terrible slaughter of the Polish Jews; the children of under-nourished mothers being born, literally, without fingernails; the torture of Norwegians in concentration camps; the death march at Bataan; the merciless beheading of our own airmen—these fill the pages of the history of World War II. We ought to know by now that we must have Brotherhood, or else. We will secure brotherhood by building up our human resources at the community level. It will cost money. But there is no alternative. We have got to find the way.

It is related that off the New England Coast a ship was hurled mercilessly against the rocks. The Coast Guard arrived, under the command of an experienced Captain. There were some inexperienced fellows on board who lacked vision and courage. One of them said to the Captain, "Captain, with that tide against us and the terrific gale, we will be able to get out there all right, but we will never be able to get back." To this the Captain responded, "Prepare the boat. We have got to go out, we don't have to come back."

And so it is with us. Despite the difficulties, we have got to find the means to conduct research in the field of human engineering. If we did not shirk in financing a war, bringing unfathomable destruction, we dare not shirk the much lighter task of financing construction. We have got to go out, we don't have to come back. Who wants to come back to Hiroshima? Who wants to come back to Nagasaki? Who wants to come back to a world on fire?

Through education and all the moral and spiritual forces at our command we must take up the continual battle against the evils of greed, bigotry and war. The future depends upon whether we learn the simple but seemingly difficult lesson of living together in a spirit of understanding and amity, regardless of differences of color, creed, political or religious convictions, or circumstances of birth. Like the animals in Aesop's fable either we must live together, or we shall perish.

Four broad but impelling objectives urge us to joint action at this historic session of the Legislature.

    I. We must build up our human resources.

   II. We must strengthen our economic resources.

  III. We must increase the efficiency of our state government.

  IV. Boldly, we must provide the necessary revenue to meet our challenging post-war needs.

I. THE FIRST OBJECTIVE

Education

In the attainment of our first objective, which is to strengthen our human resources, our school system will play a vital part. Minnesota ranks very poorly when compared with other states in the number of farm boys who graduate from high school. This is unfair to our rural youth; it is also unfair to our state. Our history sparkles with stories of farm boys who have become state and national leaders. Even though they choose agriculture as their career—and there is no more worthy vocation—they should have the benefit of at least a high school education to keep pace with an industry that is becoming increasingly scientific.

More than 27,300 students are now enrolled at our great State University, the greatest enrollment in its history. Staffs, salaries, space and equipment are plainly inadequate in the face of this unprecedented problem. The Federal Government, through payment of special tuitions to war veterans, has increased its aid to the University, and the state must do its share in providing financial assistance. Our institutions of higher learning carry on valuable research that continually penetrates new frontiers of science. The value of this research was made outstandingly clear during the war. We must do all we can to enable Minnesota institutions to carry on in research and in the training of future scientists.

We have considered our educational system, and some of the means by which it may be improved. Some may say that we cannot afford these improvements; that we have reached the limit of our appropriations. I submit this proposition: we cannot afford **not** to invest more money in education. If education is to be rescued from its present peril, we have no alternative. Courageously, in spite of all difficulties, we must launch out!

Housing

Perhaps no matter is more constantly before us these days than the housing shortage. This is not simply a problem of lumber and bricks, but is directly related to our first main objective, the conservation of human resources. Worry, broken homes, juvenile delinquency; these are but a few of the evils which follow in the train of the housing shortage. To say that our Federal Government has bungled the job of providing homes may well be true, but naming a scapegoat will not supply more homes for anyone. In the interest of veterans and all citizens who deserve and demand decent housing, we must meet the emergency by matching federal aid with state action.

Mental Hospitals

We have stated our first big objective to be the conservation of our human resources. Another aspect of this main objective is support for our mental hospitals.

Minnesota is below the average among the states in the care of the mentally ill. We should not be satisfied until we have done everything possible to assist the unfortunate individuals confined in these institutions, and to re-establish as many of them as possible as useful members of society. Consideration should be given to providing adequate psychiatric service for each mental hospital.

One of the more urgently needed improvements in our program for the mentally ill is an institution for children with serious mental and emotional disturbances who are unable to adjust themselves either in their own homes or in foster homes, and for whom no facilities are available at the present time. It is recommended that the Legislature authorize as a part of the appropriation for mental hospitals the construction and operation of such a children's institution, and until a building can be provided temporary facilities should be established for this purpose.

Youth Conservation

We come now to a problem which, as you know, is of special interest to me—the conservation of our youth. Here is one of our greatest human resources. The time has come when we must reappraise our whole philosophy in connection with the problems of youth. It deserves our special consideration and prompt action. It is essentially a problem of prevention. The factors which have caused juvenile delinquency are multiple and complex and our attack must likewise be many-sided. Every institution and agency must be used: homes, churches, schools, recreational centers, health services, child guidance clinics and every interested public and private group.

There will be submitted for your consideration a Youth

Conservation Act. By this legislation we will promote good citizenship, attack the problem of delinquency and, if all else fails and a youthful offender is brought into Court, we will provide appropriate treatment for each specific case.

This matter of youth conservation, although somewhat intangible, is desperately real. We must face it; we must attack it; we have got to launch out.

Law Enforcement

To implement our constructive program for the strengthening of those great human resources which are to be found in the youth of our state, it is my intention to do everything in my power to enforce the laws of this state fairly, fearlessly and effectively.

I favor a strengthening of the provisions and enforcement of laws relating to the sale and licensing of beer and intoxicating liquors. There should be uniform standards for licensing, uniform closing hours and uniform regulations with respect to the presence of minors.

Human Relations

As the final aspect of our first main objective, we come to the important problem of promoting good will between racial and religious groups. In the great arena of international relationships, we are all deeply concerned. Regardless of differences in ideology, we are concerned with the problem of getting along with Russia; we are concerned with the relations between colonial powers and their colonies; we are concerned with the development of friendship between Orientals and Occidentals; we are concerned that all men should learn to live together as brothers.

In this day of nuclear energy and rocket projectiles the whole human race is involved in a struggle for survival. Each one of us is a part of that struggle; the gist of the problem is individual. It is the problem of being able to live with one another in the basic relationships of life: as husbands and wives, parents and children, employers and employees, white men and Negroes, Protestants, Catholics and Jews. Every unfair discrimination a white man practices against a Negro in our community relationships; every nasty slur voiced by a gentile against a Jew; every expression of contempt against a whole nation; every act of discourtesy or prejudice makes less possible the solution of mankind's gigantic problem.

Essentially this is a matter of conscience and good will; living together cannot be accomplished legislatively, but to prevent injustice, legislation is necessary. It should provide every opportunity through investigation and conciliation to eliminate the discrimination. As a last resort any person who has suffered from discrimination and who has exhausted all the possibilities of conciliation should have legal recourse in the courts of the state. Elaborate administrative machinery is not necessary. One full-time official, assisted by the advisory group of the Inter-Racial Commission, would be able to administer such a law. We would thus make a specific contribution toward the building of a society with equal opportunity for all its citizens.

I have discussed at some length the conservation of our human resources. These are the greatest assets of our state. An enlightened citizenry, showing a concern for its handcapped and needy members, courageously attacking the problems of education, housing, public health, youth conservation and racial discrimination—here is a goal that is worthy of all the thought and energy at our command, and if the faint heart should object that the difficulties lying in our course are insuperable, our answer must be, "We have no alternative; we have got to launch out!"

II. ECONOMIC RESOURCES

Conservation

We come now to our second main objective, the conservation and growth of our economic resources. Minnesota has been fortunately endowed with a great wealth of forests, lakes, streams and minerals. We are the custodians of that wealth. I know that you concur with me in wanting to see an active campaign of conservation of these resources that will move forward on all fronts in this postwar period.

Management-Labor Relations

Another way of strengthening our economic resources is to maintain stability in management-labor relations. Minnesota has had an enviable record under its labor-relations law. I believe that law should be continued and that we should be cautious in changing it unless we are sure that amendments will improve its operation and make for greater stability.

* * * * *

I have appreciated the opportunity to talk to many of you Legislators individually concerning these important problems. I have not been able to talk to all of you. I shall welcome the opportunity during the session to consult with any member, regardless of party affiliation, on any problem that concerns the welfare of the state. Our Constitution makes clear the division of powers between the Legislative and Executive branches of government. I want you to know, at the outset of our relationship, that I shall always be cognizant of that separation of authority. Together, we shall work out a program that will best meet the needs of all the people. Accomplishment can only come through cooperation and hard work by all of us.

Although I believe in the two-party system of government, the Governor is elected to serve **all** the people. It has been well said that politics is the machinery by which society makes its moral decisions. I believe strongly in that philosophy of politics. I shall endeavor to serve you without reference to blocs or pressure groups and without regard to political consequences; I shall attempt to follow my own convictions on any matter that comes before me. I assure you that I am free to do just that. I enter upon my duties in all humility and fully cognizant of my profound obligations.

We shall be facing trying days. The type of world in which we may live for the next quarter or half of a century may well be patterned by the type of thinking and example of our leaders during the next important years. I have sensed among you an appreciation of that fact as I have discussed the problems with you. I can assure you that I am deeply sensitive to it. I would feel very insecure were it not for my faith in God, and the fact that I shall be able to rely upon Him for guidance and support when discouragement and uncertainty come. I pledge to you and the people of this great state my best efforts. I shall consecrate and dedicate myself to serve all the people fairly. Let us, with God's help, join hands to make this a truly historic session in the preservation, conservation and improvement of our economic and human resources.

Over the grave of an American Colonel in Italy, who fell in battle, a Chaplain put as an epitaph words that had been familiar on the Colonel's lips. "Always take the high ground and the enemy will flee." If we take the high ground of consecration to public service, no situation can discourage and no disappointment defeat us in reaching our goal.

Today, no less than in war time, there is a premium on fortitude. In the face of tides of apathy, pessimism and timidity, endangered by the jagged rocks of practical difficulties and amid the cross winds of selfish interests, our duty is still clear. The words of the New England Coast Guard Captain still ring true, and they are spoken to us; "We have got to go out, we don't have to come back."

INAUGURAL ADDRESS OF
GOVERNOR LUTHER W. YOUNGDAHL
DELIVERED AT A JOINT SESSION OF THE
MINNESOTA LEGISLATURE AT 12:15 P.M.,
THURSDAY, JANUARY 6, 1949

This is 1949, the great Centennial year of Minnesota.

A great painter whose hand produced many a work of art was asked "Which is your greatest painting?" The artist paused a moment. "My greatest painting? The next one!"

The people of our state, in this Centennial year, look back upon a record of achievement. 1849-1949, a century of struggle and growth, a century of toil and sacrifice, a century in which a wilderness has been transformed into a great progressive commonwealth. The Centennial year marks a luminous place along our path; a year dedicated to the people who built Minnesota, to the countless unnamed pioneers who believed enough in her future to be pioneers; to the laborers in our iron mines or in the foundries of our cities; to the tillers of the soil who cleared a wilderness and brought out of it rich farms; to the vision of countless merchants and businessmen on our thousands of main streets; to the courage of the leaders of industry who launched out to new frontiers; to the men of the various professions who helped and guided and counseled their fellowmen; to the homemakers, the teachers, the political leaders, the religious leaders—to all who have built homes, schools, churches, and better communities—to all these we pay our tribute. All these were the builders of Minnesota.

The temptation at any anniversary observance is to glorify the past at the expense of the future. We honor the past, without it there would be no great present, but our eyes are fixed upon the future. The people of Minnesota, like the famous painter, are being asked to name their greatest century. Their reply must be "The next one!"

This next century depends upon the way in which we, the descendants of these great pioneers, build for the future; the way in which we, the children of those sturdy people, maintain the security, the freedom, and the democracy which we have inherited from them.

Two years ago the fighting had just officially stopped. We then faced a great challenge; we met in a critical hour of history. Today the problems are more complex and the challenge greater than ever.

Not so long ago a group of miners were entombed in one of the Kimberly Diamond Mines in South Africa. Surrounded by unlimited riches they slowly met their death. Starving for food, thirsting for water, in need of medical assistance, deprived of spiritual comfort, diamonds were worthless.

And so it is in our world today. We are discovering that accepted values must be reappraised. We are coming to understand that our claim to distinction and progress has been based on false standards.

We have been worshipping the gods of science and material advancement until now we see ourselves trapped by the monstrous weapons we have devised. Our ability to create has surpassed our ability to utilize wisely the products of our invention.

We are learned in the art of war—we are ignorant in the art of peace. We are proficient in the art of killing—we are unskilled in the art of living. We probe and grasp the mystery of atomic fission—we reject the Golden Rule and the Sermon on the Mount. We are being entombed to our death in the diamond mine of materialism.

There must be a place in our scheme of things for those great intangible human values which cannot be represented on graphs or ledgers. Our values must stem from the Fatherhood of God and the Brotherhood of man. We must stop gauging our success by production of machines or dollars of income. We have got to understand that important as it is to produce efficiency in the factory, it is even more important to build character in its workers and to turn out a product that will strengthen our nation. No standard of living is high when jobs become drudgery and hours dreary; when rancor and bitterness exist between management and labor; when young men and women can't afford a family; when children in slums are walled off by brick from sod and sky; where there is not equality of educational opportunity for every boy and girl; where decent health conditions are not afforded to all of our people. No standard of living is high where we do not fulfill our obligation to the needy, the aged, the crippled, the blind; the dependent and neglected children; where we fail in our duty to the individuals sick of mind; when we deny equal rights to our people because of race, creed, color, or nationality.

As we face the new century in Minnesota history we are confronted by a two-fold task: first, to mark out new horizons in human goals for which we strive. Second, to provide economic means by which these goals may be achieved.

I. THE GOALS FOR WHICH WE STRIVE

1. Mental Health

First in the consideration of our human goals is the mental health of our people. There are more than 10,500 individuals of good soul but sick mind in our state mental hospitals. They are but the vanguard of a vast number to follow, in which—and mark this well!—will be represented one member out of every five families. Unless modern research and preventive measures are immediately introduced, a large percentage of these people will continue to constitute a major human resource rushing down the drainpipe of social neglect.

Most persons have accepted without much questioning the idea, so widely prevalent, that there is some stigma attached to mental illness, that nothing can be done about it and that the unhappy victims must be put away somewhere in an institution to spend the rest of their days. These ridiculed, abused, and maligned members of our social family cannot speak for themselves. They are made mute by sickness, guarded walls, and the loss of their civil rights. Their heartbroken families are rendered equally silent by the cruel stigma which false social attitudes attach to the mentally ill. Casualties of the spirit, voiceless and powerless, their very personalities—yes, their very lives—are completely dependent on the concern, wisdom, and compassion of those of us who are more fortunate.

We need not detail here the disclosures of conditions which

have shocked those of us who have visited our mental hospitals here in Minnesota; the rows upon rows of unattended human beings, regimented and neglected because of lack of help, living lives of grim monotony and deteriorating emptiness, deprived of human rights and necessities.

In other states, conditions are much the same. Nowhere is man's inhumanity to man more pronounced than in our care of the mentally ill. The mental hospital of today is only a super-structure built on the foundation of the old asylum, representing a social monstrosity which plagues the whole nation with shame and disgrace.

It fails to return to society that high percentage of patients for whom modern psychiatry holds out hope. It similarly denies the milk of human kindness to those patients who, under present levels of scientific knowledge, are incurable. I caution here against any consideration of this problem which confines its attention solely to those deemed curable; even the most hopeless patient in our hospitals has something so precious that it cannot be judged in values other than human and divine.

The mental hospital system is the only major American social institution which has remained fundamentally unchanged since the abolition of its moral counterpart, slavery.

Our system of caring for and treating these sick human beings is outmoded. To protect society from the so-called "dangerous," to confine the helpless, to furnish a roof to house those falsely thought to be incurable—for this we would need only brick and mortar. We would need only fortified buildings to lock the patients in and the public out.

* * * * *

But the time when the mentally ill could be put away in an institution, "out of sight—out of mind," must end. I propose that we inaugurate the centennial year by pioneering to make the mental hospital in Minnesota a house of hope, rather than a habitation for the living dead. I propose that we equip our mental hospitals to give our patients the best possible care and extend to those who can be cured the fullest opportunity for rehabilitation. Many of the mentally ill in our hospitals can be restored to health with proper treatment, we now know, and go home to live normal, useful lives.

Our human goal should be to make Minnesota the first state in the nation to reach the standards of decency as are reflected by the standards of the American Psychiatric Association.

You have in previous sessions shown your sympathies by generous appropriations for the type of system which has prevailed. At the last session you approved a comprehensive and progressive building program, much of which is now under way. This session, I trust, will take the decisive step to adopt a new approach for the care of the mentally ill. The modern therapeutic center, "the house of hope," would replace the traditional state hospital. Characterized by research and active training of personnel, it would have links with the home and community through clinics and social work services, which would in turn provide early detection, possible non-hospital treatment, post-hospital follow-up care of discharged patients, and consultative and other services to courts, schools, and welfare agencies.

The details of this program will be supplied in my budgetary message. It is based not on how cheaply we can maintain a patient for life, but on how early we can detect his illness, how actively we can treat it, and how quickly we can discharge him. It is intended to increase the number of citizens returning to enrich the lives of their communities. In time it would end the costly and vicious circle of building an ever expanding system of costly custodial buildings to house an ever increasing backlog of needlessly deteriorating patients.

* * * * *

Due to low quotas, low salaries, lack of training, and shortages of trained personnel, we have a psychiatric corps large enough to serve less than 4,000 of the 10,500 patients in our seven mental hospitals. The situation in the institutions for the mentally deficient and epileptic is similar. Without trained personnel, physical facilities are of no avail.

Therefore, I recommend that we establish a quota of psychiatric workers in our mental health system which would permit us to reach the standards of the American Psychiatric Association during this biennium.

How will we obtain this personnel? First, we must go out into the open market and offer competitive salaries; second, we must train people to fill vacancies. The budget message will contain provisions to establish in the state hospitals at Hastings and Rochester the first two units of a proposed teaching service for the state, for the training of doctors and other members of the psychiatric team in short supply. Third, we must establish the 40-hour work week. Fourth, we must provide adequate housing for all employees living on the grounds.

One of the most vital posts in the psychiatric team is now held by the position, which since asylum days, has been termed "attendant." The term and function of "attendant" must be changed. The psychiatric worker for this position should be more than a mere guard and housekeeper. After additional scientific training he would be eligible for more specialized and responsible tasks.

One of the major and most justifiable criticisms against American mental hospitals pertains to the vicious caste system, typified by the double standard of diet. Unless we end the double standard of diet, we cannot expect that patients will have the feeling that the institution exists for them and not they for the institution. As a necessary step to increase the recovery rate—as a factor even more important than mere nutrition the program recommends funds, equipment, and dietitians to assure every patient a decent standard of food at least equal to that of the employees.

The program calls for adequate support of occupational, recreational, and other therapies designed to end the deteriorating idleness of state hospitals. The program calls for improved living conditions, adequate clothing, linens, and other personal necessities. Certain features deal with accelerated control of tuberculosis and other communicable diseases. The death rate from tuberculosis in our institutions is twenty times that of our general population. The program also would provide for an adequate staff of chaplains to give spiritual help and counsel to the patients.

Social systems, particularly those deeply rooted in the superstitions of our asylum past, are not changed over night. The program constitutes only the bare minimum required to start us on the long road ahead. It calls only for those factors which can be absorbed administratively in the next biennium. Due to the inflationary costs of building today, as well as to the increased expenses of introducing this pioneering service, requests for capital expansion and equipment, except where vitally necessary or to complete the current building program, will be deferred.

I also recommend (1) changes in the archaic terminology and content in laws relating to mental illness, and (2) statutory provisions for transfer of the mental health authority from the Department of Health to a separate bureau in the Division of Public Institutions, in which would be organized all mental health activities.

* * * * *

Human misery knows no geographical borders. We cannot hide behind the fact that conditions in other states are comparable to ours. We cannot hide behind the fact that no one individual is solely responsible for our "snakepits" and "bedlams." **Particeps criminis.** We have all participated in a social crime. Listen to the words of a grand jury investigating similar conditions in a mental hospital in another state:

"The grand jury condemns the whole system that today allows this unholy thing to exist in our state. The responsibility is widespread and it must be met. All must share in the guilt for this social crime against these innocent and helpless people. All must share in the responsibility for instituting redress of this long standing and terrible injustice."

The advance we are proposing in the frontier of mental health is the first and one of the most crucial of our human goals. Our mental hospitals may be no worse than the national average. But we must remember this: salvation comes to human society through vigorous minorities keeping alive a zealous protest against the deification of the average. The average is not good enough. We must not rest until Minnesota achieves the pre-eminent place among the states of the nation in its ministration to those who are mentally ill.

2. Education

The second important human goal is education. One hundred years ago Horace Mann, one of the great pioneers in education, affirmed that the aspirations for and the faith in the future of the human race "... depend upon teachers, more than upon **any,** more than upon **all** other human instrumentalities united." Almost a century later James Hilton also expressed the significance of the teacher in our society when he said: "If I had a child who wanted to be a teacher I would give him Godspeed as if he were going to a war. For indeed the war against prejudice, greed and ignorance is eternal, and those who dedicate themselves to it give their lives no less because they may live to see some fraction of the battle won. They are the commandoes of the peace, if peace is to be more than a short armistice. As in a relay race, our armed men have handed victory to those who dare not stand still to admire it, but must run with it for their very life to a further and larger goal."

We have come a long way in education in this past century, but there is still much to be done. Education has lagged behind our material progress. In the next century we must stress social, civic, moral, and spiritual literacy more than the accumulation of facts and a shrewd canniness of the intellect.

In your last session you made a significant advance in the improvement of education and the people of the state have given admirable cooperation to the program.

The cost of education has increased in recent years, the enrollments have been enlarged, and there is a pressing demand for additional services. These factors require substantially greater funds to achieve this human goal. Blessed by recent years of unparalleled prosperity, we must not fail our youth.

3. Youth Conservation

The third of the great human goals for which we strive is the conservation of our youth.

A farmer was shown a gnarled and twisted tree, and was asked for his opinion as to the cause of its distortion. His answer was, "Someone must have stepped on it when it was young." In Minnesota we place prime value on our boys and girls, our young men and young women. We are determined that they shall not be "stepped on" by an unthinking and unfeeling society. You gave tangible expression to the people's determination by your enactment of our Youth Conservation Act. The operation of this measure insures that we handle the lives of our youth as human personalities and not as depersonalized problem cases. The soul of the most reprobate child is fully worthy of salvation.

The Commission, though it has been handicapped by a lack of funds, has impressive accomplishments to its credit. We must strengthen its hands. As you know, we have had to use our present institutions for diagnostic centers. This is not an ideal situation. While the institutions have cooperated fully in helping to create and maintain these centers, the necessity of having the youth placed within an institution has brought about difficulties of administration. It has also tended to some degree to label children and youth who were held in the reception center as inmates of the institutions of which they were a part.

6. Human Relations

No problem in modern life is of greater consequence than that involved in our sixth goal—the improvement of our human relations. In no area is there a more astounding difference between our technical knowledge and progress on the one hand, and our unwillingness to make application of that knowledge to harmonious living together, so absolutely essential to the functioning of a democracy.

The wonders of science are all about us, yet the wisdom to utilize these wonders in building the "Golden Age of Man" is sadly lacking. Science has progressed with dazzling rapidity; the development of our human relations has crawled along at a snail's pace. Our solemn duty is to build bridges of understanding across the tragic chasms of racial, religious, and national differences. Unless these social tensions are mitigated—

and that right soon—they threaten to wrench the fabric of our society and tear it into shreds.

We are still seeking the simple formulas which can bring world peace at the conference table, agreement in the factory and workshop, and bring tranquillity to the family circle. The ominous shadows of greed and passion hang over a world which lives in dark dread of atomic and bacteriological warfare. There is no pat remedy for our plight. Look for no miracles. Only enlightenment in human relations can bring in the new era of unity and peace. Chemists, biologists, and engineers are required to build the better world. There must be no vacation for them. But the greatest need for our day is for human engineers, human engineers who will take the products of science and use them with compassion and understanding, not to the hurt but the healing of men.

Two great wars have been fought and won in a single generation to preserve the cherished ideal of equal opportunity. This ideal we must now translate into the problems of our daily life.

Every worker in our free society has a right to be judged and selected for a job on the basis of his abilities, demonstrated skills and background of experience. Certainly, democracy suffers a tragic defeat every time a member of its society finds the doors of industry closed to him because of the color of his skin, his religious faith, or his particular race.

* * * * *

Our problem is to find the proper way by which we may successfully clear away these restrictive bonds which are crippling the effective operation of our democracy. To encourage the practice of democracy in employment requires an aggressive program of education and legislation.

7. Housing

There are few domestic problems which affect more adversely the welfare of our families and our children than the shortage of adequate housing. Its high cost and the continued existence of blighted neighborhoods impede the progress of our cities and consume their revenue. To all of us, and especially to the veteran and his family, this is far more than a prosaic problem of building materials, rent ceilings, and zoning ordinances; it affects us vitally in terms of impaired health, personality disorders, juvenile delinquency, and broken homes.

8. Law Enforcement

The people of the state have indicated in no uncertain terms their belief that our laws should be observed and enforced. The continued strengthening and support of our law enforcement program is our eighth human goal.

There still is laxity in enforcement in certain areas of the state, particularly with reference to the sale of liquor to minors. We have received a large number of letters in the Governor's office from heart-sick parents, pleading for help in relation to this problem. We have an obligation to protect our youth from the callous consciences of some unscrupulous persons in this business. I therefore recommend uniform closing hours for beer and liquor establishments throughout the state, with a twelve o'clock closing on week days and one o'clock on Saturdays. Because of the conflict of closing hours existing at the present time, we have migrations late at night from one community to another, from the earlier to the later closing establishments, with traffic hazards and all the other serious implications involved.

Secondly, I think the Legislature should provide the power of arrest for the Liquor Control Inspectors, just as the Highway Patrolmen and Game Wardens have the power of arrest in their respective fields. You will recall that when the question was considered at the last session, objection was raised that that was giving the Governor too much authority and that enforcement belongs with the local units of government. I heartily concur in the idea that enforcement responsibility belongs fundamentally in the local communities. But in many of the local communities the laws are not being enforced as they ought to be, and the people themselves are continually asking the Governor's help in bringing about effective enforcement. I submit that there is a responsibility at the state level to guide, supervise, and lead the way to better enforcement. This is a reasonable request as long as we are called upon to help the local communities.

Third, I also believe that the Liquor Control Department needs some additional personnel if it is to provide the assistance that the people expect us to give in this important field of action.

Fourth, it is also my conviction that the Liquor Control Commissioner should have the right to approve retail on-sale alcoholic beverage licenses the same as he has the supervision of off-sale liquor licenses at the present time.

The fundamental concerns which motivate me in this matter of law enforcement are now, as they always have been, twofold: first, a deep conviction as to the necessity of protecting our boys and girls; and, second, a profound respect for the sanctity of law as being the very foundation of democratic government.

I want to say in closing this message that I shall endeavor to work with all of you during this important session in a spirit of understanding and an appreciation of the difficult problems facing us.

We cannot afford to permit political differences to interfere with our common obligation to meet the needs of our people and build a stronger state. There is too much at stake.

In conclusion I should like to quote the words of a famous statesman:

"I would advise, therefore, that your legislation should be such — as will guard equally, the rights of labor and the rights of property, without running into ultraisms on either hand — as will recognize no social distinctions, except those which merit and knowledge, religion and morals, unavoidably create — as will repress crime, encourage virtue, give free scope to enterprise and industry — as will promptly, and without delay, administer to and supply all the legitimate wants of the people — laws, in a word, in the formation of which will be kept steadily in view the truth, that this Territory is destined to be a great State, rivalling in population, wealth and energy, her sisters of the Union; and that, consequently, all laws not merely local in their objects, should be framed for the future as well as the present. . . ."

Timely though they be, these words are not those of a living statesman. They are the words of Governor Alexander Ramsey as he spoke to the first Minnesota Legislative Assembly in 1849. The setting for the address of the first Governor was quite different from ours today. He spoke in no great edifice of marble, his address was delivered in a temporary capitol in the Central House, a small wooden hotel on the St. Paul river front. The hotel dining room was used for the joint session of the two legislative bodies, a flag was hoisted on the staff in front of the hotel, an Indian sat on a nearby rocky bluff and watched the proceedings.

*   *   *   *   *

Though outward circumstances are utterly changed, we need to emulate, as we face our next century, the courage, the vision, and the spirit of sacrifice which animated the founders of our state. The road before us today, as it was one hundred years ago, is rocky and fraught with peril. Too many of us fail to appreciate the hazards and are like the young American who arrived in Zermatt, Switzerland, and seeing the towering peak of the Matterhorn, asked, "What's the name of that big rock?" When told it was one of the most famous of the Alpine summits he said, "Do you think I could get up there this afternoon?" Little did he know the story of the peak's costly conquest, of the lives it had taken, of the hazards still involved in the ascent. So is liberty, a decent society, a lasting peace, each a majestic mountain peak. How much do we really want them? Do we appreciate their cost? Are we willing to pay the price for them and sacrifice for them?

The pioneers of 100 years ago did not hesitate to pay the price for a strong society. They did not allow their spiritual values to be smothered beneath the false riches of material possessions. May the high idealism, the courage, the selflessness, and the implicit faith in God which characterized the founders of Minnesota inspire us. In the same spirit of consecration may we also move ahead to our next and even greater century of advancement, building together a nobler Minnesota.

INAUGURAL ADDRESS OF
GOVERNOR LUTHER W. YOUNGDAHL
DELIVERED AT A JOINT SESSION OF THE
MINNESOTA LEGISLATURE AT 12:15 P.M.,
WEDNESDAY, JANUARY 3, 1951.

The world is in turmoil and crisis. The year 1951 and those years immediately ahead may well be the "Hinge of Fate" upon which the destiny of the world turns. We are a part of the life and death struggle of two totally opposed philosophies of life. The antagonists are communism on the one hand, which denies God and places its faith in naked force and materialistic values, and on the other the democratic way of life, which places its faith in the Fatherhood of God and the Brotherhood of Man. Under communism man is a vassal and the State is supreme. Under our philosophy each man is uniquely precious because, like an ancient coin of gold, he is stamped with the image of the King.

It seems but yesterday. It was only four years ago, in this same place, that we acclaimed the end of hostilities of World War II. We met then with a strong hope for the achievement of world peace based on the concepts of the United Nations.

Today, we do best if we resolutely face a supremely unpredictable future. We know not what the morrow may bring. It may be peace. It may be war — war of such proportions and ferocity that all previous struggles will in comparison appear as preliminary skirmishes.

In these circumstances, for us to make plans based on specific prediction of the future is both foolish and impossible, yet hazards and uncertainties must not sap our courage nor paralyze us into inaction. Any plans we make or any programs we establish which are based on eternal principles of justice and humanity will always prove valid and right as the future unfolds.

The price we shall be required to pay for freedom will be great, but the cost of slavery is infinitely greater. The price of freedom includes far more than money, materials, and military might. The intangible demands made upon us are greater than

343

these. Each of us as a citizen is charged with a personal responsibility. Our state government must reflect this sense of personal responsibility. We must discipline ourselves to absolute integrity and dedicate ourselves to the advancement of human values. Honesty and humanity in government must constantly be our goal. In times of complacence and plenty it has too often been assumed that the accumulation of material resources is sufficient for safety and survival, but in times of crisis and disaster our sense of values must change. In such times, our survival will depend not upon material resources, but upon human and spiritual values.

Many years ago a great ship sank amid the icebergs of the Atlantic. A woman passenger waiting for a life boat received permission to return to her room where she kept her diamonds and other valuables. In this moment of danger, she ignored her jewels and instead snatched three oranges and made her way back to the life boat. In a life boat oranges take priority over diamonds. At the pivot between doom or dawn, human values become more precious than material values. In times of disaster, we see with a new vividness that material things will not insure our survival.

In today's hour of peril there must be a strong reaffirmation of the utter necessity for discipline, consecration, and service.

The Legislature has in past sessions demonstrated its faith in these human values by legislation enacted in support of education, mental health, youth conservation, law enforcement, and other progressive measures.

At this session, conditions over which neither you nor I have any control make our task even more difficult. The spiral of inflation and the zooming costs of our military establishment reduce the value of the dollar and limit the sources of revenue for the operations of state government. In spite of these and other difficulties which might be mentioned, our plain duty is to bend ourselves to the task of meeting the challenges of the hour. We pledged the people to continue to work for honesty and humanity in government. We must keep this promise.

When we speak of "humanity" in government, we think of it in its broad sense as including every program by which we meet human needs and by meeting them undergird our human resources.

Similarly, "honesty" in government encompasses not only integrity in financial matters, but also a fair and equitable approach to every practical problem relating to our economic resources.

With the terms thus broadly defined, my message to you will be divided in two main divisions. The first deals with the whole area of our human and social goals. The second is concerned with the prerequisites for the attainment of these goals.

1. HUMANITY IN GOVERNMENT

1. Home and Family

Of the new proposals dealing with "humanity in government," the one closest to my heart is the one I shall now discuss, a plan for the strengthening of the home and family life.

The nation which fails to give integrity to the home will ultimately pass into oblivion.

It is in the home that the lessons of mutual responsibility, of self sacrifice, are learned. The family is the only true democracy, whose motto is "One for all and all for one." The weak and the young as well as the wise and the strong have equal claims upon the family resources. If one member suffers—all suffer with him; if one member rejoices, all rejoice with him.

It was in the patriarchal family, expanded into the clan, that humanity learned the first lessons of government and social unity. The sense of social solidarity developed slowly in society at large, but its roots lie deep in family life.

The home is the foundation of the social order. There are signs that this foundation is cracking and crumbling. The divorce rate has increased sharply. Divorces mean broken homes. Broken homes mean children who are the innocent victims. Out of these broken homes comes a tragic amount of youth delinquency and the loss of precious human resources.

It is impossible to exaggerate the calamities that befall a society in which the home disintegrates. The cost in terms of heartbreak and human wretchedness cannot be described. The economic cost defies calculation. Repercussions are felt in added relief loads, increased aids to dependent children, and additional costs of law enforcement, including the maintenance of penal institutions. Complications are felt in recreational programs, housing facilities, mental health work, in every area of social welfare. Every other social institution, including our churches and schools, is endangered.

Where family life degenerates communism and demonic schemes become rampant. Ultimately the consequences are chaos and war.

Recognizing these dangers, you provided in 1949 for a thorough investigation of this whole problem. At your direction, I appointed a committee of 26 concerned and representative citizens to study this social menace.

This Interim Committee for the study of family life has done an excellent job. Its report has already aroused widespread and favorable reaction. All the recommendations in the report deserve your careful consideration.

The report emphasizes the necessity for diagnosis and therapy in dealing with family difficulties and the use of all available facilities to remove the causes of family breakdowns.

The old adage says "Count to ten before you swing." This homespun piece of advice has prevented many a fist fight. Application of the same principle has been effective in the area of labor relations where the "cooling off" period has prevented strikes and lockouts. We may be certain that a principle which has proved effective in these and other areas will apply with equal strength to conflicts in family life.

Therefore, I favor legislation requiring a period of conciliation before a divorce action may be commenced. I also recommend the committee's proposal that judicial procedures be established to provide specialized treatment to strengthen family ties before they are broken in divorce.

You have dignified these legislative halls in past sessions by enacting farsighted and effective laws for the preservation of our state's human resources. Here again we have the opportunity to pioneer and, at relatively small cost, to undergird that basic unit of our society, the home.

2. Mental Health

In Minnesota, "snake pits" and bedlams have disappeared. We are building the House of Hope. Our official policy as a state is to recognize that mental illness is a sickness and a medical problem to which there should be attached absolutely no shame or stigma.

Having made a start, the temptation will be strong to stagnate and stop in our drive for a really adequite mental health program.

At the last session you began one of the most magnificent social structures ever put into law by this or any other legislative body in the country. You passed the mental health act and backed it up with money. By doing this, you gave a new lease of hope to tens of thousands of people who have loved ones suffering from a mental sickness.

I can report a substantial improvement in the care and treatment of the mentally ill. The health of our patients is better; mechanical restraints have been virtually eliminated; overcrowding has been relieved; increased personnel has made possible new programs of recreation and therapy. Our patients are better clothed, and the single standard of food makes them the best fed patients of any state hospital system in the nation. A beginning has been made in research in out-patient clinics and in other aspects of our mental health work.

We have laid the foundation for the House of Hope. Upon this foundation we must continue to build. It is not enough to hold the line. We must press the attack against the citadels of the asylum-past. The measure of our accomplishment must never be a smug complacency as to the rank we hold in comparison with other states. The only valid satisfaction is to be found in fully meeting the needs of these maligned and forgotten people, whose only hope lies in our compassion and action.

In mental health, Minnesota has become the symbol of the House of Hope, and the whole nation looks to us for continued leadership. We ought to pray to God that He will keep us in discontent until the day comes when every mentally sick person receives the care to which he is entitled.

3. Education

Education is of critical importance in a democracy. Thomas Jefferson spoke for America when he said, "By far the most important bill in our whole code is that for the diffusion of knowledge among the people. No other sure foundation can be devised for the preservation of freedom and happiness."

The American way of life demands that every citizen shall have the right to an education. Its enemies thrive on ignorance and illiteracy. The American ideal of educational equality is far short of attainment. We have a long way to go, and critical times such as these ought to spur us on to a new zeal to provide an education sufficient to meet the demands of the hour. Therefore, I strongly urge you to meet the costs of the educational needs in our state.

In Minnesota we have made substantial progress in public education, but Americans must be willing to devote more of their income to education than ever before. Good schools cost money. This is part of the price we are called upon to pay if we are determined to maintain our way of life. Money appropriated for schools is, I submit, an investment from which our state and nation will receive priceless returns.

We in government, as well as professional educators, ought to have a profound sense of stewardship with reference to the money which is appropriated and spent for education. The people have a right to expect that we be continually diligent and alert to improve the substance of what our boys and girls are taught. Accumulation of facts and figures and the sharpening of a shrewd and canny mind for material advantage produce neither happiness for the individual nor benefit to society. Therefore, our educators have an obligation continually to reappraise their courses of study, particularly in the fields of character development, vocational guidance and training, citizenship, and family life.

Humanity in government requires a deep concern for the true happiness of our boys and girls. To this purpose, in the "atomic age," is added the necessity of well trained and inspired citizenry to assure survival. There are only two choices:

To pay the cost or be destroyed, because, as a great historian has stated, "History is a race between education and catastrophe."

4. Youth Conservation

"If all the youth of America could speak to us, they would speak with one voice and say, 'We are the future, for in us there lies what through the ages this land shall be. Yet what we are is what you are to us. We are the question to which you make reply.' "

As legislators, you have in the past two sessions made reply to the critical needs of our boys and girls by enacting farsighted legislation which has already established Minnesota as a leader in the field of Youth Conservation. And all this at relatively small cost.

What a responsibility! What an opportunity! To salvage and repair youthful lives that have been blighted and damaged, and by positive programs to strengthen and build lives of usefulness and character among children of city and country, of every race, color, and creed, what a privilege!

Nowhere is humanity in government more dramatically illustrated than it is in our task of salvaging and conserving the lives of our boys and girls. Here, again, the cost of a positive program is infinitesimal in comparison with the price which will be exacted if we shirk our duty.

5. Human Relations

One of the most potent weapons in the arsenal of communism is the allegation that we as a people give no more than lip service to the Bill of Rights; that we loudly protest allegiance to equality, but actually practice racial and religious discrimination in our daily lives.

I submit to you as a demonstrable fact that lists of dead and wounded from our present conflict are more the result of this weapon than they are of bombs and bullets. In any future war, the potency of this weapon will become increasingly decisive. The sad fact is that, to give the devil his due, there is a kernel of truth in the propaganda.

Right here in Minnesota this problem of human relations must be faced and decided. Therefore, I plead with all my heart and soul for the passage of a Fair Employment Practices Law.

We have made a start. Our Interracial Commission has performed a real service in public education against the ignorance that breeds bigotry. At the last session you wisely appropriated money for the work of this commission.

But this is no more than a start. Surely you will reaffirm your faith in educative force of public opinion by continuing your appropriation for the commission, but the immediate crux of the problem will not be touched until not one of our fellow citizens is deprived of his right to earn a livelihood because of racial or religious discrimination.

By executive order, our National Guard has been opened to Negroes, and I thank God that as our guard units are called up for service they will not be required to be the object of insult and humiliation in addition to making the sacrifices for which they have volunteered.

In the field of civil rights talk is cheap, but our actions shout so loudly that the people of other nations cannot hear what we say.

Right here in Minnesota jobs are still being denied our fellow citizens, not because of incompetence, but because the door of opportunity is slammed in their faces by reason of racial and religious prejudice. To deny a fellow human the right to earn a living for himself and his loved ones for such morally indefensible reasons breaks faith with our American heritage.

The struggle with communism is essentially a spiritual battle. Diplomatic maneuvers and supremacy in arms will never be sufficient to win the hearts of a billion people who, shaking off the shackles of the centuries, are demanding equality as dignified human beings.

The global struggle has its application here in Minnesota.

Your action in passing an F.E.P.C. law will be a devastating blow to the armor of the forces of darkness.

6. Social Welfare

The problem of our aged citizens is one of major concern. Much of our past history in meeting our responsibility to elderly people has not been of a hopeful sort, but mainly that of keeping body and soul together. Too often the rewards of survival into old age have been poverty, sickness, humiliation, loneliness, fear, and despair.

This is a problem which grows in magnitude because of the ever-increasing life span of our people. We must overcome the tragic social consequences and the waste of human resources, and we must plan for the continued happiness and usefulness of these people to the extent that it is humanly possible.

II. HONESTY IN GOVERNMENT

1. Law Enforcement

The menace of organized crime to the life of our nation has been revealed as by flashes of lightning in the reports of investigating groups, most publicized of which have been the findings of the Kefauver Committee of the United States Senate. For my part, I am more determined than ever before that Minnesota shall take the lead in vigilant and vigorous enforcement of the law. I have never been more certain than I am now, that you and I were accurately reflecting the will of the people in ridding our state of the corrupt and degrading slot machine racket.

In order further to protect our people, particularly our youth, I once again urge that the power of arrest be granted to the state Liquor Control Inspectors. The experience of many other states indicates the wisdom of such action.

The callous indifference to the welfare of young people demonstrated in some localities by certain saloons, taverns, and roadhouses underlines the necessity of giving authority to our Liquor Control Commissioner to pass upon applications for retail on-sale alcoholic beverage licenses in the same way that he now passes on off-sale liquor licenses.

CONCLUSION

I have appreciated the opportunity to work with you during two previous sessions, and likewise the privilege of speaking to you today about the problems confronting the people of Minnesota.

The times are increasingly ominous. The world is on fire! Hiroshima, Nagasaki, and the burning villages of Korea are but mirrors reflecting the flames of greed and hatred which burn in the hearts of men.

Someone has suggested that the world has come to such a state of hopelessness that a merciful God would do well to change its orbit so as to bring it into fatal collision with a flaming star. But this is the advice of despair. Heroic men will pray that we be given the strength to direct the world affairs toward the light of a star of hope, guidance, and courage.

We do confront despair and disillusionment—but we also face challenge and opportunity.

Disappointed in many of our hopes and confused by our failures, we look about us for scapegoats. By faultfinding and accusations, we try to seek to cover up our own past apathy and neglect.

As it has been aptly said, "If, because of blindness or wishful thinking or lack of vision or courage we fail to heed the storm warnings that are flying, a conquering adversary writing the history of a vanished dream of human freedom may say with some justice that we deserved our fate."

In 1863, with the country agonizing in Civil War, Abraham Lincoln made the following statement:

"We have been the recipients of the choicest bounties of heaven. We have been preserved these many years in peace and prosperity. We have grown in numbers, wealth and power as no other nation has ever grown, but we have forgotten God. We have forgotten the gracious hand which preserved us in peace and multitude and enriched and strengthened us, and we have vainly claimed in the deceitfulness of our hearts that all these blessings were produced by some superior wisdom and virtue of our own.

The Youngdahl family at home

The Judge demonstrates his pitching technique to open a game between his alma mater and St. John's University

The Youngdahls at home at Lake Minnetonka

The Youngdahl family enjoys singing together

"Intoxicated with unbroken success, we have become too self-sufficient to feel the necessity of religion and preserving grace—too proud to pray to the God that made us. It behooves us then to humble ourselves before the offended power—to confess our national sins—and to pray for clemency and forgiveness."

That is where we need to begin today. By our attitude of self-righteousness and recrimination we accomplish less than nothing. Now if ever is the time for unity. We have all been guilty, and reparation for the past can only be found in building the future. We can build that future in America, and we can build it right here in Minnesota.

Our willingness to pay the price for constructive measures that will strengthen every force for honesty and humanity in our state government will be tangible evidence of our faith in that future.

A wealthy man took a poor boy from the slums of a great city to his lodge high in the mountains. The boy awakened in the morning. The sky was illuminated with the red and gold of the rising sun reflecting on the ice and stone of the rocky pinnacles and blazoned across the sky. The boy rubbed his eyes in wonder and a great fear filled him. Looking at the flaming splendor, he remembered the lurid tenement fires in which people he knew had burned to death. Terrified, he screamed, "Please, Sir, wake up! Something awful has happened—the whole world is on fire." His wealthy friend opened his eyes and, seeing the flame pictures of the Great Artist on the tapestried skies, replied, "Don't be afraid, my boy, everything is all right. The world is not burning up. It is just the dawn of a new day."

The world is on fire, but it need not be the holocaust of destruction. It can be and it must be the flaming dawn of a new day.

OPINION BY
JUDGE LUTHER W. YOUNGDAHL

In the Case of

UNITED STATES OF AMERICA

vs.

OWEN LATTIMORE

In the United States District Court for the District of
Columbia. May 2, 1953

Reprinted, with emphasis supplied, by the
Lattimore Defense Fund

IN THE

United States District Court

FOR THE DISTRICT OF COLUMBIA

UNITED STATES OF AMERICA

vs.

OWEN LATTIMORE,

Defendant

Criminal No. 1879-52

MEMORANDUM

[EMPHASIS SUPPLIED]

On December 16, 1952, defendant Owen Lattimore was indicted on seven counts of perjury alleged to have been committed before the Senate Internal Security Subcommittee (hereinafter referred to as the Committee). On December 19, 1952, defendant entered a plea of not guilty to said indictment and was ordered to file all preliminary motions by February 16, 1953. Trial date was set for May 11, 1953.

Defendant filed ten motions.[1] Exhaustive written briefs were served and filed in connection therewith. On March 31 and April 1, 1953, oral arguments were heard on the motions

---

[1] Motion for Inspection of Grand Jury Minutes, for Time to Prepare and File Motion for Change of Venue, for Bill of Particulars, for Leave to File Motion for Continuance, for Continuance, to Dismiss Indictment, three Motions for Production of Documents under Federal Criminal Rule 17(c) and a Motion for Discovery and Inspection.

1

2

for change of venue, for continuance and to dismiss the indictment and the various counts thereof. Arguments on the other motions were deferred pending determination of the motions herewith presented.

For an understanding of the charges against defendant and how they arose some background is necessary. Defendant, by many people, has been considered an expert in Far Eastern Affairs and a student of the problems of that part of the world. By others, he has been considered a Communist or fellow traveler. From 1934 to 1941, defendant was editor of the magazine, "Pacific Affairs." [2] For a time he was associated with the Office of War Information and the Pauley Reparations Commission. [3]

Charges against defendant were first investigated by a Subcommittee of the Senate known as the Tydings Committee. This Committee concluded there was no foundation to the charges against him. [4] Subsequently, in November, 1950, the Senate Judiciary Committee by Senate Resolution 366 (81st Congress, 2nd Session), was itself, or by means of a subcommittee, authorized to make an investigation and study of the Internal Security Act of 1950, " the administration, operation and enforcement of other laws relating to espionage, sabotage and the protection of internal security of the United States " and " effects of subversive activities in the United States."

Upon being summoned by the Committee to appear before it in executive session, defendant was questioned concerning his past life and, more particularly, his association with the Institute of Pacific Relations and as editor of its magazine, " Pacific Affairs." [5] In July, 1951, the Committee conducted

[2] P. 59, Transcript of Oral Argument. Internal Security Subcommittee, Executive Session Testimony, July 13, 1951, at p. 6.

[3] P. 15, Executive Session Testimony.

[4] Report of the Committee on Foreign Relations. S. Rept. 2108. 81st Congress, 2nd Session. July 20, 1950.

[5] Executive Session Testimony, Parts 9 and 10. Open Hearings, Internal Security Subcommittee, Feb. 26-Mar. 21, 1952.

open hearings and questioned other witnesses. These hearings terminated in February, 1952. On February 26, 1952, defendant was permitted to testify before the Committee and made his statement a part of the record.[6] In the course of making his statement, defendant was questioned further. This portion of the hearings lasted thirteen days. It is apparent from the record of the hearings and the indictment that the Committee was interested, from its study of the records of the Institute of Pacific Relations, in finding out the extent to which the Institute of Pacific Relations may have been infiltrated or controlled by Communists or those connected with the Communist movement and what influence the Institute of Pacific Relations may have had on the foreign policy of the United States of America. In his testimony, defendant denied being a Communist, a member of the Communist Party, a Soviet spy or a fellow traveler.[7]

Apparently the Committee could discover no evidence from its investigation or the testimony of the various witnesses that defendant lied in denying that he was a Communist, a member of the Communist Party, a Soviet spy or a fellow traveler. This case therefore is unlike *U. S. vs. Remington*, 191 F.2d 246, where defendant was charged with perjury in denying that he was a member of the Communist Party, and *U. S. vs. Hiss*, 185 F.2d 822, where defendant was charged with

[6] Part 9, Hearings, p. 2898.
[7] Part 9, Open Hearings, p. 2947:
    "All kinds of attempts have been made to depict me as a Communist or a Soviet agent. I have in fact been falsely identified as a fellow traveler, sympathizer, or follower of the Communist line or promoter of Communist interests. Now I want to make my position clear. I am not interested in fine or technical distinctions. I am not interested in graduations or degrees of disloyalty. I have no use for fancy, legalistic distinctions. I am none of these things and never have been. I am not and have never been a Communist, a Soviet agent, sympathizer, or any other kind of promoter of Communism or Communist interests, and all of these are nonsense. I so testified long ago, under oath before the Tydings subcommittee, and I do so again."

lying in denying that he turned over to certain people important security documents.

In the indictment under consideration defendant is not charged with lying in denying that he was a Communist or a member of the Communist Party. The indictment here charges defendant with committing perjury as to his sympathies with Communism or Communist interests (count one); whether he had been told or knew certain persons were Communists (counts two and three); whether he had published certain articles in "Pacific Affairs" by Communists (count four); whether he had a luncheon engagement with Soviet Ambassador Oumansky in July, 1941 after the Hitler invasion (count five); that he did not at the request of Lauchlin Currie take care of his mail at the White House (count six); and whether he had made prearrangements with the Communist Party to get into Yenan (count seven).

It appears from the record and the hearings of the Committee that the charges reflected in the seven counts in the indictment related to a period of fifteen to twenty years before the hearings. With this factual background we will proceed to a consideration of the several motions presented to the Court.

I.

CHANGE OF VENUE

Although defendant requested the privilege of making the motions for a change of venue and continuance at a later date, the Court ordered that the motions be argued at the hearings of the motions attacking the indictment. However, the motion to inspect the grand jury minutes, and the motions for production of documents and discovery were deferred to a date to be subsequently set by the Court should a hearing of these motions be deemed necessary by defendant.

A sufficient showing has not been made to justify a change

of venue. Title 18, U. S. C. A., Federal Rules of Criminal Procedure, Rule 21 (a) provides that a change of venue shall be granted:

> " * * * if the court is satisfied that there exists in the district or division where the prosecution is pending so great a prejudice against the defendant that he cannot obtain a fair and impartial trial in that district or division."

Charges against this defendant have received nation-wide publicity. Much has been written about this case pro and con since its inception. There is no indication or proof that defendant cannot have as fair and impartial trial here as in any other Federal Judicial District. This Court is not satisfied that " there exists in this district so great a prejudice against the defendant that he cannot obtain a fair and impartial trial." The motion for a change of venue is therefore denied. *Dennis* vs. *U. S.*, 84 App. D. C. 31; *U. S.* vs. *Eisler*, 75 F. Supp. 634.

II.

MOTION FOR CONTINUANCE

Defendant moves to continue the trial to a date not earlier than January, 1954. He bases his motion upon the decision in *Delaney* vs. *U. S.*, 199 F.2d 107. But that case is clearly distinguishable from the instant case. In Delaney, defendant was indicted for certain crimes alleged to have been committed while he was Collector of Internal Revenue at Boston. He was removed from office. Shortly before the commencement of his trial certain hearings were held before a Congressional Committee involving charges against Delaney and his conduct while in office. Much publicity adverse to Delaney was given to those charges by radio, news services and the press. The Court of Appeals held that in view of this derogatory publicity at a time so near to the trial it was error not to grant another continuance. No such factual situation appears here. There is no evidence here that would warrant a continuance based on the holding in the Delaney case. In our own jurisdiction recently, Judge Matthews in a well written opinion discussed the applicability of the Delaney case in denying a motion for change of venue. *U. S. vs. Carper*, Criminal No. 836-52, United States District Court for the District of Columbia, January 14, 1953. The Court stated that any apprehension of prejudice and inability to get a fair trial was " based upon conjecture and speculation." This the Court believes to be the situation in the case at bar.[8]

Therefore, although there is no justification for a continuance on the theory of the Delaney case, the Court feels that a reasonable continuance should be granted because of the amount of work that will be required in preparation for this case both by defendant and the Government. In fact, the Government made no objection to a continuance to early fall.

A number of additional motions are still to be argued and disposed of. The Court will require that all remaining motions be argued prior to June 1st and the case will be set down for trial on October 6, 1953. It is the Court's conclusion that the case should be tried at that time and that no further continuance should be granted.

III.

MOTION TO DISMISS INDICTMENT

The first ground upon which defendant relies to sustain his position as to the invalidity of the indictment is that it does not allege the name of the person who administered the oath to defendant. Defendant concedes that this is a technical point and voices the hope that the indictment be stricken down on the merits rather than on this technicality.[9] Since

---

[8] See *U. S. vs. Moran*, 194 F.2d 623, for a discussion of unjustified apprehension of undue publicity.

[9] See p. 97—defendant's brief in support of Motion to Dismiss.

the argument on the motions, defendant's position on this point has been fortified by the recent decision of the Fifth Circuit, *U. S.* vs. *Debrow, et al.*, Nos. 14087-14091, April 10, 1953, where the Court in a two to one decision struck down an indictment which failed to set forth the name of the Senator who administered the oath to certain defendants charged with perjury before a Committee of the Senate.

Perjury is defined in the District of Columbia by statute. The District of Columbia perjury statute,[10] as were many others, was taken from the Act of 23 George, chap. 11. Title 23, D. C. Code, § 204 is almost word for word the same as R. S. 5396 and former 18 U. S. C. §558 since dropped from the Criminal Code. It may well be true that prior to the revision of the Code and adoption of the new Federal Rules of Criminal Procedure that the name of the person administering the oath was required to be set forth.[11]

However, the purpose of the new Federal Rules of Criminal Procedure was " to provide for the just determination of every criminal proceeding. They shall be construed to secure

---

[10] 14 D. C. Code § 102:

"A person swearing, affirming, or declaring, or giving testimony in any form where an oath is authorized by law, is lawfully sworn, and will be guilty of perjury in a case where he would be guilty of said crime if sworn according to the forms of the common law."

22 D. C. Code § 2501:

"Every person who, having taken an oath or affirmation before a competent tribunal, officer, or person, in any case in which the law authorized such oath or affirmation to be administered, that he will testify, declare, depose or certify truly, or that any written testimony, declaration, deposition, or certificate by him subscribed is true, wilfully and contrary to such oath or affirmation states or subscribes any material matter which he does not believe to be true, shall be guilty of perjury; * * *."

23 D. C. Code § 204:

"In every information or indictment to be prosecuted against any person for wilful and corrupt perjury, it shall be sufficient to set forth the substance of the offence charged upon the defendant, and by what court, or before whom the oath was taken (averring such court, or person or persons, to have a competent authority to administer the same) * * *."

[11] *U. S.* vs. *Markham*, 160 U. S. 319; *Hilliard* vs. *U. S.*, 24 F.2d 99.

simplicity in procedure, fairness in administration and the elimination of unjustifiable expense and delay." [12] Furthermore Rule 52 (a) provides that " any error, defect, irregularity or variance which does not affect substantial rights shall be disregarded." Though this Court is not bound by the decision of the Fifth Circuit,[13] it nevertheless has carefully studied this opinion because of the deference that should be accorded a decision of any Court of Appeals. However, it seems to this Court that the dissent of Judge Rives has much more persuasive quality than the majority opinion. As Judge Rives points out the " holding is extremely technical and is contrary to the letter and spirit of the pertinent Federal Rules of Criminal Procedure." The dissenting Judge further aptly states that if this holding is to obtain " we are still enmeshed in the technicalities of common law pleading and the new rules have failed of their purpose."

On April 29, 1953, in *U. S.* vs. *Young,* Criminal No. 355-52, United States District Court for the District of Columbia, Judge McGuire of our Court had occasion to decide this precise point. Judge McGuire in an excellently written opinion refused to follow the majority in the Debrow case, and for substantially the same reasons stated herein, held that an indictment was not fatally defective which did not set forth the name of the Senator who administered the oath.

The indictment here alleges the defendant was duly sworn before a competent tribunal in a matter in which an oath was authorized. Whether defendant was sworn or not and by whom is a matter of proof that may be readily determined at the proper time. It is held therefore the indictment in this case is not invalid because of the failure to allege the name of the Senator administering the oath.

Defendant also contends that the indictment is invalid in its entirety because the questions and answers upon which

---

[12] Title 18, U. S. C. A., Federal Rules of Criminal Procedure, Rule 2.

[13] *Dist. of Col.* vs. *Amer. Excavation Co.,* 64 F. Supp. 19; 21 C. J. S. [Courts] § 198.

the charges are based are immaterial as a matter of law. Defendant vigorously argues that all the charges relate to ancient history and cannot possibly have any relevancy to the authorization under which the Committee was making its investigation. In support of its position defendant relies strongly upon *Bowers* vs. *U. S.*, No. 11457, United States Court of Appeals for the District of Columbia, February 12, 1953.

Aside from the reasons of invalidity as to certain counts as hereinafter expressed, there is serious doubt in the Court's mind whether any count in this indictment can finally pass the test of materiality. But the Court does not agree with the interpretation placed upon the Bowers case by defendant that it is necessary to plead in the indictment the particulars of materiality. The question of materiality like the question of pertinency is a question of law for the Court to decide when the Government's evidence is in or at the conclusion of all the testimony. Such is the holding in the Bowers case.[14]

As the Court of Appeals there stated:

" While it was the duty of the trial court to determine as a matter of law whether the question was pertinent that determination could only be made from a factual showing by the government. * * * The United States had the task of proving his guilt beyond a reasonable doubt, and a part of that task was to show the pertinency of the questions he refused to answer *since pertinency was not apparent from the questions themselves. Some of the seven questions may well have been pertinent, and it might have been possible for the government to show pertinency. But the important fact is that it did not do so.*" [Emphasis supplied.]

[14] See also *Sinclair* vs. *U. S.*, 279 U. S. 263.

Also squarely in point is the Meyers case in this jurisdiction.[15] The Court there said:

> "Under the old system of criminal pleading it was customary to set forth in detail in a perjury indictment how and why the particular question addressed to the witness was material. * * * Assuming, without deciding, that at common law such allegations were essential, the view of this Court is that such averments are no longer required under the new Federal Rules of Criminal Procedure. All that is indispensable now is a plain, concise and definite written statement of the essential facts that constitute the offense charged. There is an allegation in the indictment that the testimony sought to be elicited from the defendant was material to the inquiry. Whether it was is a matter of proof, and, of course, at the trial it will be necessary for the Government to establish the materiality of the subject matter. It is the view of this Court that under the new Rules, a general allegation of materiality is sufficient in an indictment for perjury or subornation of perjury." [p. 488.]

The Court holds therefore that the issue of materiality is sufficiently set forth in the indictment.

Because the Court has concluded that it is not now in a position to dismiss the entire indictment, the motion to dismiss the indictment in its entirety must be overruled. However, in the Court's opinion certain counts in the indictment are fatally defective and the several counts will now be considered separately. In order to determine the validity of the several counts it is necessary at the outset to consider the scope and character of the Resolution of the Congress authorizing the investigation out of which the perjury charges arose. The pertinent part of the resolution reads:

> " Resolved, That the Committee on the Judiciary, or any duly authorized subcommittee thereof, is authorized and directed to make a complete and continuing

[15] U. S. vs. Meyers, 75 F. Supp. 486, affirmed 84 App. D. C. 101, cert. denied 336 U. S. 912.

study and investigation of (1) the administration, operation and enforcement of the Internal Security Act of 1950; (2) the administration, operation, and enforcement of other laws relating to espionage, sabotage, and the protection of the internal security of the United States; and (3) the extent, nature, and effects of subversive activities in the United States, its Territories and possessions, including, but not limited to, espionage, sabotage, and infiltration by persons who are or may be under the domination of the foreign government or organizations controlling the world Communist movement or any other movement seeking to overthrow the Government of the United States by force and violence."

The Supreme Court of the United States has recently recognized " the penetrating and persuasive scope of the investigative power of Congress." In the Rumely case [16] Justice Frankfurter quoted Woodrow Wilson to illustrate " the reach that may be claimed for that power " as follows:

" It is the proper duty of a representative body to look diligently into every affair of government and to talk much about what it sees. It is meant to be the eyes and the voice, and to embody the wisdom and will of its constituents. Unless Congress have and use every means of acquainting itself with the acts and the disposition of the administrative agents of the government, the country must be helpless to learn how it is being served; and unless Congress both scrutinize these things and sift them by every form of discussion, the country must remain in embarrassing, crippling ignorance of the very affairs which it is most important that it should understand and direct. The informing function of Congress should be preferred even to its legislative function." Wilson, Congressional Government, 303.

However, the Court points out that there are limitations to that power imposed by the Constitution such as, for example, in the First Amendment.[17] Similarly the Court of

---

[16] *U. S.* vs. *Rumely*, 345 U. S. 41.

[17] " President Wilson did not write in light of the history of events since he

Appeals in the Bowers case recognizes the broad powers of Congress. It properly points out that "the questioning of witnesses customarily, and probably necessarily, takes a wide range. Committees may and do obtain vague information and receive hearsay evidence from which they form well-grounded suspicions that evils exist at which legislation should be aimed. That is to say, committees' conclusions that corrective legislation should be enacted need not be reached on the basis of relevant and pertinent evidence only." It is significant that the Court goes on to point out that "the precision of Court procedure is not required. It may be often proper, justifiable and ultimately helpful in the accomplishment of its investigative purposes for a Congressional Committee to address to witnesses questions which it cannot demonstrate to be pertinent. But in branding a refusal to answer as a misdemeanor Congress was careful to provide that the question must be 'pertinent to the question under inquiry.'" So in a perjury case arising out of a Congressional investigation, which concededly may be broad in its scope as far as determining the necessity for corrective legislation is concerned, the element of materiality must be present or the charges fall.

Count One

Having in mind the necessity of weighing the balance between the broad power of Congress to investigate and the protections afforded individuals by the Bill of

wrote; more particularly he did not write of the investigative power of Congress in the context of the First Amendment."

See also *U. S.* vs. *Patterson*, No. 11399, United States Court of Appeals for the District of Columbia, decided April 23, 1953, where Judge Bazelon referring to the Rumely case in the Supreme Court of the United States stated: "The Court recognized the possible conflict between the 'power of Congress to investigate' and the 'limitation imposed by the First Amendment' * * *."

The test most widely accepted by the Courts is that any right granted or secured by the Constitution may not be restricted unless the exercise of that right constitutes a clear and present danger. *Schenck* vs. *U. S.*, 249 U. S. 47. See also Rumely, *supra*.

Rights, as pointed out in Douds, and applying the rule to the indictment here, the Court is convinced that the first count is fatally defective. Under this count the defendant is charged with lying in denying that he had never been a sympathizer or promoter of Communism or Communist interests. It is based on a statement made by defendant to the Committee.[18]

First, this count is violative of the Sixth Amendment which protects the accused in the right to be informed of the nature and cause of the accusation against him.[19] The test has been laid down in *Sutton* vs. *U. S.*, 157 F.2d 661, where the Court held that the meaning of the Sixth Amendment was that the defendant:

> " * * * be so fully and clearly informed of the charge against him as not only to enable him to prepare his defense and not be taken by surprise at the trial, but also that the information as to the alleged offense shall be so definite and certain that he may be protected by a plea of former jeopardy against another prosecution for the same offense." [p. 663.]

Moreover this count does not meet the requirements of Rule 7 (c) of the Federal Rules of Criminal Procedure which requires that the indictment " shall be a plain, concise and definite written statement of the essential facts constituting the offense charged." [20]

[18] See footnote 7, *supra*.

[19] The Sixth Amendment provides as follows:

"In all criminal prosecutions, the accused shall enjoy the right to a speedy and public trial, by an impartial jury of the State and district wherein the crime shall have been committed, which district shall have been previously ascertained by law, and to be informed of the nature and cause of the accusation; to be confronted with the witnesses against him; to have compulsory process for obtaining witnesses in his favor, and to have the Assistance of Counsel for his defence."

[20] In *U. S.* vs. *Fields*, 6 F. R. D. 203, the sufficiency of an indictment is stated to be:

1. Whether the defendant, in ths indictment, is apprised of the charge he is called upon to answer.

2. Whether the charge is so stated that the defendant could successfully

Defendant in the first count is charged with lying in denying that he was a sympathizer or promoter of Communist interests. It seems to the Court that this charge is so nebulous and indefinite that a jury would have to indulge in speculation in order to arrive at a verdict. Sympathies and beliefs and what they mean to different individuals involve concepts that are highly nebulous and speculative at best. I presume a person could sympathize with a belief and yet still not believe. To probe the mind in a situation like this would give rise to nothing more than sheer speculation on the part of the prober. It is fundamental that a jury should not be asked to determine an issue which can be decided only on conjecture. It is clear to the Court therefore that the first count fails to meet the test of definiteness required by the Sixth Amendment and Rule 7 (c) of the Federal Rules of Criminal Procedure.

But there is another reason why count one is fatally defective. It is in conflict with the First Amendment.[21] It restricts the freedom of belief and expression which the Court in the Rumely case clearly points out is a limitation upon Congressional inquiry. In support of this count the Government cites the Barsky and Lawson cases in our Court of Appeals.[22]

In Barsky the appellant was indicted and convicted for willful failure to produce records (of the joint Anti-Fascist

plead double jeopardy if an attempt were to be made to try him again on the same charge. See also *Hagner* vs. *U. S.*, 285 U. S. 427, affirming 60 App. D. C. 335 and *U. S.* vs. *Meyers, supra.* The Meyers case also involved a perjury indictment under the D. C. Statute. For other perjury cases see *Walker* vs. *U. S.*, 93 F.2d 792; *Claiborne* vs. *U. S.*, 77 F.2d 682; *Asgill* vs. *U. S.*, 60 F.2d 776; *Kovoloff* vs. *U. S.*, 202 Fed. 475.

[21] The First Amendment to the Constitution provides that:

"Congress shall make no law respecting an establishment of religion, or prohibiting the free exercise thereof; or abridging the freedom of speech, or of the press; or the right of the people peaceably to assemble, and to petition the Government for a redress of grievances."

[22] *Barsky* vs. *U. S.*, 83 App. D. C. 127; *Lawson* vs. *U. S.*, 85 App. D. C. 167.

Refugee Committee relating to the receipt and disbursement of funds and correspondence with persons in foreign countries) before the House Committee on Un-American Activities. House of Representatives Resolution No. 5, 79th Congress, authorized the Committee to investigate the:

> " * * * diffusion within the United States of subversive and un-American propaganda that is instigated from foreign countries or of a domestic origin and attacks the principle of the form of government as guaranteed by our Constitution."

The appellant contended the questions asked in response to the subpoena and the answers might reveal that he was a believer in Communism or a member of the Communist Party. The Court of Appeals held that the Committee was authorized to make the investigation, that the resolution was not " too vague " and stated its conclusions as follows:

> " We hold that in view of the representations to the Congress as to the nature, purposes and program of Communism and the Communist Party, and in view of the legislation proposed, pending and possible in respect to or premised upon that subject, and in view of the involvement of that subject in the foreign policy of the Government, Congress has power to make an inquiry of an individual which may elicit the answer that the witness is a believer in Communism or a member of the Communist Party. And we further hold that the provision we have quoted for House Resolution No. 5 is sufficiently clear, definite and authoritative to permit this particular Committee to make that particular inquiry. We hold no more than that." [p. 136.]

In Lawson appellants were indicted and convicted of contempt of Congress for refusing to disclose whether or not they were or ever had been members of the Communist Party. The Court of Appeals said:

> " So that there may be no mistake or misunderstanding and because the point here involved has proven to be one of constant recurrence, we expressly hold herein that

the House Committee on Un-American Activities, or a properly appointed subcommittee thereof, has the power to inquire whether a witness subpoenaed by it is or is not a member of the Communist Party or a believer in Communism and that this power carries with it necessarily the power to effect criminal punishment for failure or refusal to answer that question under 2 U. S. C. A. § 192." [p. 170.]

But these cases are distinguishable from the instant case. In the case at bar defendant is not charged with lying in denying that he believed in Communism or that he was a member of the Communist Party. In count one he is charged with falsifying the fact that he was a sympathizer and promoter of Communist interests.

The Government also relies heavily on the Douds case.[23] In that case the constitutionality of Section 9 (h) of the National Labor Relations Act was before the Supreme Court. Section 9 (h) required that an officer of a union seeking to invoke the machinery of the act must submit an affidavit [commonly known as the " Non-Communist Affidavit "] that:

" * * * he is not a member of the Communist Party or affiliated with such party, and that he does not believe in, and is not a member of or supports any organization that believes in or teaches, the overthrow of the United States Government by force or by any illegal or unconstitutional methods. [29 U. S. C. A. § 159 (h).]

Three Justices did not participate in the decision. The remaining six Justices split three to three on the question whether the Non-Communist Affidavit requirement conflicted with the freedom of beliefs protection of the First Amendment.

Aside from that, however, the case is clearly distinguishable. Chief Justice Vinson speaking for the three Justices upholding the validity of the requirement of the Non-Communist Affidavit by union leaders indicated the presence in

---

[23] *Communications Ass'n. vs. Douds*, 339 U. S. 382.

that case of the manifestation of overt acts. The Chief
Justice stated that "Courts cannot ascertain the thought
that has no outward manifestation." [24] The Court discussed
the obstructions to the free flow of commerce caused by
strikes and other industrial unrest; that there was substantial evidence of obstructive strikes. All through the majority
opinion the thought is stressed that what was being sup-
pressed were overt acts which were obstructions to the free
flow of commerce and that no attempt was being made to
prevent dissemination of Communist doctrine.

Involved in the first count in the case at bar is merely
a speculation into the uncertainties of the human mind.
No overt acts could possibly emerge from this count
such as existed in the Douds case. No case has been
pointed out to the Court which sustains a perjury count
based on the speculative fathoming of the mind that will
be necessary by the trier of fact in order to arrive at a
decision under count one of the indictment.

In the discussion on beliefs in the Douds case, Justice
Frankfurter stated:

"I cannot deem it within the rightful authority of Congress to probe into opinions that involve only an argu-
mentative demonstration of some coincidental parallel-
ism of belief with some of the beliefs of those who direct
the policy of the Communist Party, though without
any allegiance to it. To require oaths as to matters that
open up such possibilities invades the inner life of men
whose compassionate thought or doctrinaire hopes may
be as far removed from any dangerous kinship with
the Communist creed as were those of the founders of
the present orthodox political parties in this country."
[p. 422.]

Justice Jackson in the same case also pointed out the
problem by stating that a trial for false swearing concerning
beliefs would "revolve around conjecture as to whether he
[the one making the affidavit] candidly exposed his state of

---

[24] *Communications Ass'n. vs. Douds, supra,* p. 441.

mind." He suggested that the intent and beliefs are determined by the Courts as incidental to deciding the legal effect to be given to overt acts.

Time and time again the Supreme Court has emphasized the freedom under the First Amendment to have opinions and sympathies, unexpressed by overt acts that show a clear and present danger to the Constitutional form of government guaranteed by the Constitution. *Schenck* vs. *U. S., supra.* Criminal sanctions cannot be imposed where we hold " beliefs and opinions concerning domestic measures and trends in national and world affairs." *Taylor* vs. *Mississippi,* 319 U. S. 583, 590.

In *Board of Education* vs. *Barnette,* 319 U. S. 624 the Court aptly said:

> " If there is any fixed star in our constitutional constellation, it is that no official, high or petty, can prescribe what shall be orthodox in politics, nationalism, religion or other matters of opinion or force citizens to confess by word or act their faith therein. If there are any circumstances which permit an exception, they do not now occur to us." [p. 642.]

The First Amendment protects an individual in the expression of ideas though they are repugnant to the orthodox. Communism's fallacy and viciousness can be demonstrated without striking down the protection of the First Amendment of discourse, discussion and debate. When public excitement runs high as to alien ideologies, is the time when we must be particularly alert not to impair the ancient landmarks set up in the Bill of Rights. " The greater the importance of safeguarding the community from incitements to the overthrow of our institutions by force and violence, the more imperative is the need to preserve inviolate the constitutional rights of free speech, free press and free assembly in order to maintain the opportunity for free political discussion, to the end that government may be responsive to the will of the people and that changes, if desired, may be obtained by peaceful means. Therein lies the security of the Republic, the very foundation of constitutional government." [25]

[25] *De Jonge* vs. *Oregon*, 299 U. S. 353, 365.

If we weaken the safeguards afforded under the Bill of Rights we impair our position with the democratic forces in the world fighting against the tyranny of Communism. "Safety of society depends on the tolerance of government for hostile as well as friendly criticism, that in a community where men's minds are free, there must be room for the unorthodox as well as the orthodox views." [26]

In our proper concern for the internal and external threat of Communism and in pursuing our efforts to strike down this threat, we should endeavor to be consistent and not attempt to require a conformity in thought and beliefs that has no relevancy to a present danger to our security. During the past few years the experts have had many conflicting and divergent views on foreign policy. Many thoughtful people and patriotic American citizens in 1938 and 1939 were not enthusiastic about our getting into the war. Violent changes in the thinking of our people occurred in a short period of time before and after Germany broke with Russia. "Attempts of the courts to fathom modern political meditations of an accused would be as futile and mischievous as the efforts in the infamous heresy trials of old to fathom religious beliefs. * * * It is true that in England of olden times men were tried for treason for mental indiscretions such as imagining the death of the king. But our Constitution was intended to end such prosecutions. Only in the darkest periods of human history has any Western Government concerned itself with mere belief, however eccentric or mischievous, when it has not matured into overt action; and if that practice survives anywhere, it is in the Communist countries whose philosophies we loathe." [27]

[26] *Rumely, supra*, Douglas, J. concurring at p. 57.

[27] *Douds, supra*, Jackson, J. dissenting in part, p. 437, 438.

Applying these guiding principles to count one, this count must fall because it is violative of both the First and Sixth Amendments.

Counts Three and Four

Count three charges that defendant perjured himself when he said he did not know that Asiaticus was a Communist. Count four charges defendant perjured himself when he stated that he, while editor of "Pacific Affairs," had not published articles by persons whom he knew to be Communists (other than Russian contributions). The question of knowledge, that is, the concept of what defendant knew is even more nebulous than sympathies. What he could have meant when he said he did not "know" gives rise to speculation and conjecture, but speculation cannot be substituted for proof "beyond a reasonable doubt" because the plain meaning of the word "reason" excludes conjecture. Defendant is the only person who will ever know what he meant when he said that he did not know that Asiaticus was a Communist. Who can say whether he meant that he did not "believe" or "suspect" or "feel" or "have reason to think." Any one or all of these still might not constitute knowledge within his own mind. Under these counts there can be no overt acts as the outward expression of the mind as were present in the Douds case.

The arguments against the validity of count one are even stronger when applied to counts three and four. Counts three and four must also be stricken down as violative of the First and Sixth Amendments.

Count Seven

Count seven is clearly defective in its plain inconsistency and indefiniteness. It charges defendant with lying when he stated that neither he nor anyone in his party made any prearrangements with the Communist Party in order to get into Yenan. The Government charges that the true fact was that arrangements had been made with *Communist authorities* [emphasis supplied]. It seems plain that defendant testified about arrangements with the Communist Party and getting beyond the line of demarcation when the Government claims the perjury involved arrangements with Communist authorities and being received at Communist Headquarters. This constitutes a fatal variance that fails to meet the requirements of the Sixth Amendment and Rule 7 (c) of the Federal Rules of Criminal Procedure. This count cannot be cured by a bill of particulars. The prosecutor cannot be substituted for a Grand Jury in helping to revive what constitutes a fatal indictment. *Jarl* vs. *U. S.*, 19 F.2d 891.

Counts Two, Five and Six

As the Court previously indicated there is serious doubt whether the remaining counts two, five and six can ultimately pass the test of materiality so as to present a jury issue. But this must await the trial.

The motion to dismiss counts two, five and six is therefore denied, without prejudice to renew the motion at the time of trial.

IV.

BILL OF PARTICULARS

The granting of a bill of particulars rests in the sound discretion of the Court. *McMullen* vs. *U. S.*, 68 U. S. App. D. C., 302.

The Federal Criminal Rules provide:

" (f) Bill of Particulars. The court for cause may direct the filing of a bill of particulars. A motion for a bill of particulars may be made only within ten days after arraignment or at such other time before or after arraignment as may be prescribed by rule or order. A bill of particulars may be amended at any time subject to such conditions as justice requires." [Title 18, U. S. C. A., Federal Rules of Criminal Procedure, Rule 7 (f)].

It must not be used as a fishing expedition. *U. S.* vs. *Kushner*, 135 F.2d 668.

It is proper in perjury cases of this type to require the Government to disclose the overt acts on which it relies to sustain the charge. *U. S.* vs. *Remington, supra.* The Allegations in counts two, five and six are so indefinite that the Court feels the defendant is entitled to a bill of particulars giving him certain information as to enable him to defend. Therefore the Court orders that the Government file a bill of particulars giving information as to counts two, five and six as follows:

As to Count Two: The Government should state the overt acts upon which it relies to show that the defendant had been told that Chi was a Communist. The word " Communist " should be defined as used here. The persons who told defendant that Chi was a Communist should be identified and the time, place and circumstances under which defendant was told this.

As to Count Five: The overt acts should be stated upon which the Government intends to rely to show that defendant perjured himself in stating that the luncheon with Oumansky was not held after the Hitler invasion of Russia and just before the defendant went out to China.

As to Count Six: The Government should state the overt acts on which it relies in proving that defendant perjured himself in saying that he had not, at Currie's request, taken care of Currie's mail at the White House while Currie was away.

In other respects the motion for a bill of particulars as to these counts should be denied.

LUTHER W. YOUNGDAHL
Judge

May 2, 1953.

Bibliography

I. Books

Aulen, Gustav, *Church, Law and Society,* New York, 1948

Beard, Charles, *American Government and Politics,* 8th ed., New York, 1939

Benson, Adolph B., and Hedin, Naboth, *Americans from Sweden,* People of America Series, Philadelphia, Pa., 1950

Berggrav, Eivind, *Man and State,* tr. by George Aus, Philadelphia, Pa., 1951

Binkley, Wilfred E., *American Political Parties: Their Natural History,* New York, 1947

Binkley, Wilfred E., and Moos, Malcolm C., *A Grammar of American Politics,* New York, 1949

Carlson, Edgar M., *The Reinterpretation of Luther,* Philadelphia, Pa., 1948

Douglas, Paul, *Ethics in Government,* Cambridge, Mass., 1952

Ebersole, Luke E., *Church Lobbying in the Nation's Capitol,* New York, 1951

Folwell, William Watts, *A History of Minnesota,* Vol. 1, St. Paul, Minn., 1952

Forell, George W., *Faith Active in Love,* New York, 1954

Graham, George A., *Morality in American Politics,* New York, 1952

Lattimore, Owen, *Ordeal by Slander,* Boston, 1950; *Solution in Asia,* Boston, 1945; *Situation in Asia,* Boston, 1949

Mattson, A. D., *Polity in the Augustana Synod,* Rock Island, Ill., 1941

Mayer, George H., *The Political Career of Floyd B. Olson,* Minneapolis, Minn., 1951

Niebuhr, H. Richard, *Christ and Culture,* New York, 1951

Niebuhr, Reinhold, *Christian Realism and Political Problems,* New York, 1953

Nye, Russel B., *Midwestern Progressive Politics: A Historical Study of Its Origins and Development, 1870-1950,* East Lansing, Mich., 1951

Ramsey Paul, *Basic Christian Ethics,* New York, 1952

Stassen, Harold E., *Where I Stand,* Garden City, New York, 1947

Voorhis, Jerry, *A Christian in Politics,* New York, 1951

II. Articles

Adrian, Charles R., "The Origin of Minnesota's Non-Partisan Legislature," *Minnesota History,* XXXIII, No. 4 (Winter, 1952)

Adrian, Charles R., "Some General Characteristics of Non-Partisan Elections," *American Political Science Review,* XLVI, September, 1952

Berle, Adolph A., and others, "National Security and Individual Freedom," the entire issue of *Annals of the American Academy of Political and Social Science,* Vol. 301, July, 1955

Billing, Einar, "Our Calling," tr., Conrad Bergendoff, *Augustana Quarterly,* XXVI, No. 2 & 3 (April, July, 1947)

Bergendoff, Conrad, "The Lutheran Christian in Church and State," *Lutheran Quarterly,* Vol. I, No. 4 (November, 1949)

Carlson, Edgar M., "Can the State Be Christian?" *Augustana Quarterly,* XXVI No. 1 (January, 1947)

Carr, Robert K., "National Security and Individual Freedom, "*Yale Review,* XLII, No. 4 (June, 1953)

"Congressional Investigations," *Congressional Digest,* XXXI, No. 5 (May, 1952)

Davenport, Walter, "Stassen's Political Gamble," *Collier's,* CXVII, May 4, 1946

Eby, Kermit, "A Protestant Political Strategy," *Christian Century,* LXVII, No. 46 (November 15, 1950)

Friendly, Alfred, "The Noble Crusade of Senator McCarthy," *Harper's Magazine,* CCI ,No. 1204 (August, 1950)

Gilbert, Brian, "Judge Youngdahl Wins His Fight," *New Republic,* CXXXIII, No. 2 (July 11, 1955)

Gilbert, Brian "New Light on the Lattimore Case," *New Republic* CXXXI, No. 26 (December 27, 1954)

Gossett, William T., "Human Rights and the American Bar," *American Scholar,* XXII, No. 4 (Autumn, 1953)

Harris, A. I., "Tories Take Minnesota," *New Republic,* CIII, No. 14, (September 30, 1940)

Helstein, Ralph, "The Packing House Workers' Case," *New Republic,* CXVIII, No. 7 (March 29, 1948)

Huie, William Bradford, "Stassen Challenges the Republican Party," *American Mercury,* LVI, No. 23 (March, 1943)

Jarman, Rufus, "The Governor and the Gamblers," *Saturday Evening Post,* CCXX, No. 24 (December 13, 1947)

Johnson, Gerald, "Lattimore's Defenders," (correspondence to editors) *New Republic,* CXXXIII, No. 2 (July 11, 1955)

Kaye, Jay, "Minnesota's First Family," *Pageant Magazine,* VII, No. 7 (January, 1952)

Krieg, Emil J., "Is Luther Youngdahl Shielding State's 'Shady Deal' Republicans?" *Minnesota Labor,* IX, No. 45 (September 26, 1952)

Lattimore, Eleanor, "What It Was Like," *Harper's Magazine,* CCI, No. 1204 and 1205 (August and September, 1950)

"Minnesota Points the Way," *Christian Century,* LXIX, No. 21 (May 21, 1952)

Moos, Malcolm, and Kenworthy. E. W., "Dr. Shipstead Comes to Judgment," *Harper's Magazine,* XCCIII, No. 1152 (July, 1946)

Motter, Alton M., "Crusading Governor," *Christian Century,* LXV, No. 7 (February 18, 1948)

Naftalin, Arthur, "The Failure of the Farmer-Labor Party to Capture Control of the Minnesota Legislature," *American Political Science Review,* XXXVIII, No. 1 (February, 1944)

Stassen, Harold E., "Democracy in the Land O' Lakes," *Christian Science Monitor* (March 23, 1940)

"The Christian Faith and American Politics," *Social Action,* XVIII, No. 2 (November, 1951)

Torkelson, W., "God's Word Is Law in Minnesota," *Magazine Digest* (April, 1948)

Williams, Howard Y., "Harold Stassen, Fake Liberal," *New Republic* CX, No. 23 (June 5, 1944)

Wingren, Gustav, "The Church and the Calling," tr. Evert Olson, *Augustana Quarterly,* XXVI, No. 4 (October, 1947)

Wright, Charles Alan

Youngdahl, Luther W., "The Christian Woman in Politics," *Women's Missionary Outlook* (July, 1948)

III   Unpublished Manuscripts

Adrian, Charles, The Non-Partisan Legislature in Minnesota (Ph.D. Thesis, University of Minnesota, 1950)

Carlson, Edgar M., The Church and the Public Conscience (Unpublished Hein Lectures delivered at Wartburg Theological Seminary, Dubuque, Iowa, 1953; Copies in possession of Dr. Carlson)

Naftalin, Arthur, A History of Farmer-Labor Party in Minnesota (Ph.D. Thesis, University of Minnesota, 1948)

IV   Speeches of Luther Youngdahl

Cen·ennial Inaugural Address to the Legislature of Minnesota (St. Paul, Minnesota, January 6, 1949)

The Challenging New Frontier in Mental Health, delivered at the Menninger Foundation, Topeka, Kansas October 4, 1949 (Copies in possession of the author)

Do Christianity and Politics Mix? delivered at the Chicago Sunday Evening Club, May 7, 1950 (Copy in possession of the author)

Farewell Address, *The Minneapolis Star* (September 26, 1951)

A Governor's Baccalaureate Sermon (Copy in possession of author)

Inaugural Address to the Legislature of Minnesota (St. Paul, Minnesota, January 8, 1947)

Inaugural Address to the Legislature of Minnesota (St. Paul, Minnesota, January 3, 1951)

Politics—A Challenge to Christian Youth (Copy in author's possession)

Putting Christianity into Practice, *Proceedings of the Thirty-Fifth Meeting of the National Conference of Catholic Charities,* 1949

Reformation Address (Copy in author's possession)

Report to the People, March 26, 1951 (Copy in author's possession)

V   Official Government Documents

Commission on the Aging, *Minnesota's Aging Citizens,* St. Paul, Minnesota, December, 1950

Commissioner of Mental Health: The Minnesota Mental Health Program, St. Paul, Minnesota, January, 1951 (Copy in author's possession)

Commission on Youth, *Governor's Second State Conference on Youth,* St. Paul, Minnesota, 1950

Congressional Record, Senate, March 30, 1950

Jackson, Carl J., Minnesota's Mental Health Program Soars Ahead, January, 1950 (Copy in author's possession)

Legislative Manual of the State of Minnesota, 1947, 1949, 1951

Minnesota Reports: Cases Argued and Determined in the Supreme Court of Minnesota, Vol. 215 (1944), Ethel Martin, Reporter (St. Paul, Minnesota, 1944)

Minnesota Efficiency in Government Commission's Recommendations— *How to Achieve Greater Efficiency and Economy in Minnesota's Government,* St. Paul, Minnesota, 1950

The United States vs. Owen Lattimore (Crim. No. 1879-52) D. C. 125 F. Supp. 295

The United States vs. Owen Lattimore (Crim. No. 1016) D. C. 127 F. Supp. 405

Youth Conservation Commission, St. Paul, Minnesota, 1949

Youth Conservation Commission Progress Report, St. Paul, Minnesota, 1949

VI   Documents of Non-Governmental Organizations

Gannon, Robert, Notes on Minnesota Tax Policy and Some Suggested Reforms (Talk given at League of Women Voters Tax Institute, November, 1949) Copies at Minnesota State C.I.O. Council office, Minneapolis, Minnesota

Gerberding, William. Reports of the Legislative Information Secretary of the Minnesota Council of Churches, No. 1-6 (Copies in files of Minnesota Council of Churches office, Minneapolis, Minn.)

League of Women Voters of Minnesota, 1953 Legislative Report (Copies at League's office in Minneapolis, Minn.)

Minnesota Association of Cooperatives Report on the 1949 Legislature (Copies in the Association's office in St. Paul, Minnesota)

Minnesota Employers' Association Legislative Digest, St. Paul, Minnesota

Minnesota Institute of Governmental Research, *State Governmental Research Bulletins,* St. Paul, Minnesota

Minnesota State C.I.O. Council, *Did You Vote for This Last November? A Report on the Minnesota Legislature and Legislators,* 1949 Session, Minneapolis, Minnesota, 1949

——*Minnesota's Unfair Taxation of Iron Ore in Comparison with Other Minnesota Taxpayers,* Minneapolis, Minnesota, 1950

——*Report on the* 1951 *Session of the Minnesota Legislature, Minnesota Labor* (September 7, 1951)

Minnesota Unitarian Conference Committee on Institutions for the Mentally Ill. A Summary of Conditions in Minnesota State Hospitals for the Mentally Ill, St. Paul, Minnesota, 1947 (Copy in author's possession)

Minutes, The Lutheran Minnesota Conference of the Augustana Lutheran Church, Annual Conventions of 1950 and 1951 (Rock Island, Illinois)

Proceedings, Annual Meetings of the Minnesota State Federation of Labor (1946-1951)

Reports, Augustana Lutheran Church (Evangelical Lutheran Augustana Synod before 1948) Annual Conventions of 1925, 1938, 1943, 1950, 1951, 1952

Report of the National C.I.O. Commission in the Matter of Minnesota Iron Ore Taxes, 1952 (Copies at offices of Minnesota State C.I.O. Council, Minneapolis, Minnesota)

Reed, Thomas H. and Doris D., *Preparing College Men and Women for Politics* (A report to the Citizenship Clearing House affiliated with the Law Center of New York University), New York, 1952

VII Brochures, Pamphlets and Statements

Gustavians for Youngdahl Volunteer Committee, Letter Endorsing Luther W. Youngdahl for Governor, Minneapolis, Minnesota, October 30, 1950 (Copy in author's possession)

League of Women Voters of Minnesota

——Ninety Days of Law Making in Minnesota, 1949

——*You Are the Government: A Handbook for Minnesota Citizens,* St. Paul, Minnesota, 1949

——Facts About Our State Constitution (Copies in League's office in Minneapolis, Minnesota)

Luther Youngdahl for Governor Volunteer Committee, S. A. Bertelsen, St. Paul, Minnesota, Chairman

——For Honesty and Humanity in Government, 1950

——Problems of the People His Concern, 1950

——Youngdahl Presents 18-Point Program, 1950

Luther Youngdahl for President Citizens' Committee, Plan for Campaign (Copy in possession of Attorney Verne Johnson, Minneapolis Minnesota)

Protestants United, Letter Endorsing Luther Youngdahl for Governor, October 30, 1950

Statement of Charles L. Schultze, Chairman of St. Paul Good Government Group, October, 1950 (Copy in author's possession)

Statement of Principles of the Republican Party of Minnesota, St. Paul, Minnesota, September 16, 1950 (Copy in author's possession)